THE QUEST FOR WHOLENESS

SUNY Series in Systematic Philosophy
Robert C. Neville, Editor

Whether systematic philosophies are intended as true pictures of the world, as hypotheses, as the dialectic of history, or as heuristic devices for relating rationally to a multitude of things, they each constitute articulated ways by which experience can be ordered, and as such they are contributions to culture. One does not have to choose between Plato and Aristotle to appreciate that Western civilization is enriched by the Platonic as well as Aristotelian ways of seeing things.

The term "systematic philosophy" can be applied to any philosophical enterprise that functions with a perspective from which everything can be addressed. Sometimes this takes the form of an attempt to spell out the basic features of things in a system. Other times it means the examination of a limited subject from the many angles of a context formed by a systematic perspective. In either case systematic philosophy takes explicit or implicit responsibility for the assessment of its unifying perspective and for what is seen from it. The styles of philosophy according to which systematic philosophy can be practiced are as diverse as the achievements of the great philosophers in history, and doubtless new styles are needed for our time.

Yet systematic philosophy has not been a popular approach during this century of philosophical professionalism. It is the purpose of this series to stimulate and publish new systematic works employing the techniques and advances in philosophical reflection made during this century. The series is committed to no philosophical school or doctrine, nor to any limited style of systematic thinking. Whether the systematic achievements of previous centuries can be equalled in the twentieth depends on the emergence of forms of systematic philosophy appropriate to our times. The current resurgence of interest in the project deserves the cultivation it may receive from the SUNY Series in Systematic Philosophy.

THE QUEST FOR WHOLENESS

Carl G. Vaught
Chairman, Department of Philosophy
The Pennsylvania State University

State University of New York Press
ALBANY

Published by
State University of New York Press, Albany

© 1982 State University of New York

All rights reserved

Printed in the United States of America

For information, address State University of New York
Press, State University Plaza, Albany, N.Y., 12246

Library of Congress Cataloging in Publication Data

Vaught, Carl G., 1939-
  The quest for wholeness.

  (SUNY series in systematic philosophy)
  Includes index.
  1. Whole and parts (Philosophy) 2. Religion—
Philosophy. I. Title. II. Series.
BS396.V38   191   81-18365
ISBN 0-87395-593-5   AACR2
ISBN 0-87395-594-3 (pbk.)

10   9   8   7   6   5   4   3   2

For Janie

Contents

Preface

For a number of years I have been convinced that the primary task of the philosopher is to think concretely about the most fundamental existential and metaphysical questions. As a result, this book has been written with the conviction that we must not be occupied with merely theoretical problems, but must focus instead upon the world as a whole and upon the most pressing questions that confront the human spirit. The professional philosopher should not address a merely professional audience, but the larger world as well, and in the end he must come to terms with himself and must make his own responses to the human predicament. In this book, my way of doing this is to discuss the quest for wholeness and the fragmentation that generates it, and to do so by focusing on some of the most significant places in experience and reflection where fragmentation is encountered and where the meaning of wholeness is first discovered. I do not expect to deal with these issues with absolute precision, for the wholeness we seek, and the process of development we must undergo in order to achieve it, are not abstractions that can be described in merely general terms. Yet I am also convinced that all of us know what human wholeness means and that we have all endured periods of disruption in between our moments of fulfillment. Beginning with this experiential "understanding," I intend to bring these concepts to articulation, if not with perfect clarity, then in whatever way can be discovered. The quest for wholeness has a mystery, a power, and a structure of its own, and it is one of the fundamental tasks of philosophical reflection to understand its significance.

In order to pursue these issues in a concrete fashion, I have built my inquiry around concrete media of expression in which story-telling and reflective discourse are connected and in which artistic, religious, and philosophical elements are interwoven. In particular, I shall discuss the problems of fragmentation and unity with reference to Melville's *Moby-Dick;* in the light of the Biblical account of the origins and the development of the Hebrew nation; in terms of Plato's dialogue about the nature of piety; and with reference to the artistic, the religious, and the philosophical elements of Hegel's speculative system. I have proceeded in this fashion because I am convinced that if the quest for wholeness is to come to life before us, it must be depicted in terms of concrete media of expression that preserve its original depth and richness, while they enable us to understand the phenomenon to which they give us access. Though abstract reflection might permit us to grasp the generic structure of human existence, it is not sufficiently rich to encompass the quest for wholeness as it unfolds within direct experience. For reflection of this kind to be possible, the concreteness of art and religion, and the human drama which they often express, must be blended with the discipline and the precision of philosophy, giving us access both to the depth and to the intelligible structure that the quest for wholeness always exhibits. The concrete media of expression that I shall consider will allow us to depict the quest for wholeness from different perspectives and will move us from the concreteness of story-telling to the comprehension of reflective discourse. However, in binding these two dimensions together and in unifying the artistic, the religious, and the philosophical aspects of human existence, each of these different frameworks will make its concrete richness reflectively accessible.

In the early stages of the philosophical tradition, Plato warns us against ever writing our deepest thoughts, and in the more recent past, Wittgenstein has claimed that philosophy is more an activity than a doctrine, more a way of thinking than a set of propositions. Separated so widely in philosophical history, and separated as well by the basic thrust of their philosophical commitments, both thinkers recognized a common problem: "How can we speak discursively about the most important issues without our words degenerating into frozen letters on a printed page?" The concrete chapters of this book and our attempts to articulate what must finally remain beyond the capacity of merely structural reflection are intended to reflect the truth in Plato's warning and in Wittgenstein's suggestion. Abstract reflection can never exhaust the richness of the quest for wholeness; it demands reflection from the reader that will never come to an end; and if it is not too paradoxical to say it, the "categories" of depth and mystery must always remain a crucial element in any attempt to articulate the meaning of the quest for unity. The quest for wholeness demands concrete reflection, forcing us to turn away from a merely structural account of the meaning of human existence. This book has been written for the artist, for the theologian, and for the philosopher, each of whom must be concerned with the question, "What does it mean to be human?" But at a deeper level, it is written for any reader who knows what it means to be fragmented, and who is willing to undertake a quest for wholeness in experiential and reflective terms.

Since this book is rooted in my own experience, perhaps I should mention briefly the stages that led me to the quest for wholeness as a philosophical problem and to the concept of concrete reflection as a way of dealing with it. This description, in turn, can make the structure of our discussion accessible by serving as an image of the reflective pattern to be traced out in the following pages. In developmental terms, my account of the quest for wholeness begins with childhood and with the power of imagination to which almost every child responds. In my own case, at least, it is clear that imagination preceded reflection, for long before I was able to understand the intricacies of reflective discourse, I was often fascinated by the story-telling of my father, where I first encountered imaginative illustrations of the human quest for fulfillment. The stories he told were sometimes taken from the pages of the Bible and were sometimes drawn from ordinary life, but in both cases they pointed to the fragmentation of the human soul, to the process of development that leads beyond it, and to the wholeness that sometimes comes, not as the result of human achievement, but as a gift that must simply be received. The stories I remember best were essentially religious, for they pointed to the inescapable conclusion that wholeness is a religious phenomenon and that the quest for wholeness finally brings us face to face with God. Yet these stories were also richly human, interwoven with expressive uses of language, and sustained by a reflective dimension that was indispensable if they were to be coherent and intelligible expressions of the wholeness they suggested. I have never been able to escape the dramatic impact of these stories, which unified experience and reflection and pointed in a concrete fashion to the wholeness that all of us seek. My recollection of them has convinced me that philosophical reflection must not abandon the richness of experience to which stories of this kind give us access, and that it must find a way of speaking about the most fundamental issues that combines the concreteness of story-telling with the clarity of reflective discourse. It is this fundamental conviction that lies behind my attempts to engage in concrete reflection and to understand a series of linguistic worlds, rich enough to depict the quest for wholeness in human terms.

Of course, wholeness at the experiential level must be distinguished from the quest for wholeness as a philosophical problem, and as is so often the case, my transition from imagination to reflection was brought about by encountering a negative moment. My first teacher of philosophy was not willing to acknowledge the integrity of the mythic world from which I had come, and he demanded instead, clarity of thought and precision of linguistic expression. I can still remember the familiar litany of his typically analytical questions: "What does the quest for wholeness mean?" "How does one know that 'wholeness' is an intelligible conception?" "What are the criteria that a way of life must fulfill in order to be whole, and how can the conception of human wholeness be related to other concepts that are presupposed in describing the structure of human existence?" In trying to answer my teacher's questions, I soon discovered that the analytical reflection he demanded stood in radical contrast with the stories I had once understood, and that the abstract discourse in which reflection of this kind was expressed cut me off from the richly metaphorical uses of language I had once been able to affirm. As a result, a tension emerged between the stories with which I began and the reflection into which I was driven, and this "contradiction" transformed my original wholeness from a religious experience into a philosophical problem. Of course, as we shall discover in the following chapters, abstract reflection has positive value, enabling us to grasp the skeletal form of experience and to make the crucial distinctions that allow us to articulate the intelligible structure of human existence. However, it is equally clear that the telling of stories, which reflect the richness of direct experience, and the demands of abstract reflection, which attempts to capture its structure, generate very different worlds. It is this contrast between experience and reflection, and between imagination and reflective discourse, that launches the quest for wholeness at the distinctively philosophical level, and it is this distinction that has led to my attempts to deal with the problems of fragmentation and unity.

After I had begun to assimiliate the techniques of analytical philosophy, I studied with a different kind of philosopher who gave me some very wise advice. He had come to the university for a semester on a visiting appointment, expecting to find a philosophy department full of theologians. Instead, he found a collection of philosophical positivists of the narrowest kind. I remember vividly the day he realized where he was. It was the third week of the term, and his back was turned to the class. He had been asking a series of questions, but having found that all the answers were the same, he finally said, "Class dismissed." At the beginning of the next hour, he came to the classroom with a list of example definitions, written on onion skin paper. At the top of the page was a merely conventional definition, equating one nonsense syllable with another, and at the bottom was the familiar claim that man is a rational animal. In between was an entire spectrum of definitions, shading off into one another in various subtle fashions. But as he moved from one definition to the next, asking each of us in turn, "What kind of definition is this?" in every case we replied, "Merely conventional." We were convinced that the attempt to understand the meaning of language was based on a set of arbitrary conventions and that the analysis of language could never lead us back to the underlying structure of the real order. Apparently, abstract reflection had already done its work, separating us from the texture of direct experience that even children seem to understand. Yet halfway down the list of definitions, the list itself convinced me that I was a fool. Suddenly, I realized that I had learned how to ask sophistical versions of the question, "What does X mean?" but that I had scarcely begun to answer those questions in a genuinely reflective fashion. Subsequent reflection convinced me that I should at least attempt to answer questions in this way and that once philosophical reflection had begun, it was necessary to pursue it to its natural conclusion. However, I also concluded that this could not be done through analysis alone and that wholeness could be achieved at the reflective level only by finding a conceptual framework rich enough to understand the world as a whole and man's place in it. Having turned away from direct experience, and having abandoned my imaginative access to it by embracing abstract reflection, I now turned back toward the world, determined to understand its structure as a unified totality. In the process, my original quest for wholeness, which had already been transformed from a religious experience into a philosophical problem, was transformed again into the philosophical attempt to understand the Whole.

In the past fifteen years I have pursued the reflective quest for wholeness by attempting to construct a philosophical system. However, in the course of my attempts to do so, discussions with beginning students have made it necessary for me to abandon a merely speculative point of view and have forced me to come to terms with the interpersonal dimension of philosophical communication. These discussions, in turn, have thrust a human element into the center of my thinking and have raised the crucial questions that have finally led to the writing of this book. Suppose a philosophical system could be constructed that described the world as a whole and gave an adequate account of the place of the human soul within it. What would be the relationship between a system of this kind and the concrete situations from which we come and to which our philosophical reflections must finally be related? Is the richness of our origins contained within the Whole we attempt to understand, or do the concrete contexts from which we spring resist incorporation into a larger unity? Can the quest for wholeness be satisfied by generating a philosophical system, or is it equally concerned with a real ground that imagination makes accessible and that can never be included in a wider context? As these questions became more insistent, I finally realized that there is a fourth level of experience and reflection, and that it lies beyond the telling of stories, the articulation of abstract distinctions, and the building of a philosophical system. It is the standpoint from which the reflective individual looks back at the place where he began and asks, "How can the quest for wholeness be affirmed as it is rooted in direct experience and as it is expressed in richly human language, and at the same time, how can it become the subject-matter of philosophical reflection?" In order to answer this question, I have developed a concrete way of thinking that stands in between imagination and reflection, experience and system, story-telling and reflective discourse and that attempts to make the quest for wholeness accessible by weaving these elements together. As I have suggested already, the quest for wholeness demands concrete reflection, and it is reflection of this kind to which the following chapters are devoted.

I want to thank James Faulconer, Elizabeth Grimbergen, and Gerald Lundgren for many helpful discussions, and I also owe a special debt to William Desmond, Brian Martine, and Jere Surber — graduate students and friends who participated in this project from the beginning. In addition, I am grateful to my colleagues at The Pennsylvania State University for their suggestions and encouragement, especially Carl R. Hausman, Henry W. Johnstone, Jr., and Stanley Rosen. I also want to thank Dean Magner and the Central Fund for Research for defraying the cost of typing and duplication; The Institute for the Arts and Humanistic Studies for appointing me a Junior Fellow and for releasing me from teaching so I could begin this work; and the other universities that have invited me to lecture about some of the topics discussed in this book — The University of Montana, The University of Denver, Brigham Young University, Western Carolina University, and Iowa State. Finally, I want to thank the editor of *The Journal of General Education* for allowing me to use an earlier version of Chapter 1 that appeared in that journal under the title, "The Quest for Wholeness: Melville's *Moby-Dick*."

Introduction:
Fragmentation, Wholeness,
and Concrete Reflection

At the deepest level of human experience, the world confronts us with a radical ambiguity. On the one hand, it sustains our existence and gives us a place to stand; on the other hand, it threatens to destroy us and to cut us off from the ground of our existence. The larger world in which we exist allows us to develop what would otherwise remain implicit in our nature, and it gives us a rich domain of content to be transformed by our own actions. Yet in doing so, it tempts us to lose ourselves in what will always lie beyond our grasp, and it lures us away from the particular context out of which we come and to which we must finally return. To be sustained, but also to be destroyed; to have our own space, but to be separated from our own ground; to be allowed to grow and to develop, but to be lured away from our origins — these fundamental contradictions constitute the inherent ambiguity of the human situation. However, in its most serious existential forms, fragmentation does not appear as a negative relationship between ourselves and what stands in contrast with us, but as an internal modification of our own nature. We are alienated from the center of human existence, and we often split apart into two competing wills, one of which affirms the meaning of human life, while the other turns away from a positive relationship with the ground of our existence. At times, the human soul even splinters into fragments, and its warring members seem to be engaged in a battle to the death. When this occurs, fragmentation becomes the central phenomenon of human existence.

Perhaps the clearest description of this phenomenon to be found in the Western tradition occurs in the eighth book of Augustine's *Confessions,* where he describes his own attempts to find wholeness against

1

the background of radical discontinuity:

> While I was deliberating..., it was I who willed and it was also I who was
> unwilling. In either case, it was I. I neither willed with my whole will nor
> was I wholly unwilling. And so I was at war with myself and torn apart by
> myself. And this strife was against my will; yet it did not show the
> presence of another mind, but the punishment of my own.

> So also, when eternity attracts us from above, and the pleasure of earthly
> delight pulls us down from below, the soul does not will either the one or
> the other with all its force, but still it is the same soul that does not will
> this or that with a united will, and is therefore pulled apart with grievous
> perplexities, because for truth's sake it prefers this, but for custom's sake
> it does not lay that aside.[1]

In this brief account, Augustine recognizes that the most basic
human problems are not to be found in the relationship between ourselves and what lies beyond us, but within the human soul itself. The
world is both positive and negative, and our relations with it are
positive and negative as well. Yet as we move back and forth between
these two dimensions, our most serious problem is to find a place to
stand that overcomes the fragmentation of our own existence and
brings wholeness to the human soul.

Of course, we might always conclude that fragmentation is an irre-
solvable problem and that the conflicting aspects of direct experience
merely cancel one another, producing a conception of the world that
remains indifferent to the deepest longings of our nature. As the
writer of the Book of Ecclesiastes reminds us in such a poignant and
unforgettable fashion:

> To every thing there is a season, and a time to every purpose under
> heaven: A time to be born, and a time to die;...a time to break down, and
> a time to build up;...a time to mourn, and a time to dance;...a time to
> keep, and a time to cast away;...a time to keep silence, and a time to
> speak;...a time of war, and a time of peace.[2]

However, the writer of this passage also implies that where the most
fundamental human interests are at stake, the individual cannot remain a mere observer, nor can he respond to his internal contradictions in a process of perpetual vacillation. Though the fragmentation
of our nature is a reflection of the objective ambiguities with which we
are confronted, and though we are often unable to find the center of
life or to discover a focal point that gives meaning to human existence,
the restlessness of our nature demands that we abandon a merely

spectatorial standpoint and that we move beyond the negative aspects of our original condition. The meaning of human existence cannot be formulated at a distance; we must face the contradictions of the human situation. Whatever our circumstances, an adequate response to the human predicament compels us to undertake a positive quest for fulfillment.

The quest for wholeness unfolds in the actual journeys of concrete individuals, who begin with fragmentation and who often struggle to overcome it by seeking a larger community in which their lives can be significant. Wholeness can never be found apart from the community, for the meaning of human existence is partly constituted by the human bonds that tie us together, first as members of an individual family, then as citizens of cities, states, and nations, and finally as members of the wider context that includes mankind as a whole. The fragmentation we experience is often caused by separation from others, and it is fragmentation of this kind that drives us toward the community to seek the fulfillment that can never be found in isolation. The person is what he is because of his relations with others, and it is relations of this kind that the quest for wholeness attempts to develop. On the other hand, the individual must not lose himself in the larger world, for to do so would be to lose the center of the fragmented self, and to abandon the hope that wholeness can be found in a fashion uniquely appropriate to oneself. If wholeness is to be accessible, it must be relevant to our particular condition, not only allowing us to be a part of something larger, but also permitting us to be ourselves as unique individuals. The quest for wholeness involves a delicate interplay between the individuality we express and the communities in which we participate, and it is the harmonious interconnection between individuation and participation that those who undertake it must attempt to achieve.[3] However, in the final analysis, the quest also requires that we move beyond the finite order and that we stand face to face with what is ultimate and unconditioned. As the word itself suggests, the quest for wholeness is a quest for salvation; but what can salvation mean apart from a source of power and meaning that can sustain our existence? This source of significance can be symbolized by the communities of which we are a part, and it can be made relevant to our particular condition. But the ground of our existence transcends the human community, and it can never be reduced to the uniqueness of the individuals within it. Though the quest for wholeness spreads outward toward the whole of humanity, and though it reaches down to the particularity of the individuals who undertake it, it also seeks a source of meaning that lies beyond the human realm. In doing so, it generates a three-dimensional space in which human beings can live.

The human space in which we exist gives us our original conception of the meaning of wholeness, and it allows the quest for wholeness to develop as a meaningful undertaking. As I have just suggested, this framework is constituted by the human community, by the uniqueness of the individuals within it, and by the ultimate source of significance that sustains our existence. In the final analysis, it is the interplay among all of these elements that makes human wholeness accessible. Yet before we attempt to undertake the journey which this framework makes possible, or indicate the method to be followed in doing so, let me emphasize another aspect of the journey which underlies the structure of the following account, but which might be easily overlooked. As the concept of a quest implies, it is to be understood as a temporal process. However, when the quest is described in temporal terms, it is tempting to assume that it moves in only one direction, transforming the fragmentation of the past into the wholeness of the future. We are often preoccupied with the goals toward which life is directed, and it is easy to conclude that wholeness is to be found at the end rather than at the beginning of a painful process of development. Just as the seed is what it is only because of the flower it might eventually become, the individual is often understood with reference to a *telos,* rather than in terms of his relation to the origins from which he emerges.[4] There is of course some truth in this account, for life is partly constituted by a forward thrust that turns our attention away from the past, making it possible for us to develop toward a greater degree of wholeness than can ever be accessible in the earliest stages of life. We cannot escape the fact that we are what we will become, and that wholeness is accessible to us only if we develop the capacities that are present implicitly at the beginning of our journey.[5] Nevertheless, it will be the thesis of this book that the quest for wholeness moves in two directions; not only driving us toward the future, but also requiring us to make contact with the past, and pointing to the possibility of a positive relationship with the sustaining ground of our existence. The quest for wholeness moves forward toward a larger, more inclusive unity, but it also leads us back to the origins of our individual existence. In doing so, it attempts to overcome fragmentation by allowing us to stand at the midpoint between an unbounded future and a determinate past that has left its individuating mark upon us.

One of the clearest formulations of this point is to be found in the first canto of the *Divine Comedy*. At the beginning of his work, Dante says,

> Midway this way of life we're bound upon,
>   I woke to find myself in a dark wood,
>   Where the right road was wholly lost and gone.
> Ay me! how hard to speak of it—that rude
>   And rough and stubborn forest! the mere breath
>   Of memory stirs the old fear in the blood;
> It is so bitter, it goes nigh to death;
>   Yet there I gained such good, that, to convey
>   The tale, I'll write what else I found therewith.[6]

As Dante continues, it soon becomes evident that he moves both forward and backward, both outward and within, both toward the larger world, and toward the origins from which he springs. In doing so, he not only affirms the importance of the future, but also acknowledges the crucial bi-directionality that the quest for wholeness always exhibits. Of course, the center of life is not confined to the midpoint of our temporal existence, and it is possible to stand in a positive relationship with the past and with the future from a variety of temporal perspectives. However, the important part to notice is that wholeness can be found, not only by moving outward toward the larger world, but also by standing face to face with the origins of our individual existence. The quest for wholeness seeks the midpoint between the larger context in which we exist and the point from which we originate, and in doing so, it attempts to hold together the inherent bi-directionality of the human situation.

The individual human family is a rather clear example of a concrete setting in which the quest for wholeness moves in both directions. A member of a family is embedded originally in a larger human matrix, and the meaning of his existence is first defined in terms of the roles he plays within this more inclusive framework. In the beginning, an individual is who he is in terms of his place within the family taken as a whole. Yet as the individual's power increases, tensions often arise between himself and other members of the family, and these tensions sometimes drive him beyond his origins to seek fulfillment in a different context. He builds a family of his own which unites two families into a larger community; he becomes a member of more inclusive social frameworks that expand the range of his participation within the human community; he moves away from the place where he began, learning how to act and how to think in ways that differ from the fashions which prevailed at home. In fact, the individual sometimes notices that the larger contexts into which he moves are merely parts of the world as a whole and that his quest for fulfillment can never be satisfied until he finds a place within this larger world. When this occurs, the quest for wholeness acquires a cosmic dimension, and the one who undertakes it ceases to be merely a particular individual, content to live in finite social settings. Instead, he expresses the deepest longings of the human spirit by orienting himself beyond the human realm. Though the quest for wholeness begins with the family, it opens out toward the cosmos; we sometimes attempt, as Socrates put it, to becomes citizens of the world. The cosmos, in turn, becomes a symbol for what is ultimate and unconditioned, and our irreducible openness to it becomes one of the conditions that makes the quest for wholeness possible in human terms.

However, as this developmental process unfolds, it sometimes causes us to sacrifice our uniqueness and to lose our identity. In turning away from the place where we began, we forfeit our particularity, and we are often tempted to lose touch with who we are. At this critical juncture we must reverse our direction and return to our origins, not to lose ourselves there, but to stand in contrast with them in positive and intelligible interaction. The quest for wholeness not only moves us outward toward the larger world, but also leads us back to the place where we began. In doing so, it allows us to stand before our origins as particular individuals and to individuate ourselves more and more clearly as we try to come to terms with who we are. Of course, we sometimes discover that our origins are too threatening for us to face them, and we turn away from them, attempting to lose ourselves in the task at hand and to insulate the future from the painful memories of past experience. In other cases our origins scarcely seem to exist, for they are often weak and ineffectual, and we seem to have no other choice but to invent our childhood and to act out the various lives we might have lived within the larger public world. In still other cases, we are orphans without origins that can be easily identified, however much we might wish for a ground upon which to stand and for a place to which we might return. Moreover, even when we have a home that is accessible to us, we soon discover that our customs and traditions will never save us, for in the moment in which we embrace them as the sustaining ground of our existence, we turn away from what we might become and are separated from other individuals with customs and traditions of their own. In all these cases it would seem that we can never return to our origins and that the salvation we seek must be found in some other way.

Yet whether our origins can be identified or not, and whether they exist in a form that can be recovered, either strong or weak, powerful or ineffectual, the particular context from which we come is important because it calls our attention to the concept of origination itself. The quest for wholeness leads us back to the place where we began, but it leads us there, not primarily to recover our finite origins, but to confront our infinite ground. It is this ground that the orphan shares with the child, and it is this foundation that can supply us with a source of originative power in terms of which the power of fragmentation can be overcome. The quest for wholeness begins with fragmentation, and it leads us outward toward the larger world, allowing us to come to terms with it by participating in the human community and by finding our place within the cosmos as the ultimate context in which our individual existence is embedded. However, the quest also requires us to return to our origins and to ask what it means to be a particular individual, living here and now as *a unique center of power* that can never be reduced to its place within a larger context. Though the past can never be recovered, we need to return to it to be reminded of the originative ground that constitutes our individuality and that allows us to stand forth as a unique and irreducible individual. The quest for wholeness moves in two directions, pointing to the Ground from which we come and to the Whole toward which we develop; and within the human space in which it unfolds, it attempts to find the center of life in between these two dimensions.

As we shall discover in the following pages, there are many ways in which the quest for wholeness can degenerate, not only failing to find the wholeness it seeks, but also exaggerating the fragmentation with which it begins. However, at this point, two kinds of degeneration should be considered that have a special bearing on our inquiry. These problems are important because they pose a threat to our capacity to speak about the quest for wholeness in a concrete fashion and because they raise questions about the possibility of reflective access to the issues before us. The first problem arises from the conviction that the way to undertake the quest for wholeness is to act rather than speak. Since the quest occurs in the real world, and since speech about it places us at a reflective distance from direct experience, it is tempting to conclude that discourse of the kind we are attempting can only be a pale reflection of the thing itself. Though we might agree that discourse can reflect the abstract structure of the quest for wholeness, we might be convinced that it can never give us access to the concrete richness of the quest from a reflective point of view. We might then conclude that if the depth and the power of the quest are accessible only in direct experience and if all that remains for reflection is the articulation of the abstract outline of the human journey, we should leave this abstract task to others, plunging instead into the immediacy of direct experience. Confronted with an absolute opposition between life and reflection, it would seem that wholeness itself demands that we choose life and that we turn away from the abstractness of merely structural reflection. However, this response to the problem overlooks the fact that the opposition between action and discourse, and the discord between experience and reflection, fragment the person in whom they occur. Just as the individual sometimes encounters discord in direct experience, splitting apart into fragments that demand reconciliation, these "higher order" conflicts divide us into aspects that cannot survive apart from one another. The conflicts between knowing and doing, and between life and reflection, involve a degenerate conception of all of these notions, and to succumb to it is to embrace a way of thinking that places fragmentation at the center of human existence. We cannot be whole unless we find a way of holding experience and reflection together, and this can be done only by developing a way of thinking that moves beyond the limits of abstraction.

Before I attempt to develop this suggestion, a second problem should be mentioned that involves a different misconception of the relationship between experience and reflection. This problem arises, not from an experiential preference for immediacy, but from the philosophical tendency to demand complete comprehension. From this second perspective, fragmentation is identified with the finitude of partial understanding, and human wholeness is equated with the capacity to give a comprehensive account of the world as a whole and of the place of the human soul within it. According to this approach to the problem of fragmentation, the quest for wholeness is primarily a reflective activity in which the mystery and the power of the quest are subordinated to our demand for absolute comprehension. As a result, the earlier opposition between experience and reflection is replaced by the conviction that reflection can comprehend experience with perfect adequacy and that the quest for wholeness can be brought to completion at the distinctively reflective level. While the first approach to the problem bifurcates the relationship between action and discourse, the second approach understands the task of reflection to be the reconciliation of this opposition within the context of reflection itself. However, we shall also discover that the reflective demand for complete comprehension is just as mistaken as the suggestion that the conflict between experience and reflection can never be mediated. Wholeness is not to be equated with completeness, and fragmentation is not a problem that can be dealt with at the exclusively reflective level. Human wholeness is finite, and it is finite precisely because it is human. But finitude must not be confused with fragmentation, and the finite character that wholeness exhibits should not force us to transform the quest for wholeness into a quest for complete comprehension. Our reflective task is not to develop a comprehensive system, but to find the midpoint between fragmentation and completeness and to articulate a conception of wholeness that is an intelligible response to the human predicament. What is needed is a way of thinking that acknowledges the integrity of the quest for wholeness within direct experience; that understands the need for a description of it within the context of reflective discourse; and that attempts to connect the two levels without subordinating experience to reflection, and without holding these two dimensions apart in absolute opposition.

In the following pages, I have attempted to develop a way of thinking that fulfills these conditions and that avoids the defects of an exclusive reliance upon either experience or reflection. The chapters of this book are to be understood as *images* of the quest for wholeness, and they are to be related to it as a series of *abstracts*, rather than as a sequence of *abstractions* that fail to capture the richness of the human journey. As a result, the chapters stand in between direct experience and abstract reflection, pointing to a middle ground from which the quest can be depicted in a concrete fashion. There can be little doubt that the quest for wholeness exists independently of our attempts to speak about it and that the primary task of reflection is to depict what actually occurs within direct experience. And it can scarcely be denied that the independent existence of the journey prevents us from giving an a priori account of its nature that circumscribes it within the confines of a completed philosophical system. However, this does not imply that reflection must become a merely abstract, structural account of what exists concretely only in actual human situations. An *abstract* of the quest for wholeness is a *concrete image* of it *from a certain point of view,* and it brings us into linguistic contact with the quest as it unfolds within direct experience. These concrete images reflect the general features that the quest for wholeness exhibits, but they also depict the individuality of those who undertake it, the communities in which it occurs, the human drama in which it is expressed, and the ultimate dimension of experience toward which the quest itself is often directed. In doing so, they make concrete reflection possible by interjecting the living character of the human journey into our attempts to speak about it. As I have suggested already, the quest for wholeness occurs in a three-dimensional space, and it involves a bi-directional development. In this same way, the following chapters are spaces in their own right, standing in between experience and reflection and attempting to reflect the power, the depth, and the intelligible structure that the quest for wholeness always exhibits. In each case they avoid the defects of abstraction and make it possible for us to forego the choice between the richness of direct experience and the lifelessness of a merely abstract account of the human journey.

The fact that the chapters of this book depict the quest for wholeness from different points of view also enables us to reject the demand for philosophical completeness and to resist the consequent transformation of the quest into a merely reflective phenomenon. The following chapters can never be welded together in an overarching system, for the points of view represented by them are *holistic versions* of the entire phenomenon in question, rather than *parts* to be included in a larger whole. As a perspective on the quest for wholeness taken as a whole, each chapter is a complex "system" in its own right, and it is the systematic character of each of them that prevents it from being included with others as a part within a more inclusive totality. In this respect, my project is more Leibnizian than Hegelian, for I agree with Leibniz that the perspectival character of discourse prevents us from constructing a system that can transcend the point of view from which it is articulated.[7] I am also convinced that there is no a priori limit to the number of different perspectives from which the world can be depicted and that experience has a depth and a richness that articulation can never exhaust.[8] The holistic character of each perspective and the fact that there is a potentially infinite number of points of view from which the quest can be described are dual reflections of the infinite richness of the phenomenon before us. Taken together, these considerations should prevent us from trying to encapsulate the quest for wholeness in a completed system. On the other hand, even though the following chapters are unique and irreducible perspectives on an inexhaustible phenomenon, they also form a *community* of images, giving us a plurality of interconnected approaches to the issues in question, and pointing in different ways to the ultimate dimension of experience that the quest for wholeness presupposes. The individual chapters are *spaces* in which the quest for wholeness unfolds, but the book as a whole is a *world of different spaces,* held together as a community of images. It is this unbounded, but unified totality that will be elaborated in the following pages.

In Chapter 1, we shall begin our detailed analysis by focusing on Melville's *Moby-Dick.* Melville's novel is an appropriate place to begin, for it mobilizes our natural sense of adventure and gives us access to the quest for wholeness by telling a story in which we can all participate. Works of art often open up a richly textured world, and when they depict the human journey in dramatic terms, they allow us to move through them in our own attempt to find fulfillment. In generating a human space in which the quest for wholeness unfolds, Melville's novel is an image of the natural development of the human spirit, beginning with fragmentation and pointing to some of the ways in which fragmentation can be overcome in the whaling venture it invites us to enter. Melville's story allows the reader to participate in the outward thrust of the human journey and to understand the wholeness that participation in a larger community often makes accessible. By contrast with this initial discussion, Chapter 2 reverses the direction of the outward journey and brings us into a positive relationship with the origins from which the quest for wholeness begins. The Biblical stories to be discussed in this chapter move us backward into a mysterious and originative past and make it possible for us to confront a real ground with which we stand in irreducible contrast. If Melville's novel opens us up to the quest for wholeness as it unfolds within the natural order, the Biblical context brings us face to face with God as the sustaining ground of human existence. In doing so, it points to the radical otherness of God, to the need to stand before him as an irreducible individual, and to the quest for wholeness as a quest for individuation. Chapter 1 traces the quest for wholeness as a natural expression of the human spirit, while Chapter 2 focuses on the emergence of particular individuals and upon their attempts to find a new kind of wholeness in response to the sustaining ground of their existence.

In the third chapter, we shall turn our attention to one of Plato's early dialogues in which the two directionalities present in the previous chapters are brought together in a common context of reflection. In a particularly vivid confrontation between Euthyphro and Socrates about the nature of piety, Plato transforms the religious quest for wholeness into the philosophical attempt to understand the Whole, while he transforms the religious response to one's origins into the theological attempt to give a reflective account of the ground of human existence. As a result, Plato's *Euthyphro* moves us beyond the context of human action into a reflective framework where the quest for wholeness can be the subject of theoretical inquiry, and where the two directionalities it exhibits can come together in a dialogue reflecting both perspectives. In the course of the dialogue, Plato transforms the religious quest for wholeness into the reflective attempt to answer the question, "What does it mean to be whole?" Yet he does so without losing touch with the concrete situations in which the problem of fragmentation arises and with reference to which the quest unfolds as a human undertaking. In Plato's hands, wholeness is not to be found in the theoretical resolution of philosophical problems, but at the point where the characters of a dialogue meet and in the dialogic interaction among alternative philosophical perspectives. It is this fact that will enable us to use the dialogue as a medium for concrete reflection and as a meeting point for conflicts that abstract reflection can never resolve.

Finally, in Chapter 4 we must confront the claims of Hegel about the quest for wholeness and must evaluate his attempt to bring the quest for wholeness to completion. Hegel claims that the two directionalities we have distinguished need not remain in conflict and that the Ground and the Whole to which they call our attention can be held together in a single system. In fact, he insists that concrete reflection is possible only in the form of a completed system and that the opposition between the two directionalities present in the dialogue can be overcome by giving them both a place within a systematic framework. The final chapter will conclude with a detailed examination of this view, for it is in this Hegelian setting that the relationship between origins and the larger world becomes most problematic and where the most careful distinctions must be drawn between the fragmentation we experience, the wholeness we seek, and the completeness we are tempted to embrace. As I have suggested already, I intend to defend the view that wholeness can be found and articulated, but I am also committed to the thesis that it cannot be bounded by a completed system. As a result, the progression of the following chapters from story-telling to reflective discourse, and from art and religion to philosophy must not be understood as a process culminating in an all-embracing Absolute. Instead, it is a journey through a series of worlds, each of which has its own integrity and within which wholeness can be found in a sequence of concrete reflections.

In his seventh letter, Plato speaks about the conditions that must be fulfilled if the philosopher is to succeed in understanding the phenomena with which he is confronted. He says that we must first name our subject-matter, then describe it, then provide an image of it, and finally give a philosophical account of its intelligible structure.[9] In this book, the subject-matter is the quest for wholeness, the description of which has occupied us already and will continue to do so throughout the entire discussion. The following chapters are living images of the journey and will allow it to unfold of itself and in a richly human fashion, while the conceptual elements that will be interwoven in this account will enable us to grasp the intelligible dimension that the quest for wholeness always exhibits. The openness of art and the otherness of religion must be conjoined with the intelligibility of philosophy if we are to give an adequate account of the human quest for fulfillment. However, what is most important is that we do what we say, and that we actually engage in the task of concrete reflection. The following pages are not merely illustrations of a philosophical point of view that has been worked out in advance and is simply being made accessible through the verbal trappings of a novel or through the pronouncements of religion and of earlier philosophers. Quite to the contrary, they are a quest for wholeness in their own right, undertaken at the level of concrete reflection. Of course, this means that the center of the book is to be found in the chapters themselves, where Ahab, Queequeg, and Ishmael; Abraham and Moses; Euthyphro, Socrates, and Hegel come to life and help to generate worlds of their own that we can never fully control. It is around these living images that I have spun my system, and it is to these worlds that my concrete reflections are intended to call us back.

1

Fragmentation and the Quest for Fulfillment

Melville's classic account of the quest for the white whale can be interpreted from a variety of perspectives. At the most immediate level, it is a work of art that addresses the human spirit in a natural, prephilosophical fashion, giving us access to a prereflective world that has not been torn apart by merely structural reflection. There can be little doubt that Melville intends for his readers to become self-conscious, for the narrator of the novel is a teacher, who attempts to convey the significance of the story he tells in a discursive and reflective fashion (p. 14).[1] However, before he teaches us anything, Melville first attempts to make us conscious of the richly textured world of our imagination and of the excitement and the dangers to be experienced when we undertake a whaling venture in the ocean that surrounds us. Melville's novel speaks to the inherent restlessness of the human spirit, and it points to our hidden wish to make contact with the mystery of nature and with the awesome power that the natural order often exhibits. Melville captures our attention by inviting us to enter an aesthetic world in which the majesty and the grandeur of nature stand in radical contrast with us, and by asking us to participate in the mystery and the power of the larger world which the ocean voyage he describes will make accessible to us.

As a work of art, Melville's novel is accessible to us all, just insofar as we are human. The story he tells gives us access to a world of adventure, and it allows us to enter an imaginative framework in which our relationship with nature can come to life in some measure of fullness. However, as the attentive reader soon discovers, the novel is not merely a story about a whale and the ocean and about the fascination that an ocean venture can provoke at the level of aesthetic immediacy. From a more fundamental perspective, it is an account of the human quest for wholeness and of the stages through which the human being must develop as he seeks fulfillment in the larger world. Having given us access to nature because it addresses us in a natural and easily accessible form, the novel asks us to undertake an ocean voyage in which the ultimate dimension of experience is expressed in religious symbols, and it invites us to make the reflective responses which the quest for wholeness always requires. Melville recognizes that the telling of stories stands at the beginning of the quest for wholeness, and he suggests that reflection stands at the end as an irreducible component. But through the careful use of classical and Biblical allusions, his story comes to focus on religion as a symbolic expression of the human longing for fulfillment. In doing so, it holds the artistic, the religious, and the philosophical dimensions of experience together in a focused unity, demanding that the reader take up the task of reflection in a world saturated already by expressive and reflective discourse.

If we are to respond to Melville's intentions, and to the quest for wholeness which he makes accessible, we must plunge into the novel as active participants, not only embracing it as a story of adventure, but also attempting to understand it as a mediated context in which the most fundamental aspects of the human journey are expressed and represented. In Melville's hands, art, religion, and philosophy interplay with one another, and in the final analysis it is this fact which allows the story he tells to be a "world" in the richest possible sense. In approaching Melville's novel, we must not vacillate between immediacy and mediation, for the novel itself is an indissoluble unity that cannot be split apart into its constituent elements. If we are to be adequate to all of its dimensions, we must engage in concrete reflection, making explicit the religious and the philosophical elements contained in it, but also re-embedding these dimensions of the story within the aesthetic framework that the story itself provides. Only in this way can we avoid an unacceptable bifurcation between story-telling and reflective discourse, and only in this fashion can the richness of Melville's account of the quest for wholeness be made accessible to the reflective consciousness. As I have suggested already, concrete reflection is a reflection of the concrete richness of the worlds in which it occurs, and it is to be distinguished from the kind of thinking that destroys its subject-matter through the power of abstraction. It is to this first kind of reflection, which lies beyond abstraction and which attempts to mirror the synthetic unity of its content, that we are committed in the following pages.

Origins

The first step in making explicit what might otherwise remain hidden in Melville's story is easily accomplished: the one who is to be the narrator of the drama, and who also appears as a central participant in it, identifies himself in the sentence, "Call me Ishmael" (p. 12). We are of course expected to understand the implicit reference to Ishmael, the son of Abraham — the child who was banished from his father's house to roam in the desert soon after Isaac was born.[2] In the Biblical account of Ishmael's origins, we are told that his father had been promised a son,[3] and that this child was to become the first member in a chain of descendants through whom the entire world would be blessed.[4] But as the years passed, and the promised child failed to appear, Abraham became impatient, and he finally turned in desperation to the handmaiden his wife had given him. It was through this union that Ishmael was conceived.[5] When Ishmael was still a child, Abraham prayed on his behalf, asking that he might become the child who had been promised.[6] Abraham was convinced that his wife would never be able to bear him a son, and he wanted his own offspring to become his chosen descendant. However, the prayer was not answered in a positive way. Instead, a son was finally born to Abraham and his wife, Sarah; and because of the virtually inevitable conflict between Sarah and her handmaiden, there was soon no room for both descendants in the household. Abraham's wife insisted that Isaac was the child who had been promised, and she demanded that Ishmael and his mother be banished from the family.[7] Because his father listened to these demands and because God himself agreed with them, Isaac, the son of Sarah, became Abraham's chosen descendant; while Ishmael, the firstborn, was compelled to wander in the desert, separated from the tribal unity that gave meaning to his life.[8]

In the ancient world and in the Biblical story to which Melville's opening sentence calls our attention, an individual was defined in terms of the role he played within the larger family context. In this context, the family and its continued existence were more fundamental than the existence of a family member, and the independence of the individual was always subordinated to the higher demands of tribal unity. This is at least one of the reasons that Abraham wanted a child, for he believed that unless he became a father, he would not be fully human. Abraham was convinced that he could fulfill his destiny and that he could preserve the unity of his family only by having children who could carry forward the family tradition. Abraham's conception of wholeness was defined by his genetic relation to his ancestors and his progeny, and it was for this reason that he was committed so strongly to the continuation of his tribal heritage. For Abraham, to be human was to have a place within a family, and to be whole was to be a part of this larger human world. However, after the birth of Isaac, a crisis arose within the family which forced Abraham to make a choice. Abraham was compelled to choose between the unity of his family and the life of Ishmael, and it was this anguished choice that separated Ishmael from his origins and cut him off from the ground of his existence. From his tribalistic perspective, the continued existence of Abraham's family as a coherent unit required that one of its branches be cut away. In this case, tribal unity demanded that Ishmael be detached from his family and be forced to wander in the desert, separated from the unity he had once enjoyed.

The relationship between the Biblical Ishmael and the Ishmael of Melville's novel is too subtle to be examined in a merely cursory fashion, and a discussion of it will be necessary at various stages in our treatment of Melville's larger intentions. At this point, however, we should notice that the implied reference to the wanderings of the Biblical Ishmael suggests that the Ishmael of the novel is also a wanderer. In fact, having identified himself, Melville's Ishmael makes his status as a wanderer explicit at the beginning of his narrative:

> Some years ago — never mind how long precisely — having little or no money in my purse, and nothing particular to interest me on shore, I thought I would sail about a little and see the water part of the world. [p. 12]

The trip, he says, "is a way I have of driving off the spleen and regulating the circulation" (p. 12). But then Ishmael continues, perhaps a bit more ontologically, in a fashion that reflects his eternal condition as a wanderer:

> Whenever I find myself growing grim about the mouth; whenever it is a damp, drizzly November in my soul; whenever I find myself involuntarily pausing before coffin warehouses, and bringing up the rear of every funeral I meet; and especially whenever my hypos get such an upper hand of me, that it requires a strong moral principle to prevent me from deliber-

ately stepping into the street, and methodically knocking people's hats off — then I account it high time to get to sea as soon as I can. [p. 12]

Ishmael concludes that there is nothing surprising in this wish to turn toward the sea. He says that if we but knew it, "almost all men cherish very nearly the same feelings toward the ocean with me" (p. 12).

In giving us his reasons for turning toward the ocean, Ishmael points to the particularity of his condition. He says that he has decided to undertake an ocean voyage in order to drive off the spleen, to regulate the circulation, and to escape from the boredom and the poverty of life on shore. However, he also speaks of his hypochondria, and he calls our attention to the "damp, drizzly November in his soul." Apparently, the illness with which he is afflicted is not merely one among many; it does not pertain simply to an aspect of his existence, nor is it subject to precise and determinate treatment. Ishmael's original condition exhibits a dimension of depth which points beyond his finitude, and its negative character drives him outward toward the larger world in which his quest for wholeness can develop. Of course, at this point we must not overlook a crucial distinction between the Ishmael of Melville's novel and the child of Abraham. In the Biblical account, Ishmael was not responsible for his fate and was thrust out into the desert through the choice of his father. By contrast, Melville's Ishmael chooses to respond to his hypochondria by undertaking a journey of his own, not across an "ocean" of sand, but through a less resistant "sea" of water. However, even in the novel, the alienation Ishmael experiences reaches down into the depths of his existence, and his hypochondria suggests that he will not be able to satisfy his longing for unity by finding a finite resting place. If Melville's Ishmael is to have a family, it must be absolutely universal, for a context less universal than mankind as a whole will not be sufficiently rich to overcome the fragmentation of his original condition. It is no accident that he tells us nothing about his immediate family but tells us instead about his longing for fulfillment in the larger human world. Ishmael's initial responses to his negative condition point beyond themselves to the ultimate dimension of human existence, thrusting him outward toward a larger community that can bring wholeness to the human soul.

In this description of his initial condition, Ishmael does not confine his attention to the special character of his individual situation. The

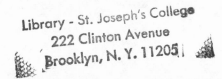

pervasive nature of his illness, and the dimension of depth it exhibits, permit him to implicate his readers in his journey. In fact, he suggests that the quest to which he is committed exhibits a universal range of reference, and that in this respect, he represents us all. For example, he tells us that on Manhattan Island, we find that right and left, the streets take us toward the water. On the shore, we see the waves "which a few hours previous were out of sight of land" (p. 12). He invites us to look at the crowds of water-gazers there. They are "posted like silent sentinels all around the town,...thousands upon thousands of mortal men fixed in ocean reveries" (p. 12). In every case, their gaze is directed beyond their immediate situation toward the boundlessness of the ocean that stretches out before them. But Ishmael is not content to describe the water-gazers in merely static terms. Some of the participants in the sketch he draws not only look at the water; they strain toward it. And he indicates that nothing will content them but the extremest limits of the land:

> Loitering under the shady lee of yonder warehouses will not suffice. No. They must get just as nigh the water as they can without falling in.

> Inlanders all, they come from lanes and alleys, streets and avenues — north, east, south, and west. Yet here they all unite. [p. 13]

Since the inlanders converge at the water, it might seem appropriate that we focus our attention on the ocean itself and that an account be given of this larger context to which the crowd of water-gazers seeks to respond. Yet as ultimate and unlimited, and as a symbol for the eternal dimension of experience in the midst of time, we should scarcely expect a bold, direct, unmediated description of its nature. Instead, Ishmael describes what the water has meant to a variety of those who have sought to confront its mysteries. First, an ironic reference to metaphysics:

> Say, you are in the country;...let the most absent-minded of men be plunged in his deepest reveries — stand that man on his legs, set his feet a-going, and he will infallibly lead you to water, if water there be in all that region. Should you ever be athirst in the great American desert, try this experiment, if your caravan happen to be supplied with a metaphysical professor. Yes, as everyone knows, meditation and water are wedded forever. [p. 13]

Somewhat higher on the chain of being stands the artist, and Ishmael points to his commitment to the water by describing a particular example of his work:

He desires to paint you the dreamiest, shadiest, quietest, most enchanting landscape in all the valley of the Saco. What is the chief element he employs? There stand his trees, each with a hollow trunk, as if a hermit and a crucifix were within; and here sleeps his meadow, and there sleep his cattle; and up from yonder cottage goes a sleepy smoke. Deep into the distant woodlands winds a mazy way, reaching to overlapping spurs of mountains bathed in their hill-side blue. But though the picture lies thus tranced, and though this pine-tree shakes down its sighs like leaves upon the shepherd's head, yet all were vain, unless the shepherd's eye were fixed upon the magic stream before him. [p. 13]

Ishmael then refers to the poet, who is often drawn to the sea, and he asks whether upon our own first voyage as a passenger we did not feel, along with the poet, "a mystical vibration, when first told that you and your ship were now out of sight of land" (p. 13). It is this mystical vibration that opens us up to a world of adventure and that gives us access to the journey Ishmael intends to describe. Finally, however, Ishmael focuses on the ocean more directly, asking the questions that lead to the heart of our inquiry:

Why did the old Persians hold the sea holy? Why did the Greeks give it a separate deity, and make him the own brother of Jove? Surely all this is not without meaning. And still deeper the meaning of that story of Narcissus, who because he could not grasp the tormenting, mild image he saw in the fountain, plunged into it and was drowned. But that same image we ourselves see in all rivers and oceans. It is the image of the ungraspable phantom of life; and this is the key to it all. [p. 14]

The sea becomes the mirror in which Ishmael finds the depths of his existence reflected. The problem of self-discovery to which his reference to Narcissus calls our attention defines the nature of his quest: Ishmael undertakes the quest for wholeness in order to come to terms with his hypochondria and to replace the fragmentation implicit in his initial situation with the stability that often results from self-discovery. However, Ishmael knows that the boundlessness of the ocean to which he turns for fulfillment is reflected in the ungraspable mystery of the person, and he understands that this mysterious dimension can never be fully articulated. In fact, he suggests that the poet, the artist, and the metaphysician, in descending order of richness, all seek to articulate a common mystery. They all attempt to focus our attention upon the ungraspable phantom of life in its relation to the ocean that surrounds us. Yet Ishmael also knows that if he is to respond to the lure of the ocean and to the depths of his own existence, he must not remain a mere observer. An adequate response to human fragmentation and to the longing for wholeness it generates demands active participation. As a result, Ishmael contrasts himself with idle passengers, and with the officials of the typical American sailing ship — on the one hand unengaged, on the other far too occupied with tasks on board. Differing from them, he goes to sea as an ordinary sailor, "right before the mast, plumb down into the forecastle, aloft there to the royal masthead" (p. 14). Of course, Ishmael's willingness to become a deck hand on an ocean vessel does not imply that he is not resentful of his superiors, and in this respect, his irony is biting: "What of it," he asks,

> if some old hunks of a sea-captain orders me to get a broom and sweep down the decks. What does that indignity amount to, weighed, I mean, in the scales of the New Testament? [p. 15]

Or he asserts:

> True, they rather order me about...and make me jump from spar to spar, like a grasshopper in a May meadow. And at first this sort of thing is unpleasant enough. It touches one's sense of honor, particularly if you come from an old established family in the land, the Van Rensselaers, or Randolphs, or Hardicanutes. [p. 14]

Of course, the Ishmael of the novel does not trace his ancestry back to the children of Abraham. However, even if he had insisted on the dignity of his origins, it is unlikely that he would have demanded a radical change in his station. "It is quite as much as I can do," he says, "to take care of myself, without taking care of ships, barques, briggs, schooners, and what not" (p. 14). Apparently, Ishmael's active relation to the ocean continues to be the focus of his concern.

In spite of its intrinsic indeterminacy, Ishmael knows that the journey to which he is committed must be articulated more explicitly. Otherwise, the mystery of the ocean would engulf him, and he would be unable to transform it into a framework in which the quest for wholeness can unfold in an intelligible fashion. The quest cannot take place within the ocean as a whole unless it also comes to rest upon a specific object in terms of which its goal can be defined. As a result, Ishmael is careful to indicate that he has determinate intentions and that it is a whaling venture in which he is soon to become engaged. Yet even here he insists that the quest always involves an interplay between mystery and determination and that the whale himself is the intersection of these two dimensions. In his description of him, Ishmael points to both dimensions simultaneously:

> Such a portentous and mysterious monster roused all my curiosity.... The wild and distant seas where he rolled his island bulk; the undeliverable, nameless perils of the whale; these, with all the attending marvels of a thousand Patagonian sights and sounds, helped to sway me to my wish. [p. 16]

Nevertheless, Ishmael also makes it clear that Moby Dick is to be the focus of his journey:

> The flood-gates of the wonder-world swung open, and in the wild conceits that swayed me to my purpose, two and two there floated into my inmost soul, endless processions of the whale, and, midmost of them all, one grand hooded phantom, like a snow hill in the air. [p. 16]

The quest for the white whale is the guiding theme of Melville's novel, and I shall return to this theme presently. At this point, however, it might be instructive to describe the quest for wholeness in more explicitly philosophical terms and to indicate some of the ways in which Melville's account of Ishmael's situation illustrates these general features. As I have suggested already, the quest is developmental in structure and begins with the fragmentation which often characterizes the human condition. In fact, it is the individual's recognition of his original alienation from what is ultimate that prompts him to undertake the quest for fulfillment. However, it is also important to notice that the quest can begin *anywhere*; that it must begin *somewhere in particular*; and that it always begins *nowhere*. Formulated in somewhat different terms, the quest is a temporal process that is *universal* because it can begin with anyone; *particular* because it must begin with the one who actually undertakes it; and *ultimate* because it always makes reference to a point beyond the temporal dimension. This reference to what transcends the human realm makes it possible for the alienated individual to participate from the outset in the ultimate dimension of human existence. As Melville's novel suggests, the quest for wholeness does not begin in a merely negative fashion, but as a blending of three positive dimensions, and in Ishmael's case, the universal call of the ocean, the particularity of his original condition, and the virtual boundlessness of the sea serve to illustrate these three conditions. Taken together, these elements constitute the human "world" to which Ishmael commits himself and within which he attempts to bring his quest to progressive fulfillment.

The universality with which the quest begins suggests that anyone can become engaged in the attempt to transform his alienated condition into a positive form. This aspect of the journey points to our universal desire for wholeness and to our wish to participate more fully in the positive dimensions of experience which human wholeness makes accessible. In addition, this dimension of the quest often leads to a collective participation in what is ultimate, allowing it to unfold within a larger community of participants. This will certainly be the case with Ishmael, for he shares his life with other individuals who undertake the whaling venture with him and upon whom the success of his journey will ultimately depend. However, the presence of this larger community does not obliterate the fact that an individual's own particularity must be taken into account in the attempt to understand the quest in developmental terms. What is unique about an individual qualifies his participation in the ultimate dimension of experience, and it is his uniqueness that must be developed if the individual is to be given access to the meaning of his own existence. Ishmael is merely one among many of those who are fascinated by the ocean, and a number of them set out for the water's edge as though they intend to undertake the journey with him. However, Ishmael emerges from the group in the full measure of his own particularity. Though the quest may begin anywhere, it begins, in fact, with him. Ishmael goes on board the ship; he moves out into the ocean; and he attempts to transcend his original condition. From the crowd of water-gazers clustered at the ocean's edge, Ishmael alone chooses to act decisively. Only after the voyage has been undertaken does a larger community begin to develop, and even then, Ishmael remains detached to some degree, affirming the integrity of his own existence. If we ask why he responds in this fashion, it is only possible to say that he recognizes his participation in the positive aspects of experience that constitute the "structure" of the quest for wholeness. The fact that the quest can begin anywhere makes participation *possible*; that it must begin somewhere makes it relevant to our *particular condition*; and because it always begins nowhere, we are given an initial access to *eternity*. Fragmentation is related to a plurality of positive dimensions, and if we share Ishmael's journey, they will serve as a framework in which our own quest for wholeness can be fulfilled.

Perhaps the indispensable role of all the elements reflected in our analysis can be expressed more concretely if we compare Ishmael's response to his condition with other responses which also are possible. These alternative responses are defective because they fail to acknowledge the importance of one or more of the elements which constitute the "structure" of the quest for wholeness. At the beginning of his narrative, Ishmael mentions Narcissus, the legendary character who plunged into the water and was drowned in the attempt to grasp his own essence (p. 14). Narcissus was unwilling to understand the relationship between himself and "the ungraspable phantom of life" in gradualistic terms and sought to bring that relationship to immediate closure, thus annihilating himself. In this case, the fulfillment of the self was rendered impossible because Narcissus ignored the indispensable role to be played by his own particularity. The temptation to which Narcissus succumbed is an ever-present possibility. In the middle stages of the story, Ishmael warns us that a sailor at the top of the masthead who looks out across the water might easily topple into the sea:

> There is no life in thee now, except that rocking life imparted by a gently rolling ship; by her, borrowed from the sea; by the sea, from the inscrutable tides of God. But while this sleep, this dream is on ye, move your foot or hand an inch; slip your hold at all; and your identity comes back in horror. Over Descartian vortices you hover. And perhaps, at midday, in the fairest weather, with one half-throttled shriek you drop through that transparent air into the summer sea, no more to rise forever. Heed it well, ye Pantheists! [p. 140]

Ishmael also mentions Cato, who threw himself upon his sword in response to his sickness and in response to the pervasive illness of his culture (p. 12). Unlike the case of Narcissus, Cato's action was a matter of deliberate choice, resulting from self-hatred rather than self-love. He chose to resolve the problem of man's relationship to what is ultimate by canceling one of its terms. Ishmael contrasts his own intention to undertake an ocean voyage with both of these attempted resolutions. Unlike Cato and Narcissus, he undertakes the much more precarious task of transforming his own particularity into a quest for progressive fulfillment.

Prior to the voyage which Ishmael undertakes, it was necessary for him to find a ship and to offer himself as a member of the crew. A few days before, Ishmael had met Queequeg, a savage covered with tattoos. Queequeg had decided to go with him on the journey but was on the surface scarcely acceptable to the owners of a whaling ship. The owners of the ship in fact responded with great reluctance to the prospect of accepting Queequeg as a member of the crew (pp. 82–83). In this way, they sought to restrict the range of those who were to set out together on the whaling venture. Only when Queequeg demonstrated his competence with the harpoon did they agree to hire him (p. 84). Had they refused to do so, they would have lost a man who became one of the harpooners in the quest for Moby Dick. Ishmael would also have not survived the chase, for at the end of the voyage, he is saved from destruction by clinging to a coffin which the ship's carpenter made for Queequeg during the course of the journey (pp. 396–397, 470).

Finally, we should consider the character of Ahab, the most dramatic example in the novel of one who fails to acknowledge the indispensable role to be played by all the elements reflected in our analysis. Ahab recognized his lack of wholeness. It was symbolized by the fact that he had lost his leg in an earlier encounter with Moby Dick (pp. 77, 159–160). Ahab also recognized the part to be played on the voyage by a rich variety of men. He not only welcomed the participation of a cannibal, but also smuggled onto the ship his own harpooner — one far darker and more mysterious than Queequeg (pp. 91–92, 187). However, Ahab's own response to the voyage did not consist in a progressive quest for self-discovery. Instead, he attempted to annihilate what he took to be the source of his malady. As he cried at one dramatic moment on deck, "Death to Moby Dick" (p. 146). Cato and Narcissus responded to the problem of fragmentation through self-destruction, while Ahab responds by attempting to destroy the symbol of the eternal dimension of his own existence. Both attempts are inadequate, for they finally result in the destruction of the individual to whom the riddle of life is addressed.

The Power of Negativity

At the inception of a quest for wholeness, the lure of the goal, the particularity of the participants, and the universal call of the ultimate dimension of experience are present as equally fundamental. These irreducible elements are the necessary conditions that make the quest for wholeness possible and that allow it to unfold in an intelligible fashion. However, as the individual attempts to respond to what is ultimate, he often discovers that his own particularity is not always a positive aspect of his development. The characteristics that distinguish one individual from another often set him in radical contrast with others, and they sometimes serve to accentuate the fragmentation that compels him to undertake the quest for fulfillment. The individual who shares Ishmael's journey soon discovers that his own self-development will always remain incomplete. The journey he undertakes is directed toward a goal that is extraordinarily elusive, and it occurs within a context whose infinite dimensions he cannot fully appreciate. In addition, the developing power of the individual, and the incompleteness from which it springs, sometimes bring him face to face with aspects of experience that have a power of their own and that constitute a positive threat to his development. In many cases these external elements merely reflect the alienation with which the quest for wholeness begins, but they often do so in an accentuated form and in a fashion that disrupts the progress of the one who undertakes it. In fact, in the present context, the disruptive character of these negative elements can be illustrated in a striking fashion in terms of Ishmael's own self-development.

Ishmael's initial description of his decision to set out on an ocean voyage contains only the slightest hint of negativity: it is merely present indirectly in his ironical reference to his own hypochondria and in his strictures against the passengers and the officials of the typical American sailing ship. However, the presence of radical discontinuity is revealed more clearly when Ishmael begins to make active preparations for the journey. He first leaves Manhattan for New Bedford, planning to sail from there to Nantucket in order to finally board a whaling ship. Yet when he arrives in New Bedford, he discovers that the ship on which he had planned to book passage has already sailed and that he must wait three days before he can hope to arrive at the port from which the sailing venture can be undertaken (p. 17). Such a slight delay might seem negligible, but it is the first direct suggestion of a pervasive negativity that threatens to impede the progress of Ishmael's journey. The voyage Ishmael undertakes is intended to liberate him from illness, but his circumstances in New Bedford require that he wait three days for the beginning of this process of redemption.

Ishmael encounters further resistance in New Bedford when he searches for a place to spend the night: "I now by instinct followed the streets that took me waterward, for there, doubtless, were the cheapest, if not the cheeriest inns" (p. 18). But then he exclaims:

Such dreary streets! Blocks of blackness, not houses, on either hand, and here and there a candle, like a candle moving about in a tomb. At this hour of the night, of the last day of the week, that quarter of the town proved all but deserted. [p. 18]

Earlier, Ishmael had been drawn toward the water as a context in which his quest could be fulfilled. Now he turns toward it to find a lodging place, but encounters blackness at the water's edge. At this stage of his journey Ishmael finds that the water is not a place to live, but a medium through which he is required to move. If he is to overcome his illness, he cannot remain in the tomb on this last day of the week, but must endure the power of negation in order to be resurrected through a process of positive development. The quest for wholeness not only presupposes the demand for fulfillment, but also occurs against the background of radical opposition. Moreover, this negative moment must be confronted directly as the journey unfolds.

The image of negation is sustained when Ishmael stumbles by mistake into a Negro church. First, he overturns a pot of ashes set inside the door. Then he notices "a hundred black faces turned round in their rows to peer" (p. 18). Beyond, he sees "a black Angel of Doom... beating a book in a pulpit" (p. 18). Finally, he tells us that the preacher's text is about the blackness of darkness, and the weeping and wailing and teeth-gnashing there. In his attempt to evade these images of blackness, Ishmael rushes quickly from the church and makes his way to the place where he will eventually find lodging. However, the sign over the door of the establishment disturbs him: it reads, "The Spouter Inn — Peter Coffin." The suggestion of a negative dimension, now all too obvious, is of course not lost on Ishmael. He mutters to himself, "Coffin? — Spouter?" "— Rather ominous in that particular connection, thought I" (p. 18). Nevertheless, Ishmael crosses the threshold of the door and asks the proprietor for a place to spend the night. Apparently, he intends to continue with his active preparations for the journey, even in the face of opposition. At first, the innkeeper tells him that all the rooms are taken, but somewhat later he says that a place is available if he will share a room with another (p. 22). The owner knows that one of the rooms has been rented to Queequeg, the cannibal, and seeing the possibility of a joke at Ishmael's expense, he of course has Queequeg's room in mind.

Ishmael gives us a detailed description of his initial glimpse of Queequeg: "I was all eagerness," says Ishmael, "to see his face, but he kept it averted for some time...." Finally, however,

> he turned round — when, good heavens! What a sight! Such a face! It was a dark, purplish, yellow color, here and there stuck over with large, blackish looking squares. Yes, it's just as I thought, he's a terrible bedfellow; he's been in a fight, got dreadfully cut, and here he is, just from the

surgeon. But at that moment he chanced to turn his head so towards the light, that I plainly saw that they could not be sticking plasters at all, those squares on his cheeks. They were stains of some sort or other. At first I knew not what to make of this; but soon an inkling of the truth occurred to me. I remembered a story of a white man — a whaleman too — who, falling among the cannibals, had been tattooed by them. I concluded that this harpooner, in the course of his distant voyages, must have met with a similar adventure. And what is it, thought I after all! It's only his outside; a man can be honest under any sort of skin. But then, what to make of his unearthly complexion, that part of it, I mean, lying about, and completely independent of the squares of tattooing. To be sure, it might be nothing but a good coat of tropical tanning; but I never heard of a hot sun's tanning a white man into a purplish yellow one. However, I had never been to the South Seas; and perhaps the sun there produced these extraordinary effects upon the skin. Now, while these ideas were passing through me like lightning, this harpooner never noticed me at all. But, after some difficulty having opened his bag, he commenced fumbling in it, and presently pulled out a sort of tomahawk, and a seal-skin wallet with the hair on. Placing these on the old chest in the middle of the room, he then took the New Zealand head — a ghastly thing enough — and crammed it down into the bag. He now took off his hat — a new beaver hat — when I came nigh to singing out with fresh surprise. There was no hair on his head — none to speak of at least — nothing but a small scalp-knot twisted up on his forehead. His bald purplish head looked for all the world like a mildewed skull. Had not the stranger stood between me and the door, I would have bolted out of it quicker than I ever bolted a dinner. [pp. 28–29]

In his initial responses to Queequeg, Ishmael attempts to interpret his strangeness in familiar terms: "Perhaps this harpooner was captured by cannibals and tattooed by them as was the case with another sailor I had once heard about." "Perhaps the sun of the South Seas tanned his skin a purplish hue." "Despite outward appearances, it's the inside of a man that counts. He could be honest underneath." However, these initial interpretations are scarcely sufficient to mediate the strangeness of Queequeg; and when he reaches for his tomahawk, takes off his hat, and stuffs a shrunken head into his pouch, Ishmael almost bolts for the door. Though he has finally found a place to spend the night, Ishmael is surprised to find that he must share the bed of a cannibal whose radical otherness is not to be transcended by familiar and reassuring interpretations. Queequeg comes from another world, and it is not yet clear that this radically different realm can be incorporated within the life and world of Ishmael. In fact, at every stage of his active preparation for the journey,

Ishmael has encountered blackness, and in each case, blackness has failed to yield to his attempts to comprehend it. It is true that Ishmael's quest begins with what is ultimate and with his own attempts to find fulfillment in the larger world. Yet as his journey unfolds, he discovers that he must confront the power of what stands in contrast with him and that he must accept the fact that he can come to himself only by standing face to face with what is radically distinct from his own nature. Though the ocean beckons to him at the beginning, and though it opens itself up to his attempts to find fulfillment in a whaling venture, the perils of the deep must also be confronted. In Ishmael's case, these perils are represented by the one who sleeps by his side.

At this point in Ishmael's journey, the presence of negativity has been confined to its inception, and only hints have been given to indicate that Ishmael's goal is not to be understood in positive terms alone. However, one of the most striking indications that the goal of the journey also exhibits its own mysterious negativity is to be found in Ishmael's description of one of the sailors he encounters in the Spouter Inn. In describing his companions gathered around the dinner table, Ishmael says that

> one of them held somewhat aloof, and though he seemed desirous not to spoil the hilarity of his shipmates by his own sober face, yet upon the whole he refrained from making as much noise as the rest. This man interested me at once; and since the sea-gods had ordained that he should become my shipmate....I will here venture upon a little description of him. He stood full six feet in height, with noble shoulders, and a chest like a coffer-dam. I have seldom seen such brawn in a man. His face was deeply brown and burnt, making his white teeth dazzling by contrast; while in the deep shadows of his eyes floated some reminiscences that did not seem to give him much joy.... When the revelry of his companions had mounted to its height, this man slipped away unobserved, and I saw no more of him till he became my comrade on the sea. In a few minutes, however, he was missed by his shipmates, and being, it seems, for some reason a huge favorite with them, they raised a cry of "Bulkington! Bulkington! where's Bulkington?" and darted out of the house in pursuit of him. [pp. 23–24]

One might be tempted to conclude that on an earlier voyage Bulkington had become an image of the white whale, and that his shipmates were attracted to him because they found the mysterious dimension of their journey and the mystery of their own nature reflected in his character.

Yet Melville suggests in even more forceful terms that the mystery of the quest for wholeness is not to be restricted to the preliminary stages of the journey. In fact, one of the purposes of the sermon Ishmael hears soon after his initial encounters with Queequeg and Bulkington is to suggest that the mysterious aspects of experience are definitive elements of the goal toward which the quest is directed. The setting in which the sermon is delivered exhibits the power of negativity in terms that are both ultimate and unconditional. On the walls of the chapel, plaques are to be found commemorating sailors who have died in the course of whaling voyages. One reads,

SACRED

To the Memory

OF

JOHN TALBOT

Who, at the age of eighteen, was lost overboard,
Near the Isle of Desolation, off Patagonia,
November 1st, 1836

THIS TABLET

Is erected to his Memory

BY HIS SISTER　　　　　[p. 39]

At the beginning of his journey, Ishmael had longed to see and hear the Patagonian sights and sounds. Now it appears that Patagonia may also be a place of human destruction.

Father Mapple's sermon brings the theme of potential and actual human destruction to focus. For his text, he chooses the story of Jonah, and in the sermon itself, he gives a detailed account of Jonah's refusal to obey the voice of God and of his subsequent encounter with the great fish (p. 45). Of course, the text reflects the interest of the audience in the ocean and in the whaling ventures which make their interest determinate, and for this reason alone, it seems to be related to our central theme. Yet the story of Jonah does not appear to bear any further relation to Ishmael's situation or to the condition of those in the audience whose friends and family had died in the course of their ocean voyages. Those who died, and Ishmael himself, had committed themselves to search for the whale. By contrast, Jonah was attempting to evade a mission for which God had appointed him and had encountered the whale in his abortive attempts to escape. In the first case, the audience is oriented beyond the land, swayed by the wish to sail around the world and to undertake a whaling voyage into distant seas. In the second case, Jonah was satisfied to remain on shore, and finally sailed in the opposite direction from the goal that God had preordained.[9] As a result, we must ask what Jonah has to do with Ishmael, and how his wish to turn away from what is ultimate is related to Ishmael's positive quest for fulfillment.

At the most immediate level, the story suggests that the power of negativity appears in the guise of punishment. Jonah incurs the wrath of God because of his failure to obey the divine command, and when the story is understood in this fashion, Jonah's punishment is rational. It represents a divine response to deliberate human failure, and in these terms, it is perfectly intelligible, by analogy with our experience of duty to a law or to a power higher than ourselves. We might wonder, then, whether this way of understanding Jonah's situation can be extended to the case of Ishmael, and by implication, to the universal human situation. Can the negative dimension to be encountered in the quest for Moby Dick be understood in terms of human failure, or can we perhaps understand it in terms of hybristic elements that sometimes characterize our nature? The story of Jonah seems to suggest this kind of interpretation, and in doing so, it offers the reader the final hope that discord and discontinuity can be understood in rational terms. The story assigns the blame for encountered darkness and discord to the human being, and it presents a model in terms of which the power of negativity can be understood in a positive and intelligible fashion. However, for the careful reader, Father Mapple's response to the story conveys a warning that the negative elements of experience are not to be rationalized so easily. At the conclusion of his sermon, the preacher reminds us that when Jonah repented, God saved him; and he is careful to speak about man's positive relationship with God in customary and traditional terms (p. 51). Yet he also suggests that human goodness is finally of no avail in relation to the divine mystery:

Eternal delight and deliciousness will be his, who coming to lay him down, can say with his final breath — O Father! — chiefly known to me by thy rod — mortal or immortal, here I die. I have striven to be thine, more that to be this world's, or mine own. Yet this is nothing; I leave eternity to thee; for what is man that he should live out the lifetime of his God. [p. 51]

At the conclusion of a story which interprets the negative dimension of experience in moral terms, Father Mapple refers to his own possible mortality. He indicates the nothingness of his attempts to measure up to the standard that God lays down, and he points to the abysmal mystery of God, stretching out beyond the life of any man. We must surely conclude that if the power of negativity is to be made intelligible in the case of Jonah, the mysterious darkness of the divine abyss remains present nonetheless.

Having listened to the warning implicit in the sermon, Ishmael finally goes on board the *Pequod* with a group of men who will become his companions in the quest for Moby Dick. In this way, the universal call of the ocean contracts into a microcosm, and the whaling ship becomes a bounded context in which the quest for wholeness can unfold. However, it soon becomes evident that the darkness to which the chaplain calls our attention cannot be overcome by the companionship of a larger community committed to a common venture. As they board the ship, Ishmael and Queequeg meet a man who calls himself "Elijah," reminding them of the Hebrew prophet who warned the kingdom of Israel of their impending destruction, and who prophesied that the rulers of Israel would die and that the dogs would lick their blood in the streets.[10] In the Biblical story, Ahab and Jezebel encroached upon the mystery and the power of God, worshipping instead the gods of the earth and the harvest, and finally calling down divine condemnation in a fire from the heavens.[11] In a similar fashion, the appearance of "Elijah" at the beginning of Ishmael's voyage suggests that Ahab and his crew will encroach upon the divine mystery and will attempt to comprehend what lies beyond their understanding. In fact, insofar as Moby Dick is Melville's way of pointing to what remains beyond our grasp, the mystery and the power that he embodies will become the "objects" that the *Pequod's* crew attempts to conquer. Yet, as we might expect, the power and the mystery of the whale will also become instruments of divine retribution in response to this expression of human willfulness. Just as in the Biblical account, this attempted conquest of what is ultimate will not succeed and will finally lead to the destruction of those who undertake it.

In his brief description of the white whale, Ishmael makes it clear that its mystery and power are irreducible elements. For example, he claims that for some time past, though at intervals only, Moby Dick had haunted the seas most frequented by the sperm whale fishermen. Not all of them knew of his existence; only a few had knowingly seen him; and the number who had actually and knowingly given battle to him was small indeed (p. 155). Yet Ishmael tells us that the reputation of the white whale did not remain confined to narrow circles: from only a few encounters, wild rumors spread about the nature of Moby Dick. These rumors became the bearers of the initial mystery, and in the end, they incorporated "all manner of morbid hints, and half-formed foetal suggestions of supernatural agencies, which eventually invested Moby Dick with new terrors unborrowed from anything that visibly appears" (p. 156). Some sailors claimed that Moby Dick was ubiquitous and that he had been seen at opposite latitudes at one and the same time. Others maintained that he was not only ubiquitious, but also immortal (p. 158). As the rumors spread, the mystery of the initial inaccessibility of Moby Dick was reflected in the godlike qualities that the sailors attributed to him. However, in such explicit form, mystery can easily be interpreted as superstition, and as Ishmael himself suggests, superstitious rumor is an inadequate vehicle for the expression of what is genuinely ultimate. As a result, Ishmael tells us that even stripped of supernatural formulations, "there was enough in the earthly make and incontestable character of the monster to strike the imagination with unwonted power" (p. 159). The white whale was larger than other whales of his kind. His brow was furrowed, and on his back was a high pyramidical white hump. But of all the whale's characteristics, his whiteness was the final and the most fundamental source of his mystery. Whiteness, says Ishmael, is itself "a dumb blankness, full of meaning" (p. 169). Ishmael also reminds us that the whiteness of Moby Dick is conjoined with tremendous power and that it is because of his power that the whale does not finally remain inaccessible. In fact, Captain Ahab had encountered Moby Dick already, for in an earlier battle, the monster had severed his leg. The negativity to be encountered in the goal of Ishmael's quest reveals itself as active power, and at least in the case of Captain Ahab, the mystery of the white whale is transposed into the power of negativity itself.

The accessibility of Moby Dick is due to the fact that the whale confronts the men who seek him as an individualized center of power: he stands forth as a distinct "individual" from the ocean context out of which he emerges. However, the possibility of an encounter with him also depends upon the fact that he swims in patterns — patterns that his pursuers can attempt to trace (p. 172). Ishmael describes in some detail Ahab's attempts to trace them:

> Had you followed Captain Ahab down into his cabin...you would have
> seen him go to a locker in the transom, and bringing out a large wrinkled

roll of yellowish sea charts, spread them before him on his screwed-down table. Then seating himself before it you would have seen him intently study the various lines and shadings which there met his eye; and with slow but steady pencil trace additional courses over spaces which before were blank.

Almost every night they were brought out; almost every night some pencil marks were effaced, and others substituted. For with the charts of all four oceans before him, Ahab was threading a maze of currents and eddies, with a view to the more certain accomplishment of the monomaniac thought of his soul. [p. 171]

Ishmael is careful to mention that the patterns Ahab traces are not invariant, and he acknowledges the fact that they do not exhaust the richness and the complexity of the whale's behavior. On the other hand, these patterns remain as clues to the one who seeks him, and they comprise an irreducible dimension of his nature.

At various stages of his narrative, Melville interrupts the temporal flow of his story with detailed attempts to classify a great variety of whales and to specify certain crucial features of their anatomy and physiology (pp. 116–128, 224–233, 278–286, 376–385). This dimension of the novel is often regarded as an unnecessary series of digressions, and as an indication that Melville sometimes fails to maintain the quickened pace required of an adventure story. However, the apparent digressions are vitally important, for they point to the author's awareness of the intrinsic nature of the whale and of its crucial role in giving an intelligible account of the quest for Moby Dick. The patterns Ahab draws on his sea charts mirror the patterns of morphology and of process to which Melville calls our attention in these sections. In addition, his references to them not only point to the unification of the morphological and the living aspects of the whale, but also to the possibility of relating them both to the geometrical designs that Ahab traces on the maps spread out before him. Of course, Melville knows that Moby Dick is a mysterious center of power that cannot be confined to a merely structural account of his nature. However, he also reminds us that where mystery and power are present, *logos* must be present as well. In fact, Moby Dick is the unification of *mystery, power,* and *structure,* and in the following section, I shall speak about our relationship with him in terms of these fundamental conceptions. In more human terms, I shall also characterize this complex relationship, first from the perspective of Ahab; then from the perspective of Queequeg; and finally, from the standpoint of Ishmael himself.

Dispersion and Unity

Power and self-annihilation

Among the characters in Melville's novel, the one who most deliberately attempts to bring the white whale to focus is Captain Ahab. Early in the voyage, he gathers the crew on deck and announces that the chief object of their common venture will be the destruction of Moby Dick. He brandishes a gold coin that he promises to give to the first sailor who sights the white whale, and standing in their midst, he nails the coin to the masthead. He then produces goblets filled with grog and passes them among the crew. The goblets go round and round. "Drink and pass," says Ahab. Finally, Ahab summons the harpooners and arrays them before him, their lances crossed in solid phalanx. Then he shouts from their midst: "Drink ye harpooners! Drink and swear, ye men that man the dreadful whaleboat's bow — Death to Moby Dick!" Once again the goblets are lifted and "to cries and maledictions against the white whale, the spirits are quaffed down with a hiss." "Once more...the replenished pewter goes the rounds among the frantic crew...." Only then are the sailors, who have been swept up into the cosmic vision and the hatred of Ahab, finally dispersed; only then does the captain retire into his cabin (pp. 145–156).

During the early stages of this dramatic encounter with the crew, Starbuck, the first mate of the ship, objects in the most stringent terms to Ahab's wish for vengeance. He claims that to be enraged with a dumb brute is madness and that to seek vengeance upon a dumb thing seems blasphemous. However, Ahab replies by attempting to make clear his own conception of his relationship with Moby Dick. "All visible objects," he says,

> are but as pasteboard masks. But in each event — in the living act, the undoubted deed — there, some unknown but still reasoning thing puts forth the mouldings of its features from behind the unreasoning mask! How can the prisoner reach outside except by thrusting through the wall? To me, the white whale is that wall, shoved near to me. Sometimes I think there's naught beyond. But 'tis enough. He tasks me; he heaps me; I see in him outrageous strength, with an inscrutable malice sinewing it. That inscrutable thing is chiefly what I hate; and be the white whale agent or principle, I will wreck that hate upon him. [p. 144]

In this brief description, Ahab defines the white whale as an inscrutable center of power. It is this inscrutability that he hates, and he responds to it by attempting to circumscribe the mystery of Moby Dick in terms of the concept of power. Ahab wishes to strike the white whale; it had once struck him. He seeks to thrust through the wall of mystery and make living contact with the source of his misery. And Ahab wishes to do this whether the white whale be agent or principle. In either case, inscrutability must be overcome. Yet Ahab ultimately rejects responsibility for himself and for his actions, for he posits one power against another and does not accept his obligation to plunge into the mystery of which power is an outward manifestation. Moreover, there is no logos in his posture toward himself or toward the whale, for he fails to acknowledge the ultimate intelligibility of nature which the mystery and the power of the whale invite us to explore. As strong as he is, Ahab does not grow beyond the stage where he recognizes power as brute force. He rejects the mystery and the logos which give power its ultimate significance, and in doing so, he makes a choice which finally condemns him to his fate. In the end, an unmediated opposition defines the meaning of Ahab's existence: the raging power of Ahab is to be pitted against the power of the whale.

It is possible to understand Ahab's relationship to Moby Dick as a quest for wholeness. However, as his conversation with Starbuck suggests, Ahab believes that wholeness is accessible to him only if inscrutability can be eliminated and if the power that maimed him can be destroyed by a power of his own. Ahab transforms the quest for wholeness into a quest for completeness, refusing to allow the white whale to preserve its mysterious independence and insisting that its power be subordinated to his own demands for absolute comprehension. The voyage of the *Pequod* is Ahab's attempt to accomplish this transformation, and in the process, the death of Moby Dick becomes the sole condition under which Ahab can live. On the other hand, it is important to notice that Ahab's quest is not directed simply beyond himself, but that it has a bearing on his conception of the meaning of his own existence (pp. 160–161). In the case of Ahab, the meaning of human existence is mediated by the concept of power, and he is able to participate in what is ultimate because he discovers a center of power that does not remain confined to a point beyond himself.

Ahab's participation in the power that Moby Dick represents is reflected in the fact that he acquires some of the whale's characteristics and in the process becomes a microcosm of his own demand for completeness. In the early stages of the voyage, Ahab remains in his cabin, inaccessible to the members of his crew (pp. 108–109). But as the journey unfolds, the mystery of his inaccessibility is gradually replaced by the presence of Ahab. He takes his stand on deck with increasing frequency, placing his wooden leg within an indentation on the floor (p. 110). Finally, in a sudden fit of rage Ahab reveals himself directly. He calls the second mate a dog and threatens to kill him, and he advances upon him with such overbearing power that Stubb retreats involuntarily (p. 113). Unlike Ahab, Stubb does not strike back. That evening, however, he dreams about his captain, and imagines that Ahab is of monstrous size, looming up before him as a giant pyramid (p. 115). Later, we find that Moby Dick is described as a great white monster with "a peculiar...wrinkled forehead, and a high, pyramidical white hump" (p. 159).

The similarities between Ahab and Moby Dick are sustained by the fact that Ahab's power waxes and never wanes, and that it reaches a crescendo on the final day's chase for the whale. On that final day, Ahab shatters his sextant, abandons his sea charts, and leaps into the whaleboat to lead the chase himself. And when the whale confronts him directly with its own inexhaustible power and with the inscrutable mystery that he was never able to accept, Ahab hurls the final lance; he makes the final attempt to conquer his enemy (p. 468). In the end, the power of Ahab reflects the infinite power of his own self-accentuation: with a lunge he becomes one with his goal; in that final moment, the white whale snatches him up from his surrounding context. At this stage, however, there is a sense in which reference to a goal is both unnecessary and misleading. In fact, the termination of Ahab's quest for completeness can be understood as the end of a process of development that swells up from within (pp. 160–161). Ahab attempts to develop his power to infinite proportions in response to his own incompleteness, and he seeks to transform his incompleteness at the point of its origins. However, in Ahab's case, these origins do not lie outside himself. Rather, they are to be found at the point of intersection between man and what is ultimate and in the longing for wholeness that man's fragmented relationship with what is ultimate often generates. At the end of his journey, the original opposition between Ahab and the white whale is internalized and given a purely immanent reference: his hatred for Moby Dick is transformed into an instance of infinite power and turns back upon itself. In the end, Ahab's enemy becomes his own incompleteness, and it is this incompleteness that he attempts to conquer. Yet the power he accentuates in doing so cannot be bounded by other aspects of his nature. Finally, Ahab explodes. He identifies himself so completely with power alone that he loses his identity. Ahab reaches the goal of his quest for completeness, but he does so only by sinking into the depths of the ocean, strapped to the back of the object of his hatred. At the end of his journey, Ahab vanishes into the sea, bound to Moby Dick by a rope that is attached to his own harpoon (p. 468).

Mystery and self-acceptance

An alternative mode of development to be found in the story is exhibited by Queequeg, the cannibal. In fact, Queequeg's way of life is so rich and constant that to speak about it in developmental terms is to overlook from the beginning its most fundamental characteristic. From the outset, Queequeg keeps a wooden idol close beside him (pp. 30, 51, 66); from the beginning, he appears to be at home within an alien environment. For example, on one occasion Queequeg sits beside a wooden table in the Spouter Inn, fascinated by the printing in a book he is unable to read. He passes his eyes over the pages again and again, incapable of understanding their significance. However, the cannibal is oblivious of those about him who regard him as strange, concentrating instead upon the task that is immediately at hand (p. 51). Though he can neither read nor write, and though he will never be able to decipher the meaning of the quest for wholeness in verbal terms, there is an easy and fluid relationship between Queequeg and what surrounds him. He is related to the world in a fashion that is both natural and immediate, and he is not concerned to strive for fulfillment or to seek participation in a way of life that lies beyond his present mode of existence. Of course, this does not imply that Queequeg does not sometimes respond to those about him in fear or anger. For example, when he first discovered Ishmael sleeping in his bed, he brandished his hatchet, demanding to know the reason for Ishmael's presence (p. 31). Yet this response was spontaneous and unaffected because it was called for by the situation in which he was involved.

Perhaps a more dramatic example of Queequeg's fundamental orientation is exhibited on the brief voyage that Queequeg and Ishmael were forced to undertake in order to reach Nantucket. In the course of that one-day journey, one of the passengers fell overboard. He was the same person who minutes before had mimicked Queequeg behind his back, provoking his indignation. Yet when this passenger fell into the sea, Queequeg, stripped to the waist, dove in immediately to save him. After some minutes, he succeeded (pp. 65–66), and upon his safe return, Ishmael described his friend somewhat ironically as follows:

Queequeg, he says,

did not seem to think that he at all deserved a medal from the Humane and Magnanimous Societies. He only asked for water... something to wipe the brine off; that done, he put on dry clothes, lighted his pipe, and leaning against the bulwarks, seemed to be saying to himself — "It's a mutual, joint-stock world in all meridians. We cannibals must help these Christians." [p. 61]

Queequeg's rather mild and balanced way of life can perhaps be understood most adequately in terms of the concept of *finite self-acceptance*. He accepts himself and his place in nature, just as he is able to accept the mysterious and the unexpected dimensions of his immediate environment. At the same time, his openness and self-acceptance are grounded in his relationship to the idol that he carries with him. The constant presence of the idol makes a quest for wholeness unnecessary, for it symbolizes his participation in a way of life that makes human significance immediately accessible. As a consequence, Queequeg is unconcerned about which ship is to be chosen for the voyage he plans to undertake. He asks Ishmael to select the ship, while he remains inside his room, fasting before his wooden god (p. 66). Queequeg's silent fasting suggests the intensity of his relationship to the primordial dimension of his own existence, and it implies that the vertical relationship in which he stands is more fundamental than any process of development in which he might become engaged. The fact remains, however, that Queequeg does become a member of the *Pequod*'s crew and that he shares the quest of Ahab and Ishmael, at least by implication. What then is the relation between the quest in which he participates and the primordial relationship in which he stands? Why does Queequeg undertake a voyage, the projected end of which is present to him from the beginning in some measure of fullness?

Part of the answer is suggested in Ishmael's brief account of Queequeg's early history. Ishmael tells us that Queequeg was the son of a king and that his uncle was a high priest. He even implies that it was Queequeg's destiny to become a king himself. Yet Ishmael says that from his early days, there had lurked within him the strong desire to visit Christendom. Queequeg wished "to learn among the Christians, the arts whereby to make his people still happier than they were; and more than that, still better than they were" (p. 57). For this reason, Queequeg left his homeland to come to the Western World. Unfortunately, he soon discovered that life was no better in Christendom than it was upon his native island. "The practices of the whalemen soon convinced him that even Christians could be both miserable and wicked; infinitely more so, in fact, than all his father's heathens" (p. 57). In fact, Queequeg came to the conclusion that association with Christians had made him unfit to ascend his father's throne. "By and by, he said, he would return, — as soon as he felt himself baptized again. For the nonce, however, he proposed to sail about, and sow his wild oats in all four oceans" (p. 57). Christians had made a harpooner of him, and the harpoon served now as his scepter.

Queequeg proposes to sail about the oceans in order to sow his wild oats, and he implies that he had become a harpooner through a process of degeneration. He had wandered away from his origins to search for a better world, only to find that no better world was accessible. As a consequence, he claimed that it was necessary for him to be baptized again — to be related once more to his origins in a fashion which was both positive and sustaining. On the other hand, Queequeg does not force the issue to an immediate resolution, nor does he assume that rebaptism is possible through an effort of his own. Rather, he accepts the fact of his degeneration, just as he accepts the other dimensions of his existence. He commits himself to the task at hand, but does not formulate his work in terms which suggest an orientation toward a final consummation. In fact, the absence of an orientation of this kind is the foundation of Queequeg's own self-conception. Unlike Ahab, Queequeg does not formulate the ultimate object of his concern in determinate fashion, nor does he attempt to overcome the mysterious dimension of what is ultimate by transforming the quest for wholeness into a quest for completeness. Queequeg accepts himself as a wanderer in the ocean at large and does not fasten his attention exclusively upon the whale. Rather, the water as the medium through which it swims becomes the focus of his existence. The meaning of Queequeg's life must be formulated in terms of his participation in the ocean taken as a whole and not in terms of the water as a context in which the quest for wholeness unfolds. In fact, his "spatial" and "verticalized" relationship to the water constitutes his rebaptism and becomes the vehicle through which he recovers his origins.

The nature of Queequeg's rebaptism becomes explicit in the manner of his death. On the final day's chase for the whale, he does not take his accustomed place in the whaleboat. Instead, he remains on board the *Pequod,* standing on the masthead. When Moby Dick attacks the crew and the ship begins to sink, Queequeg remains at his post. He looks out across the water; he folds his arms in silence; and he vanishes into the sea (p. 469). Though Queequeg is fascinated with language, and though he knows how to communicate with his comrades in the quest for Moby Dick, when the ultimate moment comes, he is cut off completely from the possibility of verbal articulation. Nevertheless, Queequeg becomes a microcosm of the ocean and of its inexhaustible mystery, and the power of this larger context is reflected in the dignity with which he confronts his death. Self-acceptance and acceptance of the mystery and the power of existence is Queequeg's final self-defining act. It is true that his rebaptism does not consist in a recovery of his tribal origins, and in this respect, he fails to achieve the wholeness he seeks. Yet the death of Queequeg brings fulfillment to his soul: his rebaptism occurs in relation to the ocean as a whole and is in this way elevated to eternal significance.

Salvation and self-discovery

Sometime prior to his death, when he had been ill aboard the *Pequod,* Queequeg asked the ship's carpenter to build him a coffin. It was to be made after the fashion of a canoe and was to serve as his burial place, in imitation of the burial customs of the whale fishermen of Nantucket (p. 396). However, before the voyage reached its culmination, Queequeg recovered from his illness. In fact, it soon becomes evident that unlike Ahab and Ishmael, he had regarded his illness from the outset as a merely natural phenomenon (pp. 398–399). As a result, he was able to understand it simply as a part within a larger whole, and more fundamentally, was able to understand death itself as the final stage of life. Queequeg dies in a fashion which bears no positive relationship to the coffin that had been constructed for him; and he does so, unfettered by the customs and traditions to which the existence of coffins calls our attention.

As the *Pequod* sank from view below the surface, the coffin of Queequeg vanished in the ocean. He was not buried in it. Yet the coffin's role in the story is not restricted to its original function, for it also has a positive bearing on the life of Ishmael. Ishmael tells us that as he was being drawn down with the others into the whirlpool created by the sinking ship, suddenly "the coffin life-buoy shot lengthwise from the sea, fell over, and floated by my side" (p. 470). He adds that he was buoyed up by the coffin, and that for almost one whole day and night, he "floated on a soft and dirge-like main.... The unharming sharks... glided by as if with padlocks on their mouths; the savage seahawks sailed with sheathed beaks" (p. 470).

This unexpected and somewhat apocalyptic reference to the coffin as a symbol of life stands in stark contrast with our usual conceptions, and in contrast with the earlier references to coffins that are interwoven in the story. At the beginning of his journey, Ishmael set out to sea in order to escape the coffin warehouses around him and in order to avoid the funeral processions in whose train he was tempted to follow. He shuddered at the name of Peter Coffin, displayed above the door of the Spouter Inn; and in the church, he stood before a series of plaques, commemorating the death of whale fishermen in distant seas. Yet in spite of his wish to escape the symbols of death and illness, Ishmael crossed the threshold of the door into a new and richer existence. He made friends with a cannibal; he became a member of a whaling crew; and he plunged actively into the ocean, participating fully in the quest for Moby Dick. Yet at the termination of this risk of participation, a coffin emerges unexpectedly from the ocean into which he had plunged. Ishmael's outward movement is met by a counterthrust from the ocean itself, and it is through this unexpected reversal that salvation finally comes.

As the emergence of the coffin suggests, we might regard Ishmael's participation in the ocean venture as a way of dying. Ishmael had been a teacher, and his natural tendency was to remain aloof from an active involvement in the quest for Moby Dick. But when he became a member of the *Pequod*'s crew, and the quest for wholeness began to unfold, he plunged into a concrete context of encounter and interaction. In doing so, he laid aside his merely private standpoint and was able to participate both in the life and world of Queequeg and in the erotic quest of Ahab. In both cases he was snatched up into a domain that lay beyond his grasp. But even though Ishmael transcends his merely private point of view, he does not die in the sense of Ahab and Queequeg: he is neither consumed by the quest, nor simply resigned to a life and death of self-acceptance. Ishmael attempts to keep both the whale and the ocean in view, and he seeks to bring Ahab's quest for the whale into a positive relationship with the ocean context to which Queequeg returned in resignation. Formulated in somewhat different terms, Ishmael abandons his merely private standpoint, but he also keeps his distance in order to bring the whale and the ocean to focus in intelligible discourse. Ishmael's quest for wholeness moves from the natural human bond that he shares with other men, through the alienation and radical discontinuity that he encounters at the water's edge, to a moment of wholeness, and to his own attempts to articulate its significance. He moves from a "spatial" beginning, through a "temporal" journey, to a "spatial" consummation, finally floating on a coffin that had once been intended for his friend. However, his wholeness is not achieved until he begins to speak about the mystery and the power of the quest for wholeness, and until he attempts to articulate the meaning of his journey. In speaking about the journey, Ishmael recovers his origins as a teacher, and in describing the interplay between the whale and the ocean, he reveals their role within the story in a rich and living discourse.

Ishmael is the narrator of Melville's novel, and the coffin that emerges from the whirlpool is the foundation for his speech. Ishmael is also a central participant in the account he gives, for he could scarcely speak about the whale and the ocean, and about their mystery and power, had he not plunged into the context which these themes provide. However, Ishmael's most important task is to tell the story that reveals the structure of the quest for wholeness. His act of speaking is the logos of narrative discourse, binding together the power which makes the quest possible and the surrounding mystery that makes it necessary. In fact, there is a three-fold logos involved in the account Ishmael gives of his journey: the logos of the narrative itself; logos taken as the structure of the story; and logos understood as the sustaining ground from which the speech itself emerges. Taken together, these elements constitute the intelligible aspect of the story Ishmael relates. The openness and the power of Ishmael are not finally the openness of Queequeg to the inexhaustability of the ocean, nor the surging power of Ahab which drives him toward completeness, but are instead the mystery and the power of living language — an open-ended context which points to the act that produces it; to the ground that sustains it; and to the structure of the story that unfolds in Ishmael's own process of self-discovery.

In telling us his story, Ishmael becomes an image of narrative intelligibility, just as Queequeg is an image of the ocean taken as a whole, and just as Ahab is finally to be identified with a center of power from which his fragmentation had initially separated him. In the final analysis, it is the intelligibility of Ishmael's narrative discourse that binds Melville's story together and gives us access to the mystery and the power of the journey which would otherwise remain beyond our grasp. However, we must not forget that the intelligibility of Ishmael's speech depends upon the emergence of the coffin from the depths of the ocean, and that the coffin itself is a reflection of the customs and traditions of the whalemen of Nantucket. Ishmael is able to speak about the quest for wholeness because he participates in the customs and traditions which make the journey possible, recovering in this way the human origins from which the whaling venture is an outward extension. Standing as he does upon the coffin, Ishmael discovers that the quest for wholeness must not only take place within the world as a whole, but that it must also enable the individual to recover the human ground from which the quest itself originates. It is to these human origins, and to the customs and traditions which make them determinate, that the emergence of the coffin directs our attention. Yet the coffin upon which Ishmael stands is not only a positive ground, but also a symbol of death, suggesting that he can recover his origins only if he "loses himself" within the journey that sustains his existence. In accepting Ahab and Queequeg as his companions and in relating their story, Ishmael sacrifices his simple particularity, and it is finally as a concrete reflection of this sacrificial act that the coffin provides the foundation for his speech. By acknowledging the integrity of his compatriots and by giving himself over to his story, Ishmael abandons his insistence on the primacy of his own existence. Yet in doing so, he paradoxically saves his own life and recovers his own ground. It is from the balance that he maintains among the power, the mystery, and the meaning of existence that his speech emerges, and it is upon this ground that the novel itself unfolds.

At the conclusion of his narrative, Ishmael tells us that he is finally rescued by a ship named the *Rachel.* As we should remember, Rachel was the wife of Jacob, the grandson of Abraham, and a living participant in the religious tradition from which the Biblical Ishmael had once been ejected. Borrowing once more from his Biblical origins, Ishmael says that the *Rachel,* looking for her lost children, merely found another orphan. However, this concluding remark forces the attentive reader to ask about the real identity of Ishmael and about the relationship between the larger world in which the ocean venture occurs, and the Biblical tradition of which it sometimes seems to be a metaphorical extension. Does Ishmael's salvation depend upon a world of strangers, or is it a function of the origins from which he had once been ejected? Is the wholeness he seeks to be found within the larger world, or by returning to the Biblical context from which his quest originates? As if to emphasize the inherent ambiguity of his situation, Ishmael tells us that he alone has come to relate the story of the fate of his friends and of his own salvation. In doing so, he reminds us of the Book of Job, where four separate individuals say to the suffering man, "I alone have come to tell thee."[12] This final Biblical reference, with its tantalizing multiplicity, throws the reader back upon himself, forcing him to make his own responses to Ishmael's story. What is the difference, we must ask, between Ishmael's adoption by strangers and his cosmic readoption by his original family; and what is the difference, if any, between being an orphan and being a child? It is to these questions that we shall turn in the following chapter.

2

Revelation, Individuation, and the Recovery of Origins

As Melville's novel suggests, the quest for wholeness is a natural expression of the human spirit, which begins with alienation and with the longing for unity that all of us share. Though his story points to the ultimate dimension of experience and though it brings us face to face with aspects of the natural order that sometimes threaten our existence, its initial concern is to give us access to the natural stages of the human journey and to the human matrix from which it originates. In Melville's novel, the quest for wholeness is universally accessible, and his narrator speaks for us all in tracing the pattern of his own development and in articulating the significance of his quest in the face of natural opposition. However, we should also notice that in building his account around the life of Ishmael, Melville's ultimate intentions are radically ambiguous. For example, it remains unclear whether the Ishmael of the novel represents the human condition in an unrestricted form or whether he is related more intimately to the Biblical tradition from which his name is derived. Is Melville's Ishmael merely a symbol for us all, pointing to the universal aspects of the human situation; or is he also an analogical extension of the son of Abraham, calling our attention to the origins of the Hebrew tradition and to the religious implications of the context in which the life of Ishmael develops? As a novelist who remains true to his art, Melville refuses to answer these questions. In fact, he heightens their intensity by allowing Ishmael to undertake an outward journey, only to reverse its directionality by having a coffin emerge unexpectedly from the ocean, and by permitting his narrator to be rescued by a ship that represents a particular religion. Is Ishmael to be taken at his word when he claims that the *Rachel*, looking for her lost children, merely found another orphan, or does the wholeness he achieves depend upon his readoption by the family from which he had once been ejected? Again Melville refuses to answer. However, in allowing us to ask the question, he leads us into the middle ground where this complex Ishmael stands, inviting us to notice the difference between an adoption by strangers and readoption by the ground of one's existence.

In this chapter, we must respond to this ambiguity in a decisive fashion. Having permitted Melville to develop an account of the quest for wholeness as a universal task and having plunged into the journey as an undertaking that all of us share, we must now reverse this process of development and return to the ground from which it originates. In the process, we must also trace Melville's own reversal of directionality back to its roots, for it is only in this way that we can emphasize the origins of his account and can grasp the second directionality that remains implicit in his story. As I have suggested already, the quest for wholeness moves in two directions: though it moves outward toward the larger world and permits us to come to terms with our alienation through a process of natural development, it also moves backward to a real ground, allowing us to return to our origins and to the power of the place where we began. The artistic immediacy of Melville's novel permits us to immerse ourselves in an outward journey and to develop our self-conscious particularity as we participate in an ocean venture that leads beyond our original condition. Yet as this outward journey comes to an end, we are reminded by the forceful interjection of a coffin that wholeness is in part a function of our own particularity. As the novel itself suggests, it is the relationship between an individual and the coffin upon which he stands that serves to individuate him and that allows him to return to the origins of his individual existence.

On the other hand, the attempt to understand this second directionality and to bring it into an intelligible relationship with our earlier discussion raises problems of its own. For example, how can we move from the artistic world of Melville's novel to the religious world that it finally invokes, and how is the religious tradition to which Ishmael returns at the end of his story to be connected with his outward journey? In more general terms, what does it mean for a wanderer to return to his origins, and how is it possible for the alienated individual to stand in a positive relationship with his family or with other finite symbols of the ground of his existence? More generally still, how is the concept of origins to be understood, and how is it to be related to the quest for fulfillment, both as a human undertaking and as an attempt to respond to the ultimate dimension of human existence? All of these questions reverse the directionality implicit in Ishmael's ocean venture and point beyond the artistic context that has given us access to the quest for wholeness. In fact, they lead us back to the existence of a particular religious community and to its relationship with the larger human world; they bring us face to face with our own past and with the intimate connection between the concept of origins and the concept of God. At the most fundamental level, however, they demand that we undertake the reflective task of grasping our own particularity and of understanding its relationship to the real ground with which we stand in contrast.

Yet before we take up the issues implicit in these assertions, we must ask a further series of questions that move us even closer to the heart of our inquiry. Why, we might wonder, is a shift of directionality necessary, and if it is, how can it be effected? How can we be certain that the reversal we contemplate is not merely an accidental result of Melville's artistry and is thus of no essential religious or philosophical significance? What does Melville's reversal of direction have to do with the structure of the quest for wholeness, and given its occurrence, why must we turn our attention away from nature to ourselves, and from the world as a whole to the concept of a ground that sustains our existence? Of course, when these questions arise, it should be evident that they cannot be answered in merely general terms, for they presuppose a conception of individuality that can never be exhausted by discursive speech. We must admit that the transition from an outward to an inward journey is never necessary, precisely because our origins can never appear as a category that we are forced to acknowledge at the merely theoretical level. In religious terms, we are never forced to hear the voice of God, and at the philosophical level, we cannot be compelled to attend to the uniqueness of our own existence and to the irreplaceability of the particular context from which our outward journey begins. On the other hand, our origins always speak to the one who attempts to listen, and it is by responding to what they say that we can finally return to the sustaining ground of our existence.

In this chapter, we shall develop this theme by focusing on the Biblical tradition, not because of an accidental relationship between the Ishmael of Melville's novel and the children of Abraham, nor because a transition to it has been forced upon us, but because the religion of the Hebrews brings the concepts of uniqueness and particularity to focus more clearly than does any other tradition in our history. Of course, we must not expect the Biblical account of Hebrew religion to be as universally accessible as Melville's account of the quest for the white whale. The world of Abraham, Isaac, and Jacob is individual, not universal, and it receives its concrete expression in the historical existence of a particular religious community. However, it is important to focus on this tradition because it emphasizes the particularity that is always involved in man's relationship with what is ultimate and because reflection upon it will make it possible for us to acknowledge the particularity to be experienced in our own case. As I have suggested already, there is no natural transition from the artistic dimension of experience and from the outward quest for wholeness to the existence of a particular religious community. Nevertheless, through an imaginative identification with Abraham and his descendants, we can cross the space that separates us from the concept of origins, and in the process, can stand face to face with ourselves and with the originative ground of our existence. The Biblical story points beyond itself to a real ground, and it exhibits a dimension of depth that must always be acknowledged in silence. Yet we shall also find that appropriate reflection upon it will allow us to break beyond the bounds of universality and will permit us to make an intelligible response to what is unique about our own existence.

The Radical Reversal of Tribalism

Abraham's journey

When we return to the origins of the Hebrew tradition and to the place where Ishmael's outward journey begins, we are led at once to the Biblical account of Ishmael's father and to the fact that he once undertook a journey of his own. The Book of Genesis tells us that before the birth of Ishmael, in an absolutely unmediated fashion, God appeared to Abram in a vision, demanding that he leave his country; that he turn away from his family and from his father's house; and that he go into a new land that God himself promised to show him. Moreover, God promised that if he would do this, Abram would become the founder of a new nation and would be a blessing to all the nations of the earth. Without further discussion, the Biblical record says that Abram departed, taking his wife, his nephew, and other members of his household with him, together with all he had accumulated in the land of Haran. The Bible then describes the journey in a single sentence: "They went forth into the land of Canaan, and into the land of Canaan they came."[1]

It is important to notice that the Biblical account of the quest for wholeness begins with a contrast between the divine and human realms and with a response to an antecedent encounter with what is ultimate. In this special case, God speaks; and he suggests that Abram can find wholeness for himself and for his descendants, only if he cuts himself off from his past and takes up the task of founding a new nation. The obvious contrast between the starkness of this command and the seductive fashion in which Melville's novel begins underlines the difference between two conceptions of the quest for fulfillment. The novel begins with the universal human situation, and it lures us toward the ocean in an attempt to elicit our participation in Ishmael's outward journey. By contrast, the divine command comes unexpectedly to a single individual, and the absence of a detailed description of the journey emphasizes the radical particularity of Abram's response to the divine interjection. Ishmael's outward journey also begins without explicit reference to his family, while the journey of Abram requires that he reject the tribal context in which his life had been embedded. When he hears the voice of God, Abram stands face to face with the creative ground of his existence, and in response to it, he undertakes a journey that leads beyond the familiar world of his original tribal situation.

As I have indicated already, to be an individual in the ancient world was to be a part of a larger family. In fact, to be a person was not to be an individual at all, but to be a *function* of a larger context in which one had a specific role to play. In the ancient family, wholeness was achieved by enduring the rites of initiation that marked the transition from childhood to the adult world and was sustained by one's capacity to perform an appropriate function within the family as a larger totality. To be a person was to be a member of a tribe, and to be whole was to play one's role within this larger context. It is reasonable to assume that Abram shared this ancient understanding of the nature of the "individual," and as a result, we must not overlook the anxiety he must have experienced when he was told to leave his family and his father's house to go into an unknown land. The journey into Canaan was not merely a geographical transition, but was also the initial stage in the redefinition of Abram's humanity. When he responded to the divine command, Abram ceased to understand himself simply as the child of his father and began to grasp the fact that wholeness could be achieved in his own case only if he became the father of a new world. Yet Abram also understood that his outward journey was not primarily an attempt to reach beyond the family to the larger world, but was instead a return to the origins of existence itself. Abram's "outward" journey occurs in obedience to a real ground, understood as a creative source that requires a new creation from the one who hears it speak. In this special case, these primordial origins demand that Abram abandon the security of his family; that he embrace the task of founding a new nation; and that he interpret God's unexpected interjection as a sign that the ground of human life does not provide a resting place within a larger context, but requires a creative response that reflects the ground of creation itself.

As our discussion develops, we will compare Abram's understanding of the quest for wholeness with our earlier account of Ishmael's journey and will distinguish the two conceptions of the quest which will emerge from this comparison. At this point, however, we should first return to our story and should emphasize the inherent difficulty involved in Abram's radical reversal of tribalism. This difficulty is reflected in the fact that Abram falls away from what is ultimate, failing to obey at least a part of God's commands. Though he left his country and his father's house, as God had commanded, Abram took his possessions and the other members of his family with him,[2] attempting in this way to remain true to the tribal context out of which he emerges. At this stage of his journey, Abram is apparently of two minds about the nature of his situation. On the one hand, he abandons his past and the house of his father to go into an unknown country that God promises to show him; on the other hand, he attempts to preserve the tribal framework in which he had lived by taking it with him, attempting to impose the patterns of the past upon a radically different situation. However, Abram's attempt to understand his journey in customary terms does not succeed. As understandable as it might be from the human perspective, the wish to stretch the tribal past into an unknown future is a symptom of fragmentation when it is understood in the light of an encounter with the originative ground of human existence. By refusing to obey the voice of God completely, Abram preserves a semblance of tribal unity at the expense of a vertical separation from the creative origins that had addressed him in the desert. When he reaches the land of Canaan, Abram is a divided consciousness, torn apart by the attempt to mix the past and the future and to integrate two distinguishable models of human fulfillment. On the one hand stands the ancient family and on the other stands an unknown world; in between stands Abram, fragmented by his commitment to incompatible conceptions of his own humanity.

Abram's fragmentation will not permit the promises of God to be fulfilled in a simple and straight-forward fashion. God had promised to make him the father of a great nation and to make his name great, and in addition to his original command, he had said unequivocally: "I will bless them that bless thee, and curse him that curseth thee: and in thee shall all the nations of the earth be blessed."[3] However, Abram's natural attachment to his tribal past made it impossible for him to respond unambiguously to the reversal of tribalism that God's promises demanded. No doubt, Abram believed that the new nation he would bring into existence would be an extension of his tribal heritage and that God intended for his family to expand from its tribal beginnings into tribal completeness. Yet God's original command makes it evident that Abram was not being asked to continue his family tradition, but was being told to create something new. In demanding that he leave his country, his family, and his father's house, God wishes to create a new nation, and the price Abram must pay for his positive response to this command is his willingness to abandon the tribal conception of his own nature. But granted that he does not understand the implications of his original act of obedience and granted that we also would not have understood had we been in his place, how can Abram be taught the meaning of his positive task, and how can we understand the newness of the new creation that the creative ground of existence wishes to generate? If it is perfectly natural for him to bring his tribal past with him on the journey, how can his attachment to the past be overcome so that he can become the source of something new? God responds to Abram's failure to understand his intentions in a paradoxical fashion: instead of calling his attention to a mistaken conception of the past, and of his own relationship to it, God focuses Abram's attention on the future by allowing him to live for a number of years in the new land without any descendants. Of course, this shift toward the future finally leads him to ask the inevitable questions: "How can I become the father of a great nation, if I cannot become the father of a single offspring?" "How can my heritage that stretches from Ur of the Chaldees to the Promised Land be continued if I am not only separated from my father's house, but must also live in a strange land, separated from my own future?" "How can a great nation come into existence through me if my life's journey not only negates the past, but negates the future as well, leaving me imprisoned with the memory of an isolated encounter with God?" These questions, in turn, make us wonder how the vertical encounter with an originative source can be translated into a transformed conception of human wholeness. In Abram's case, we must ask how a new nation can be created that has nothing to do with his tribal past and with his tribal expectations, and in the process, how human wholeness can be understood in terms of the relationship between a particular individual and the creative ground of his existence.

One night as Abram sat beside his tent in the desert, God began to answer these questions by addressing him directly. The voice that had first spoken to him in his homeland spoke to him again, saying, "Fear not Abram: I am thy shield, and thy exceeding great reward."[4] Yet separated from his country and from his father's house, Abram does not respond joyfully to this second interjection, but speaks instead in terms of his own grief and out of a deep concern for his own future:

> Lord God, what wilt thou give me, seeing that I go childless, and the steward of my house is this Eliezar of Damascus?...Behold, to me thou hast given no seed: and lo, one born in my house is my heir.[5]

At this decisive moment, God responds in a fashion that acknowledges Abram for the first time as a genuine participant in a conversation between the divine and human realms. Instead of making a further demand that requires instant obedience, God makes a promise that binds him to his creature and that will eventually transform Abram's conception of the meaning of his life. On this occasion, God promises that an adopted child will not become his heir, but that his descendants will be his natural successors.[6] Of course, anyone familiar with the story knows that before this promise can be fulfilled, Abram must suffer again and again until he plumbs the depths of his origins and one day stands face to face with his originative ground, finding there a new conception of human wholeness and the transformation of his own fragmentation into the newness of a new community. Nevertheless, God's promise of a child to a specific individual is itself an individuating act, and it reflects the individuation that will result when Abram finally returns to the ground of his existence. Even at this early stage of his journey, Abram no longer wants a great nation to emerge from the tribe out of which he comes — through him as a vehicle of tribal continuity — but instead, he expects a child of his own who will be the fulfillment of a promise made to him alone. In the Hebrew tradition, it is this promised child who will bring a new community into existence and who will be the bearer of a new conception of human wholeness.

The Book of Genesis tells us that Abram trusted the promises of God.[7] Though he had attempted to bring his customary way of life with him into the new land and though he was fragmented by the contradiction between his tribal past and his creative origins, Abram now believed that one day he would have a child and that this child would be the first link in the chain of descendants through whom his destiny would be fulfilled. Having first turned away from his country and from his father's house in a merely geographical sense, Abram now turns away from the past altogether toward a promised future. In doing so, he takes a decisive step beyond tribalism, ceasing to think of himself as a function of a larger family, and beginning to understand that he will become the father of a child who will be distinctively his own. God's promise to Abram individuates him, allowing him to transcend his role within the family and to become an individual who will produce a nation of individuals, all of whom must stand before God. Abram now turns toward the future, not simply as a framework that can replace tradition, but as a temporal expression of the newness his creative origins require. It is within the newness of an incomplete future that his quest for wholeness unfolds, and it is the originative act which this incomplete future demands that binds him to the creative ground of his existence. Yet we must not forget that even after God had promised him a son, Abram's first step into the promised future was inherently ambiguous. As we have discovered already, Abram's oldest child was not the offspring of his wife, but the son of an Egyptian handmaiden; and despite Abram's earnest entreaties, this son never became the child who had been promised.[8] God rejected Ishmael as Abram's chosen descendant, and he made it inescapably clear that this child would not fulfill Abram's destiny or become an expression of the originative act that God required of him. When Abram asked God "Why?" the answer he received remained ambiguous,[9] for part of Abram's task was to penetrate the mysterious intentions of the creative Ground of his existence. However, God's ambiguous answer also pointed to an earlier mistake that Abram had made during the course of his journey and to the fact that he still did not understand the full implications of the kind of journey God required.

The mistake upon which this failure depends occurs at the end of Abram's journey from his father's house into the new land. The Biblical record tells us that when Abram and his family reached their destination, they found that there was a famine in Canaan. As a result, they decided to go into Egypt to escape the hunger they were beginning to experience in the Promised Land.[10] In human terms, this response to the promised future was perfectly intelligible, for the famine was understood as a threat to the family, demanding that they move beyond it toward the larger world. What had begun as a response to a divine interjection thus became a human attempt to transcend the negativity of the new world and to find salvation out beyond the place into which they had been called. While Abram and his family lived in Egypt, his wife acquired an Egyptian handmaiden, and they incorporated her into the family in accord with ancient tribal customs. Having abandoned their tribal past and having journeyed into a new world, Abram and his wife now fall away from newness, first by leaving the land that God had given them, and then by grafting what they found beyond it onto their family in a merely customary fashion. When Abram and his wife returned to Canaan, they took this symbol of another country with them, and as a result, their promised future was tainted by the presence of a stranger in their midst. In fact, years later, the stain created by her presence became the ground for Abram's most radical mistake. Knowing that he had been promised a child, and fearing that his aging wife would not be able to bear it, Abram decided to use the handmaiden as a way of fulfilling God's promise through his own action. According to the traditions of the ancient family, a first born son would become his father's natural heir, even if he were the offspring of a handmaiden. In producing a child through the Egyptian woman, Abram attempts to guarantee the future in a merely customary fashion, hoping that this child will be accepted as his chosen descendant. And having fallen once more into a customary tribal pattern, Abram stands before God, praying that his own product might live before Him as the child who had been promised.[11]

However, God again refuses to allow Abram's family to develop in a natural tribal pattern. Having demanded that he leave his country for an unknown land and having promised him a child that for many years failed to come, God now refuses to acknowledge Ishmael as Abram's chosen descendant. Instead, he appears to him a third time, establishing a covenant with him and promising that a second child will be given as a "gift" from God himself. As a symbol of this promise, God changes the names of Abram and his wife to Abraham and Sarah, calling their attention to the fact that he is seeking to transform their nature by giving them a child who will not be the expression of tribalism, but instead, a child who will express the newness of a new world. The son of Abraham and Sarah is not to be the natural offspring of tribalism, but an individual born of two individuals, all of whom stand before God as the origin from which they spring. Abraham finally learns that the originative ground of existence will not share itself with him unless the outward thrust of his temporal journey is interrupted and until each temporal moment is subordinated to the origins that lie beyond it. The unnatural birth of Isaac to parents too old to bear children is the birth of a new world, and it is a decisive step toward a transformed conception of the human quest for wholeness. In this case, what is ultimate shatters the natural tribal context, separating Abraham and his descendants from a merely natural and continuously developmental conception of human existence. God requires that Abraham abandon his natural origins, and that these origins be replaced by an originative response to the ground of creation itself. In addition, God makes it clear that the future into which Abraham moves is not to be used as an occasion to repeat the tribal way of life that he had already abandoned in principle, but is to be seen instead as an incomplete future, symbolizing the new world that God himself wishes to create. In the vertical space between Abraham and God, a new nation is to be forged; and within this context, nature, custom, and natural temporal development are to be transformed into a new creation.

In the Hebrew tradition, the unnatural birth of Isaac was the first concrete expression of the triumph of a new conception of human wholeness. Abraham and his family had originally found wholeness in their life together as a tribal unit, where each member of the family was a function of this larger, more inclusive unity. In the ancient family, to achieve wholeness was to play one's role within this larger context, and wholeness itself was a function of the part–whole relationship that obtained between the tribe and its members. In tribal terms, Abraham and his wife, Isaac and their servants, Sarah's handmaiden and Ishmael are all included in the same totality, and wholeness is accessible to each of them as parts within a larger context. Yet we have also discovered that two other conceptions of the quest for wholeness can arise out of this original tribal unity, and it is these branching conceptions which form the basis for our own discussion. On the one hand, when God rejects Ishmael as Abraham's chosen descendant, he is alienated from his family and is ejected outward toward the larger world. It is here that Melville picks him up, allowing him to seek a new form of wholeness within the world taken as a whole. Melville transforms Ishmael's ejection from his family into the hypochondria of his soul, and it is finally the depth of his illness which enables him to see beyond the finite boundaries of his family and to undertake a quest for wholeness within the larger world that he shares with us all. Ishmael's outward journey is universally accessible, and he invites us to undertake it with him, assuming that we share his alienation, and that to some extent, at least, we have all been "ejected" from the unity we once enjoyed. Ishmael moves beyond his family toward the larger world, and he asks us to come to terms with our alienation by seeking the meaning of human existence within the larger "ocean context" that surrounds us.

On the other hand, the emergence of the coffin at the end of the story and Ishmael's readoption by his original family move the attentive reader backward toward his origins, finally calling our attention to the ground of human existence. As the Biblical tradition reminds us, tribalism is not only interrupted by an outward thrust resulting from alienation, but also by a backward movement resulting in individuation. Ishmael's father was asked to undertake a journey which leads beyond tribalism, not through outward expansion, but through an inward contraction in which he finally comes to stand before God as a unique individual. In this case, the *universality* of the tribe is interrupted by the unexpected interjection of what is *ultimate,* and the *individuality* of Abraham emerges in his encounter with the ground of his existence. Of course, we must not forget that Abraham's "backward journey" also has an outward moment; his second child is a product of unexpected and unpredictable novelty and is the first stage in the creation of a new community of individuals, all of whom stand together because they stand before the same originative source. However, in the final analysis, this outward moment is a response to an originative ground, and issues in a journey that returns us to the origins of our existence. If the Ishmael of the novel finds salvation through participation in a larger context, his Biblical "ancestor" finds it through a process of individuation. It is this individuation process, and the new kind of community to which it leads, which underlies the structure of the Biblical tradition, and which we must develop in more detail in the following pages.

The sacrifice of Isaac

As our discussion develops, we must attempt to answer an inevitable question about the intelligibility of Abraham's journey, and we must bring our account of human particularity and divine individuality into a positive relationship with the universality from which we have apparently turned away. We must also ask about the struc-

ture of the human situation when it is understood according to the
Hebrew pattern, and about the ways in which the voice of God can be
connected with our earlier attempt to understand the quest for wholeness as an outward journey. At this point, however, let us return to the
story of Abraham and ask these questions in a concrete fashion. For
example, what does Abraham's journey mean from his own perspective, and how is he able to universalize himself on the basis of an
individual encounter with the ground of his existence? Having moved
away from his family toward uniqueness and individuality and toward
the wholeness that individuation brings, how does he escape the
prison of his isolated individuality and participate in the outward
development that the quest for wholeness always exhibits? It might
seem that these questions have been answered already in the birth of
Isaac, for when Abraham receives the promised child, he is no longer
an isolated individual, but the father of a new nation that will eventually contain a great number of other individuals who owe their lives
to him. The new nation is itself the universalization of Abraham's
individual existence, and it is the birth of this new world that gives
Abraham's journey its outward modality. However, Abraham's offspring within this new community are not only his genetic successors,
but are also real *individuals*. In fact, the new community he brings
into existence is a *community of individuals* which does not repeat the
ancient tribal pattern of genetic succession. We must remember that
Isaac is not Abraham's son in the same way that Ishmael was, and
that as a result, he cannot become his father's heir through a process
of natural generation. If Isaac is to become the second member of the
new nation, he must endure what Abraham was the first to experience: Isaac must stand before his creative origins and become an
individual himself before he can take his place within the universal
community that is to emerge from Abraham's faith.

The story of Isaac's individuating experience is a familiar one, but it
is scarcely ever understood. In fact, as Kierkegaard suggests, the
story itself is absurd,[12] at least if intelligibility is equated with a set of
general principles that have a universal application. However, there is
a sense in which we can all understand it, if we endure the pain
involved in imagining ourselves in Isaac's place. To understand the
story of Abraham and Isaac is to undertake their journey and to stand
with them on the mountain where their tribal consciousness is finally
transcended. In its account of this moment of transcendence, the Book
of Genesis tells us that after Isaac had become a man and after
Abraham was able to envisage the fulfillment of all that God had

promised, a voice suddenly demanded that he take Isaac up into the mountains and that he offer him to God as a sacrifice.[13] Having asked Abraham to leave his family for an unknown land and having finally given him a son that broke beyond his natural expectations, God now demands that Abraham be willing to sacrifice his future. But what is it that God wishes to destroy? It is the natural possessiveness of a father who is inclined to say, "This is *my* son, and *I* will be fulfilled through him." But what does God demand instead? God says, "Isaac, your son, is *mine,* and neither you nor he can be fulfilled apart from a vertical relationship with the sustaining ground of your existence." If Isaac is to become something new, he must be allowed to stand alone before what is ultimate; and if he is to be Abraham's first descendant in the new world, he must be permitted to stand before the ground of human existence in his own uniqueness. The quest for wholeness demands individuation, and in the Biblical account, the wholeness Abraham and Isaac achieve separates them from one another so they both can stand before God as unique individuals. It of course seems strange that the creative ground of existence should demand the destruction of Abraham's natural expectations, insisting that he relinquish his desire to bring a great nation into existence. But if a new nation is to be created that transcends the ancient tribal pattern, it must be permeated at every juncture with newness. The natural relationship between father and son must be shattered so that both can become individuals, for the new world that Abraham is being asked to create is a *community of individuals,* all of whom are related individually to what is ultimate and unconditioned. The emergence of this new community depends upon a prior moment of radical individuation, and within the Hebrew tradition the concept of community presupposes a series of individual encounters with the ground of human existence.

When God speaks to Abraham to subject him to his most severe test, Abraham replies simply, "Here am I."[14] The earlier interchange with God about the promised child is never mentioned, nor does Abraham protest that all is lost. He simply fastens his gaze upon what is ultimate and indicates by his actions that he is willing to leave the promised future in God's hands. Abraham had been snatched out of the larger, more universal context of tribalism to endure a lonely journey into an unknown land, and in the process he had gradually become an individual, no longer a member of an overarching community. Now he stands at the threshold of a new world, finally beginning to realize that newness cannot be of his own making, but must be allowed to emerge in ways that can never be fully controlled. Abraham's silent obedience to God's command is his tacit acknowledgment that the newness that had been promised cannot be mediated by his own intervention and that he must finally sacrifice Isaac as a symbol of his natural expectation. But as our attention shifts to this silent act of obedience, what shall we say about Isaac himself? How shall we understand his role in the story? What is his relationship with his father, and what are the stages in his own painful process of individuation? The Book of Genesis tells us that Abraham took Isaac on a three-day journey and that during those three days, they scarcely spoke to one another. Yet the account also says that they went on the journey *together*, bound from the outset by their natural affection for one another.[15] Father and son have a common destination, and they are linked indissolubly by their relation to it. At this point, however, the Midrashic commentaries add something absolutely essential: the commentator insists that Isaac was not a child taken on a journey he did not understand, but a mature man, who must have understood that his father's ultimate orientation was not toward his "child," but toward the sustaining ground of his existence.[16] What does the story mean, then, when it says that they went up into the mountains together? Certainly it means that they shared something at the level of natural affection, but it also suggests that they shared something far more fundamental. In the course of their upward journey, both had their eyes fixed upon God, who shatters natural tribal patterns and in the process, creates a new world. Otherwise, the two lonely travelers could not have traveled together. Didn't Isaac, the mature man, have a glimpse of the individuating act that would take place on the mountain when he asked, "Father, where is the lamb?" And when his father replied that God would provide it, didn't Isaac see that their life together depended upon their existence as individuals before the origins of their existence? However this may be, Isaac was not an innocent victim.[17] To the contrary, he was a man, just beginning to share the loneliness of his father and beginning to understand that the bonds of natural affection must be transcended if he was to stand beside his father as a unique individual. All of this, and more, is contained in the sentence, "And they went up the mountain together."

But notice also the dimension of depth reflected in the journey, shared by a father who was coming to the end of the individuation process, and by a son, standing on the threshold of individuation himself. As Erich Auerbach has reminded us, God's original command comes from nowhere, or rather, from some unknown height or depth.[18]

In addition, we are not told where Abraham and Isaac are, nor even who they are. They are simply present before God, standing alone. The journey they undertake also occurs in darkness, and we are told nothing about it except that it took three days.[19] To be sure, the Bible tells us that the journey is not merely horizontal, but has an elevated destination, and Abraham lifts up his eyes to see it from afar.[20] Yet the journey itself takes place in a vacuum,

> like a silent progress through the indeterminate and the contingent, a holding of the breath, a process which has no present, which is inserted, like a blank duration, between what has passed and what lies ahead....[21]

In the Biblical description,

> the decisive points of the narrative alone are emphasized, what lies between is nonexistent; time and space are undefined and call for interpretation; thoughts and feelings remain unexpressed, are only suggested by the silence and the fragmentary speeches; the whole, permeated with the most unrelieved suspense and directed toward a single goal..., remains mysterious.[22]

However, we must not forget that within this mysterious context, the goal itself remains unambiguous. At the beginning of the journey, God had commanded Abraham to sacrifice his son, and it is this sacrificial act that stands at the center of the new world that is to be forged at the top of Mount Moriah.

When Abraham and Isaac reach the mountain, the aging father builds an altar, and having arranged the wood, he binds his son and places him upon it.[23] Abraham and Isaac had been bound together on their journey by a curious mixture of natural affection and by a common commitment to their divine source, but at this point the natural order falls away, and the binding has an exclusive reference to Isaac's relation to the ground of his existence. When this cord has been secured between Isaac and God, and when Abraham raises the knife over his son to destroy him as the natural extension of himself,[24] Isaac looks up and focuses his attention on what lies beyond. In that instant Isaac becomes an individual, separate from his father, now bearing for the first time a relationship of his own to what gives unique and unified integrity to the human spirit. Of course, at this point God speaks, saying that it is no longer necessary for Abraham to slay his son.[25] Indeed, he has already slain him as a natural extension of himself, but having done so, he now receives him again as a man who can stand *with* him before the creative origins of his existence. This new Isaac *cannot* be killed, for the meaning of his life no longer depends upon his relationship with the natural order, but upon his own relation to the individuating source of his existence. In sacrificing his son, Abraham brings his own process of individuation to completion, and in being sacrificed, Isaac becomes an individual with his own irreducible uniqueness. When the sacrifice has been completed, to be Abraham's son is not to stand in a *genetic relationship* with the father who comes before, but to stand *with* him before the originative ground that allows the individual to become a new creation. What now binds Abraham and Isaac together is the relationship they share with what is ultimate, and it is this shared relationship that allows the Hebrew tradition to generate a community of individuals, all of whom have experienced the wholeness that an encounter with what is unconditional often brings.

After the sacrifice has been completed, Abraham comes down the mountain alone, and there is no further reference to the fact that Abraham and Isaac traveled together.[26] We might be tempted to conclude that the father and the son could no longer bear to be together,[27] and we might be inclined to read the subsequent accounts of Isaac as the story of a man cursed by rejection, unable ever to rise to the heights of his father.[28] However, to proceed in this way would be to make a radical mistake. Abraham and Isaac come down the mountain separately because they *are separate* and because both have discovered that the quest for wholeness sometimes produces individuals whose wholeness is not simply a function of their natural relationship. Though he can never be another Abraham, Isaac comes down the mountain as an individual who is able to stand alone, and he comes down, having risen to heights that will place him alongside his father in the subsequent list of the patriarchs. Abraham and Isaac traveled toward the mountain together, and they came down separately; but they are united in their separateness, and united more fundamentally than they ever were before. In this case, father and son stand together because they both have stood alone and because they share a concept of origins that will allow a new community of individuals to come into existence. In the Hebrew tradition, wholeness is achieved when a plurality of distinct individuals are bound together by their common obedience to an originative source. However, the paradox of this tradition consists in the fact that only having stood alone is one allowed to enter the community of those who have been alone as well.

In the final analysis, what binds these individuals together is not a common outward venture, but the fact that they all have returned to their origins and are in this fashion connected in a universal nexus.

In our earlier account of Ishmael's outward journey, we began with the universal call of the ocean and with the particularity of Ishmael's original condition, and we described his outward journey as the development of the natural human consciousness in the face of natural opposition. We also saw how Ishmael's quest came to a culmination within the ocean as a whole and at the point of intersection between the ocean and family from which he had once been ejected. In the present chapter, we began instead with a backward journey from Ishmael's family toward an individuating ground, and as we have just discovered, this originative source requires a sacrifice of tribal continuity. However, we have also found that the destruction of Abraham and Isaac's tribal consciousness issues in a *universal community* of *real individuals* and that in this case, universality depends upon a series of individual encounters with the ground of human existence. Of course, this means that the two directions in which the quest for wholeness develops produce two distinguishable conceptions of human wholeness: the first begins with fragmentation and finds wholeness through reinclusion in the family, while the second begins with an individual's encounter with God and finds wholeness by generating a new conception of the human community. However, we should not forget that this second kind of journey must also face the threat of fragmentation. In the Hebrew tradition, fragmentation consists in the tendency to fall away from an individuating relationship with God and to turn back to the standpoint of the natural tribal consciousness. The radical contrast between one's natural family and the individuating context into which we are sometimes called poses a permanent problem, and it is for this reason that subsequent members of the Hebrew tradition must recapitulate the suffering of Abraham. The moment on Mount Moriah is an achievement against the background of a radical contrast between Abraham's natural expectations and his relationship with God, and as we shall see in the following pages, this same opposition is present at every moment in the tradition he generates.

Abraham's children

The perpetual conflict between tribalism and the new community Abraham brings into existence is revealed most clearly in the way in which later generations reflect the earlier contrast between Isaac and

Ishmael. Just as Isaac and Ishmael moved in opposite directions, pointing to the two directionalities in which the quest for wholeness can develop, Isaac himself had twin sons who were oriented in radically different ways. In fact, the Book of Genesis tells us that Jacob and Esau struggled with one another even before they were born, and that at the moment of their birth, the "younger" Jacob came into the world holding onto Esau's heel.[29] As the story develops, we find that Jacob's initial act was merely the first in a series of attempts to displace his older brother, and that throughout his life, Jacob was a trickster. [30] In fact, his very name means "one who attempts to supplant,"[31] pointing to his efforts to displace his brother, just as his father had once displaced Ishmael. One day when Esau was tired and hungry, Jacob persuaded him to sell his birthright for a bowl of pottage.[32] Later, Jacob and his mother also tricked his aging father into believing that Jacob was Esau, and in this way he received his father's blessing.[33] Thus, the radical reversal of tribalism continues into the second generation, this time mediated by the deliberate efforts of the younger brother himself. In this case, however, there is a two-fold difference from the earlier story of displacement: in the first place, Isaac was willing to follow the ancient tribal pattern of behavior, subordinating the younger son to his older brother. Though he had stood on Mount Moriah to participate in the radical reversal of tribalism, he is nevertheless prepared to make his older son his natural heir. As a result, Isaac regresses to the tribal customs of the past, falling away from the reversal of tribalism which had occurred on the mountain. Abraham, his father, had moved away from his tribal consciousness toward a new creation; by contrast, this new creation now moves backward into the tribal origins from which he had emerged. Yet Jacob's attempts to displace Esau as his father's heir also differ from the story of Isaac and Ishmael in another crucial respect. In the earlier story, God's unexpected appearances to Abraham are the reasons for the radical reversal of tribalism, while in this second case, God remains in the background, and the subordination of the older brother is accomplished by a merely human act. At this point, there is no explicit indication that Jacob's displacement of Esau is the will of God, nor that it reflects the reversal already accomplished in the earlier account.[34]

It was not until the end of his life that Jacob finally understood the vertical space within which the existence of his own people was to be established. Having been a trickster all his life and having been alienated from his brother for a number of years, Jacob lay down in the fields one night to sleep; and in those sleepless hours he struggled with an angel. All night he tried to insist upon his own particularity and to preserve his natural tendency to arrange things in the world to his own advantage. But when morning came, Jacob finally capitulated to a source of power that lay beyond his own will, and in that moment his name was changed from Jacob to Israel, reflecting the fact that his nature had been transformed from one who attempts to supplant to one who strives with God.[35] Though he walked with a limp which was inflicted during the struggle, from that day on Jacob's new name pointed to the eventual existence of a new nation that would emerge from God's decisive acts. The creation of the nation of Israel is prefigured in the transformation of Jacob, and in both cases this transformation depends upon a positive encounter with the ground of human existence. We should also notice that it was in the light of his encounter with God that Jacob was finally reconciled with his brother.[36] Because of the natural hatred he felt toward Jacob, Esau had decided to kill him. As a result, the day after Jacob's struggle with the angel, Esau advanced to confront him by the river where his nature had been transformed.[37] However, when he saw Jacob limping along to meet him, he was unable to raise his hand against him. Instead, the Book of Genesis tells us that Esau ran to meet him, embraced him, and fell on his neck and kissed him.[38] Of course, in human terms, this reconciliation is predicated on the reemergence of natural affection that had long been suppressed. However, at the most fundamental level, it occurs because Jacob has become a new creation. It is because of his transformed nature, which even Esau acknowledges, that reconciliation is achieved, and it is on this basis that God can finally say of him, "I am the God of Abraham, the God of Isaac, and the God of Jacob."

Jacob's discovery of the vertical dimension of existence places him alongside Abraham and Isaac in the list of the patriarchs. These three men — father, son, and grandson — form a genetic succession, and they are bound together by the ties of birth and tradition that connect them into the wider nexus of an emerging community. However, what is most fundamental in their experience is that each of them stands in a vertical relationship with what is ultimate, and in the final analysis, each is related to the other because of this fact. God not only appears to Abraham, but also to Isaac and Jacob, and in each case he renews his covenant with the new community that each of them is asked to bring into existence.[39] The intelligibility of the Hebrew tradition is grounded in the analogy between Abraham and

Isaac, and between Isaac and Jacob, and in both instances the analogy consists in a *similarity of relation* to the origins of human existence. The structure of this new community rests upon the analogies that bind its members together, and it is these analogies between vertical relationships that allow a community of individuals to come into existence. The analogy between one individual and another not only permits each of them to be a unique center of power, but also allows them to be related to one another in a larger context. However, the copresence of uniqueness and relation also forces us to move beyond the tribal consciousness from which the Hebrew tradition once emerged. In the tribe, to be a person is to be a *part* of a *larger whole;* while in the Hebrew tradition, to be human is to be an *individual* who can *never be reduced* to a *function of a larger totality.* God first deals with Abraham, Isaac, and Jacob as individuals, and it is on this basis that the new community they are asked to bring into existence is constituted.

As the Hebrew community develops, we find that Jacob himself had ten sons who were the offspring of Leah, his first wife, and of the two handmaidens who had been given to him.[40] In this way, the original duality of the Hebrew tradition begins to widen out into a larger family of participants. However, the contrast between Isaac and Ishmael, and between Jacob and Esau, is still reflected in the fact that the son Jacob loved most was not one of these ten children, but the child of Rachel — the wife who finally gave him a son after these other children were born.[41] However unconsciously, Jacob is prepared to act on the radical reversal of tribalism which has already been effected, for it is to Joseph, the child of his old age, that he gives the many-colored coat as an expression of his fatherly affection.[42] Of course, neither understanding nor accepting the radical reversal that their father's act reflected, the older brothers were jealous, and one day when Joseph came to visit them while they were tending their sheep, they took their revenge upon him by selling him to a caravan bound for Egypt.[43] As a result, the natural hostility of Joseph's brothers sent him into slavery, and it also sent them back to tell their father that he had been killed by a wild animal on his way to meet them in the desert.[44] Once again, two prongs of the children of Abraham split apart, and the one who was to become the vehicle through whom the family would eventually be made whole was forced to endure the pain of radical negation.

For a number of years, Jacob believed that Joseph was dead. However, when he was an old man, and his family was suffering from famine, he sent the ten older brothers to Egypt to buy grain. Of course, after they arrived, they discovered that Joseph was not only still alive, but that he had also become a ruler in the Egyptian government.[45] Moreover, when they were finally reconciled with him, and after they had returned to tell their father about the fate of their younger brother, Jacob and his family moved down into Egypt at Joseph's invitation.[46] In this way, the family was saved from destruction by the mediation of one of its children. In our earlier account of the quest for wholeness as an outward journey, Melville's Ishmael was rescued by a ship named the *Rachel;* in this case, Rachel's son saves the members of his own family from starvation. Instead of insisting on the difference between his life as an Egyptian and his previous life within the family, Joseph acts decisively to reclaim his origins. In doing so, he asks his family to share his royal status, canceling out the negativity which they had once forced him to face. It took an entire lifetime for Abraham to stand face to face with God on Mount Moriah. Moreover, at the decisive moment, Isaac, the "victim" of the sacrifice, became the second member of the Hebrew nation, and in that instant ceased to be Abraham's merely natural offspring, standing alongside him as God's adopted child. Jacob, in turn, attempted to secure a favored status for himself by his own acts, deceiving his older brother and his aging father; but as he neared the end of his life, he finally stood in the presence of God, entering the vertical dimension which would undergird the developing nation that would come forth from his own children. Both his name and his nature now pointed to the new nation that would come into existence through him and suggested that God wishes to reveal himself to a larger community of participants. Finally, Jacob acted in a vertical fashion by giving his special favor to a younger son, only to find that this son must first be lost before he could move into the vertical domain and could take his family with him to a higher level of existence. Like all of those who had come before him, Joseph stood alone in the presence of God, but out of this moment of separation, he rescued his family and allowed them to stand with him in the vertical space that he had entered. In this developing human tradition, wholeness is once again a function of *particularity* and *ultimacy* rather than the product of *a universal quest,* but in this case, *universality* finally emerges in the development of a family as a *concrete plurality.*

When Jacob and his family arrived in Egypt, they lived with Joseph for a number of years, sharing the official favor of the royal household.[47] In fact, for 300 years or more, the Hebrews found a home in

Egypt, and it appeared that the original discontinuity with which this tradition had begun had finally issued in the relative continuity of a unified and peaceful existence. However, the Bible tells us that as time passed, a Pharoah came to the throne who did not remember Joseph, and since the intruders were beginning to multiply and to pose a threat to the Egyptians, the Pharoah finally ordered that they be reduced to the status of slaves. In a radical attempt to limit the expanding population, he even demanded that all the male children of the Jews be cast into the river.[48] As a result, the Hebrew people as a whole were confronted with the radical negation that their father, Joseph, had once experienced. Yet unlike Joseph, they concluded that God's promises to Abraham had been forgotten and that the entire nation would be destroyed in the very land to which they had come to find salvation.

In a situation in which radical discontinuity had been overcome, it now breaks out again in a more radical form. On this occasion, the positive contrast between the patriarchs and God, which had been reflected in the pairs of brothers, is transposed into a master–servant relationship between the Egyptians and the Jews. As a result, what had been an internal discontinuity within the family is now universalized and becomes an opposition between one nation and another. Of course, this leads us to wonder how this new form of radical discontinuity can be mediated and how it can be brought into a positive relationship with the original contrast between man and God. Moreover, we must ask how the master–servant relationship should be understood and how it is to be related to the Hebrew attempt to return to the origins of human existence. However, in the remainder of this chapter the answers to these questions will not be developed in general terms, but by considering the life of Moses, for as the Bible tells us, it is Moses who was born as the liberator of his people. In the Hebrew tradition, the life of Moses is the central element in dealing with the problem of human fragmentation and is the decisive step in the emergence of the Hebrew nation as a new community. Moses' special task is to universalize the relationship between the patriarchs and God and to establish a positive relationship between God and the entire nation of chosen people. To be sure, the pathway that leads from Abraham to Moses is punctuated with episodes of radical discontinuity, and this will be true in Moses' case in an intensified form. However, in every case, these moments of discord are transposed into a positive form by listening to a source of meaning that lies beyond the human realm and by attempting to bring human existence into a positive relationship with the ground of existence itself. In the life of Moses, the radical reversal of tribalism and the positive interplay between God and man reaches one of its highest expressions, and it exhibits a structure in terms of which the Hebrew community transcends the opposition between master and slave.[49] In the crucial episodes of his life, Moses returns to his origins, and in doing so he sets his people's feet on a path that leads from bondage to freedom.

Moses and the Burning Bush

When Moses is born into a Hebrew family, the discontinuity present in the earlier stages of the Hebrew tradition is recapitulated in the life of a single individual. In fact, the original duality between Abraham and God, and the radical contrasts between Isaac and Ishmael, Jacob and Esau, and Joseph and his brothers are brought to an even clearer focus in the dyadic character of Moses' origins. Though Moses was a direct descendant of Abraham, he was born a slave in Egypt; and though he was born a slave, he was educated as an adopted member of Pharoah's court.[50] The story is a familiar one: rather than have him cast into the river because of the Pharoah's murderous decree, Moses' mother placed him in a basket by the river's edge. Soon after, the daughter of the Pharoah came to the river to bathe, found the boy hidden there, and having looked into his face, decided not to leave him, but to take him with her to become an adopted child in her father's household.[51] In this way, Moses transcends the slavery of his origins and moves beyond the fragmentation of his original condition. However, before Moses entered Pharoah's court, his sister, who had been hiding by the river to protect him, offered to find a nurse for him from among the Hebrew women, and when Pharoah's daughter agreed, she brought her mother to the river to reclaim her child.[5] Thus, at the beginning of his life, Moses is not only elevated to a royal status, but is also returned to the family from which the command of Pharoah had separated him. Of course, the difficulty that Moses must face is that the duality of his salvation is reflected in the ambiguity of his origins: is Moses to be regarded as the child of a Hebrew slave, or is he to be understood as the adopted son of Pharoah's daughter? Is he a child of the family from which he had come and to which he returns, or is he an adopted member of Pharoah's court? It is this crucial ambiguity that must be resolved as Moses develops toward maturity.

Moses was educated in the household of Pharoah, and for forty years he remained in Egypt as a prince in Pharoah's court. It has even been suggested that he was to become the ruler of Egypt, for the historical record indicates that Pharoah's daughter had no children of her own to become her father's heir.[53] However, one day an incident occurred that made it impossible for Moses to remain in Pharoah's household. As Moses was walking among his original people, he saw an Egyptian taskmaster with a whip in his hand, beating one of his "brothers." He then looked to the right and to the left, and when he was convinced that no one else would observe what he did, he struck the Egyptian and buried him in the sand.[54] Of course, in that decisive instant, Moses not only identified himself with the slave, but also made a choice between the two sides of his origins: in that moment he reclaimed his original family and turned away from his adopted home. However, the Book of Exodus indicates that Moses was also unable to find a home among the Hebrews, for his ambiguous status as both a ruler and a brother made the slaves suspicious of him.[55] As a result, when the Pharoah sought revenge upon him for the death of the slave master, he was forced to flee from both dimensions of his nature. Moses was not only alienated from his origins, but was also cut off from his adopted home; as a consequence, he was thrust out from both his "families" to wander as a stranger in the desert.[56] More than 300 years before, the children of Abraham had crossed that same desert to seek salvation from famine and had become the children of slaves. Now the slave who was an adopted child of Pharoah's daughter crosses it again, only to become an alien in an alien land.

Moses wandered in the desert alone until he reached the land of the Midianites. In this new land, he married a foreign wife; produced a child; and called his son Gershom, for he said, "I have been a stranger in a strange land."[57] The opposition between Moses' original status as a descendant of Abraham and his birth as a slave; the contrast between the facts surrounding his birth and the royal character of his education; the internal conflict which is finally expressed in a violent act that separates him from his origins and from his adopted home — this pervasive discontinuity is reflected in the name Moses gives his own child. In fact, the tangled past from which he comes makes the strangeness to which the name refers even more ambiguous: is it the strangeness of Egypt or the strangeness of slavery? the strangeness of adoption into Pharoah's court or the strangeness of the alien land into which he had wandered? There is perhaps no unequivocal answer to these questions, but the crucial question that must be answered is this: "How is it possible for the slave who became a ruler, and then a stranger, to become a child of Abraham again?" "How can Moses untangle the strands of his ambiguous heritage and recover his origins in a positive and unifying fashion?" "How will he be able to return to his origins, when these origins are themselves inherently ambiguous?" As the name of his child suggests, these questions haunt Moses in the desert, but it is just these questions that must be answered if he is ever to come to himself as a unified individual.

The fragmentation which Moses experiences is as radical, if not more so, than the alienation to which the Ishmael of Melville's novel is subjected. As I have suggested already, Moses is afflicted by a double alienation, not only separated from his family, but also cut off from his adopted home. In addition, he wanders aimlessly in the desert without intending to undertake a quest for fulfillment. Moses lacks the positive orientation toward the future which characterizes Ishmael's journey, and he is apparently unaware that his alienation can be overcome by his active participation in the ultimate dimension of human experience. In Ishmael's case, the quest for wholeness presupposes a vague and indeterminate longing for salvation: it is an expression of his own hypochondria and is a symptom of the "damp, drizzly November in his soul." However, in Moses' case, the moment of negativity is much more abrupt and discontinuous. His separation from the court of Pharoah was thrust upon him by an act of violence, and this moment of separation was as direct, unmediated, and unexpected as was the decree that had separated him already from his original family. As a result, Moses wanders in a strange land as an isolated individual, cut off in a dual fashion from the sustaining ground of his existence. If this dual alienation is to be overcome, it cannot be transcended by developing an initial participation in what is ultimate of the kind that sustained Ishmael's journey. Unlike Ishmael, Moses' problem is defined by the fact that he lacks this kind of positive participation, and it is this fact that makes his alienated condition so desperate. If Moses is to recover his origins, these origins must come to him, for his separation from them is so radical that he can never hope to return to them by an act of his own. As he tells us once more: "I have been a stranger in a strange land."

Yet one day when Moses was tending the flock of his father-in-law near a mountain which the local inhabitants called "the mountain of God," the radical isolation into which he had fallen was cancelled by a direct encounter with God. As the Book of Exodus tells us:

The angel of the Lord appeared unto him in a flame of fire out of a bush: and he looked, and, behold, the bush burned with fire, and the bush was not consumed. And Moses said, I will now turn aside, and see this great sight why the bush is not burnt. And when the Lord saw that he turned aside to see, God called unto him out of the midst of the bush, and said, Moses, Moses. And he said, Here am I. And he said, Draw not nigh hither: put off thy shoes from off thy feet, for the place whereon thou standest is holy ground.[58]

God reveals himself to Moses in a dramatic and unexpected fashion: he appears in a bush that burns, but is not consumed. God then waits to see that Moses has turned aside to marvel at the sight before he addresses him, and he speaks to him even then without first identifying himself. It is to this forceful, but unidentified interjection, that Moses first responds. Yet Moses' initial response is equally direct and forceful: He says, simply, "Here am I." Of course, it is not yet clear who Moses is or what he will become, for his origins remain ambiguous and his destiny has not been made explicit. However, in standing before the bush and in confronting God face to face, he takes the first step that will finally enable him to recover his origins and to undertake the task that will define his future. Just as Abraham, Isaac, and Jacob had done, Moses listens to a speaking logos, and it is his willingness to respond to what he hears that allows him to transcend his original condition. Of course, at this point in the story, it also remains unclear who God is or what he intends to accomplish by addressing Moses in such a strange and mysterious fashion. At the outset, He simply reveals himself as a mysterious center of power to which Moses must respond if He is to manifest his nature and intentions. However, even at this stage, two centers of individuality confront one another across the vertical space that holds them apart, and a context is generated in which these two "individuals" can eventually be bound together in harmonious interaction.

In order to preserve the depth and the mystery present in this original encounter and to point to the distance that always separates the divine from the human realms, the voice from the bush prevents Moses from drawing too near to the bush itself. The religious significance of this command is then developed when God demands that Moses remove his shoes, saying that the ground upon which he stands is holy ground.[59] Apparently the speech that will bind Moses and God together will never allow them to merge with one another or to overcome the moment of discontinuity that holds them apart. Though God addresses Moses and Moses responds in turn, each stands on his own ground, and it is the ground that separates them from one another that is said to be holy ground. Of course, the ground where Moses stands is holy because God is there, manifesting his presence in all its mystery and power. However, this ground is also holy for another reason: communication between individuals that allows intelligible discourse to occur, but which also refuses to use language to enslave or to subordinate, is a kind of discourse that transforms the space in which it occurs into a sacred region. It is this region which the voice at the bush invites Moses to enter, and it is the speech that will occur within it that will eventually bind Moses and God together. At the burning bush Moses stands before God and confronts the fullness of the divine individuality. Yet in addressing him as an individual in his own right, God does not swallow him up, but allows him to come to himself as a person standing face to face with the Ground of his existence.

The ground upon which Moses stands is said to be holy prior to any attempt to specify the nature of the mystery that reveals itself to him, and the encounter between Moses and God presupposes that he first reveals himself as holy and mysterious. However, Moses is not left with a merely vague impression of the nature of God, nor is he asked to undertake a journey in which its significance will be developed more fully. Rather, the mystery and the power that Moses encounters at the bush develops *itself*: as Moses stands face to face with God, God addresses him and says, "I am the God of thy father, the God of Abraham, the God of Isaac, and the God of Jacob."[60] At this point, we are told that Moses hides his face, for he is afraid to look upon God.[61] Yet we should also notice that Moses' initially vague impression of the nature of God is mediated by the suggestion that the mystery he encounters here is also the God of his father. In this way, what would have otherwise remained a merely private experience of mystery is transformed into an occasion upon which Moses recovers his past. However, this occasion also enables Moses to recover his dignity, for the voice tells him that he is not only the God of his own father, but also the God of Abraham, Isaac, and Jacob. In this way, God reminds him that he is not primarily a slave, but a member of an ancient family tradition and a link in the chain of descendants through whom Abraham was to become the father of a new world. Moses had been alienated from his original family, first by being born a slave in Egypt; then by being snatched up from the river and adopted as a child of Pharoah's daughter; and finally, by being thrust out into the desert to wander as a stranger, at home neither in his own family, nor in Pharoah's household. However, the experience at the bush enables him to reestablish a relationship between the present and the past and to come to terms with himself, both as the child of a slave and as the bearer of a noble heritage. In the process, the momentary experience of Moses acquires an initial measure of self-transcendence, pointing beyond itself to aspects of his origins that it was essential for him to recover if he was ever to return to the ground of his existence.

When this moment of self-transcendence occurs, the voice from the bush immediately attempts to extend it to the single temporal dimension that is yet to be considered, and it does so by calling Moses' attention to a task that is to be performed. God says,

> I have surely seen the affliction of my people which are in Egypt, and have heard their cry by reason of their taskmasters; for I know their sorrows; And I am come down to deliver them out of the hand of the Egyptian, and to bring them unto a good land and a large, unto a land flowing with milk and honey; unto the place of the Canaanites, and the Hittites, and the Amorites, and the Perizzites, and the Hivites, and the Jebusites. Now therefore, behold, the cry of the children of Israel is come unto me: And I have seen the oppression wherewith the Egyptians oppress them. Come now therefore, and I will send thee unto Pharoah, that thou mayest bring forth my people the children of Israel out of Egypt.[62]

God asks Moses to resolve the ambiguity of his heritage by identifying himself with the slaves still living in Egypt; by repudiating his role as a prince in Pharoah's court; and by leading his people to a new land in which they can become the children of Abraham again, rather than the children of slaves. Yet at a deeper level, God also asks him to come to terms with himself by standing in the vertical space where Abraham once stood; by gathering up the tangled threads of his own past; and by undertaking the task of liberating his people as an expression of the sacred space that had been established already at the vertical level. In doing so, he asks him to move both forward and backward, gathering up the past and the future into the wholeness of a unified life. The task of the patriarchs had been to move away from their human origins and to return to the ground of their existence at the primordial level. Years later, Moses encounters this same ground, but this time, the Ground itself allows him to recover his origins in human terms and asks him to undertake a task that will lead him beyond the present into an unknown future. At the burning bush, Moses is asked to move in two directions at once, holding together the two directionalities that are to be found in the human quest for fulfillment.

Moses responds to God's command, not by calling the reality of his present experience into question, nor by questioning the connection which has been established between the present and the past. Instead, he chooses to focus upon himself and upon his own finite particularity. "Who am I," says Moses, "that I should go unto Pharoah, and that I should bring the children of Israel out of Egypt?"[63] Having first responded, "Here am I," he now attempts to separate himself from the context he had entered, retreating to the standpoint of his original isolation and attempting to free himself from the intersection between the divine and human realms. In this way Moses falls away from God, seeking to extend his isolation as an alienated individual to the vertical plane of his existence. However, God's reply quickly reinvokes the relationship between time and eternity. God says,

> Certainly I will be with thee; and this shall be a token unto thee, that I have sent thee; When thou hast brought forth the people out of Egypt, ye shall serve God upon this mountain.[64]

The future into which Moses is projected is sustained by the fact that it also stands in a positive relationship with the presence of God. Thus, God suggests that his presence spans all the modes of time and that he will reveal himself in the future, just as he had revealed himself already in the past and in the present. God had revealed himself to Abraham, Isaac, and Jacob in order to separate them from their tribal existence and in order to found a new nation as a community of individuals. But once this nation had come into existence and had tasted the bitter negation of slavery, he now reveals himself to Moses in order to gather up the past, to affirm the present, and to establish the future as a unified *"community"* of temporal moments. At the most fundamental level, the community of patriarchs is a visible expression of this community of moments, and it is finally God's presence throughout the modes of time that grounds his presence to them as a sequence of individuals. God's appearances to Abraham, Isaac, and Jacob suggest that he spans the past, the present, and the future, and it is this suggestion that comes to focus in Moses' experience at the burning bush. As we have discovered already, God not only asks Moses to return to his origins, but also to move outward toward the future as the liberator of his people. And God suggests that it is his own presence throughout the whole of time that will finally make it possible for Moses to recover his past, to participate in the mystery of present experience, and to affirm the value and the significance of his own future. In the Hebrew tradition, the wholeness of a community of individuals is reflected in the wholeness of the person, and the inherent bi-directionality of Moses' journey is mirrored in the temporal moments that the individual is asked to gather up into a unity.

At first, Moses refuses to gather up these temporal moments by doubting his ability to carry out the task to which God had called him. But he also tries to overcome his hesitation by asking God a further question:

> Behold, when I come unto the children of Israel, and shall say unto them, the God of your fathers hath sent me unto you; and they shall say to me, What is his name? What shall I say to them?[65]

This question might seem to convey the impression that Moses did not know the name of God — a name well known already to the Hebrew people. Moses' question might then be construed as an attempt to overcome his ignorance of the traditions of his people and to certify his mission by mentioning a name familiar already to the children of Israel. On the other hand, Moses' question might also be interpreted as an attempt to uncover the nature of God — a nature which had already been partly manifest, yet partly hidden. He could then be construed as attempting to establish a more profound conception of the nature of God than had been available to those who had worshipped him simply as the God of their fathers.[66] However this may be, it at least seems to be clear that the answer Moses receives to his question serves to advance the tradition from which he comes and to bring that tradition to a more coherent focus. This focus is achieved when God says:

> I am who I am:...Thus shalt thou say unto the children of Israel, I AM hath sent me unto you.... Thus shalt thou say unto the children of Israel, the Lord God (Yaweh) of your fathers, the God of Abraham, the God of Isaac, and the God of Jacob, hath sent me unto you: this is my name forever, and this is my memorial to all generations.[67]

In the remainder of this chapter, we must attempt to understand the meaning of this answer, for it is the focal point of the experience of Moses and the center of the religious experience of the Hebrew nation as a whole. It is also the crucial place where our outward movement toward the world as a whole experiences its most radical counter-thrust and where the notion of wholeness comes to focus upon a more profound conception of origins than we have yet been able to express. The wholeness of the Hebrew tradition is grounded in the name of God, and the wholeness that finally comes to Moses' life presupposes that he understands the nature and significance of the ground to which this name gives us access. At this point, however, let us simply notice that the unveiling of the name of God to Moses confirms His earlier claim to be present throughout all the modes of time. In the reference to Abraham, Isaac, and Jacob, God reinvokes the past; in addressing himself to Moses, he points to the significance of the present moment in Moses' experience; and in promising to be present in the future he promises to sustain Moses in the task he asks him to perform. In fact, in responding to Moses' claim, "Here am I," with the corresponding claim, "I AM," God interjects himself into the center of the human quest for wholeness; he collects all its temporal moments into a unity; and he points to the fact that his presence can be revealed in the two temporal directions in which he asks his servant to move.

God's universal presence throughout the modes of time is represented in the symmetrical chronology which the Old Testament attributes to the life of Moses. Moses lived for forty years in the court of Pharoah; he spent forty years in the desert prior to his experience at the burning bush; and he was to live another forty years as the leader of the Hebrew people in the wilderness.[68] Thus, the modes of God's temporal presence are also symmetrical within the concrete context of Moses' life. However, it must not be forgotten that the symmetry present here does not cancel the original discontinuity between the divine and human realms. In the lives of the patriarchs and in the life of Moses as well, human wholeness is always established through a free act of divine self-disclosure; and it is established from the side of man only due to his willingness to respond to what God reveals about his nature and intentions. As a result, it is vitally important that a conversation develop between Moses and God. The questions Moses asks reveal the dimensions of his freedom, and the fact that God chooses to answer demonstrates his willingness to disclose himself, in spite of the discontinuity between them. Yet we should also notice that this original duality is accentuated by the fact that Moses not only asks questions, but also exhibits a reluctance to obey God's commands. Even after God has revealed his name, Moses seeks to avoid his mission by claiming that he is slow of speech and that he is unfit to speak to Pharoah on behalf of his people.[69] The logos of the divine command is met by Moses' counterclaim that he is incapable of logos, and that for this reason he cannot become a vehicle for the salvation of his people.

As we shall discover in the following pages, the intelligibility of the divine ground will be a crucial element in the life of Moses, and in his attempt to lead his people into the region where they can also hear the voice of God. However, at the beginning, God requires obedience from his servant, and he responds in righteous anger to Moses' reluctance to obey. In almost a mocking whisper, he asks,

> Is not Aaron the Levite thy brother? I know that he can speak well. And also, behold, he cometh to meet thee: and when he seeth thee, he will be glad in his heart. And thou shalt speak unto him, and put words in his mouth: and I will be with thy mouth, and will teach you what ye shall do. And he shall be thy spokesman unto the people: and he shall be, even he shall be to thee instead of a mouth, and thou shalt be to him instead of God.[70]

Yet even when God addresses Moses in the power of his divine wrath, as he clearly does in this passage, he refuses to permit a complete separation between himself and his people. By claiming that he will teach Moses what he should say, he reiterates his promise to be present throughout the whole of Moses' life; by subordinating Aaron to Moses, the younger brother, he recapitulates the radical reversal of tribalism; and by interposing Aaron between Moses and his people, he allows Moses to become a finite image of his own transcendence. In the final analysis, it is as *an image of God* that Moses becomes a unified individual and is able to undertake the task of obedience that will make the divine logos accessible to the people of Israel. However, just as Moses is himself an image of God, we shall also find that the name of God is a universal image that brings all the dimensions of his nature to focus in a single context. The wholeness Moses achieves is grounded in the wholeness of God, and God's wholeness, in turn, is made visible in the image of his own nature that his name expresses. In the final section of this chapter, we shall turn to the interpretation of this image and to the ways in which it binds the two directionalities of Moses' life together. In doing so, we shall attempt to uncover the structure of the linguistic space where Abraham once heard the voice of God; where Isaac accepted his destruction as the offspring of tribalism; where Jacob wrestled with the angel; and where Moses stood in order to become whole and in order to be reconciled with the temporal directionalities that define the structure of human existence.

The Name of God

At the beginning of the Hebrew tradition, the role of language as an expression of intelligible structure is relatively insignificant. For example, God first speaks to Abraham only to demand obedience and to promise that he will be the father of a new nation; and apart from his objection that he has no offspring, Abraham responds to God's commands and promises in silence. This is especially clear when God demands that he sacrifice Isaac, for on that occasion Abraham does not respond at the verbal level at all, but only by taking a journey into the mountains where he will stand alone before God, unsupported by a larger community or by the mediation of intelligible discourse. On the other hand, when a community of individuals begins to develop on the basis of Abraham's original act of obedience, the role of language as a vehicle of intelligibility also begins to expand. For example, when Jacob wrestles with the angel, he makes verbalized demands upon him, and a dialogue occurs which finally issues in the transformation of his name from Jacob to Israel. This name, in turn, becomes the name of the children of Israel, so that the linguistic result of the conversation between Jacob and the angel is an image of an emerging community, the name of which will serve to separate the chosen people from all other nations. Of course, the final step in this moment of separation occurs only when Moses responds to God's command and returns to liberate his people from slavery. However, this response is also mediated by linguistic interaction, for Moses not only listens to the divine commands, but also engages in an extended dialogue with God, the center of which is his request that God reveal his name. One of the most striking facts about Moses' experience at the burning bush is that he is unable to come to terms with himself and to discover who he is until God reveals his nature in a logos that mediates the abruptness of the divine interjection. Moses' initial fascination with the mystery and the power of the burning bush is not sufficient to bring unity to his experience; and unity finally comes, only when God holds his mystery and power together in a speech about his nature and intentions.

In attempting to interpret the meaning of the name of God, we stand on the same ground where Moses once stood, confronting the demand that we bring our thoughts into accord with the content that God himself reveals. The name of God is his living image, and it requires an interpretive response that bears an intrinsic connection with Moses' original response to God himself. If the quest for wholeness cannot be formulated at a distance because it concerns the meaning of human existence, the interpretation of the name of God is equally impossible in merely objective terms. The name has to do with who we are, and it has a direct relationship with the particularity of our own individual experience. On the other hand, in attempting to interpret the name of God, language as interpretive discourse becomes more important than it was in Moses' original experience. In asking God to reveal his name, Moses receives an answer that is the foundation of subsequent interpretations, but the interpretation itself must make elements within the name explicit that are not immediately evident in God's original response. If intelligibility is to be achieved, the logos of the divine command and the logos of dialogue and revelation must be supplemented by the logos of interpretation and by the quest for a structure that can reflect the original content that the name itself exhibits. The quest for understanding brings the Hebrew quest for wholeness to fulfillment, for in the final analysis it is the intelligible element present in the name of God that underlies the journey of the Hebrew people from Ur of the Chaldees to the conquest of the Promised Land. The Hebrew tradition moves from the particular encounter of Abraham with God to an affirmation of God's universal presence throughout all the modes of time, and it is the acknowledgment of this universal presence that provides the reflective ground of this tradition.

In making an interpretative response to the name of God and in moving from the logos of revelation to the logos of intelligible structure, there are two kinds of interpretation that it is important to distinguish. The first is a complex mixture of philosophical and theological components that articulates the meaning of the name in categorial terms and relates this meaning to the wider context of human existence. We have adumbrated this kind of interpretation already by discussing the modes of time and their concrete unification and by indicating the ways in which these concepts are helpful in illuminating the meaning of Moses' experience. However, a practical mode of interpretation is also possible in which rites and rituals are established to express the meaning of the name in human terms and to give the larger human community concrete access to the structure that the name itself exhibits. Though Moses does not attempt the first of these kinds of interpretation, he does attempt the second, for he mirrors the nature of his encounter with God in the rites and rituals he establishes for his people to obey. In doing so, he generalizes his individual experience and makes its context accessible to a wider range of participants. In this final section, our task will be to develop both kinds of interpretation and to indicate the ways in which the structure of each of them reflects the structure of the other. However, we shall also attempt to show how both modes of interpretation reflect the experiential unity to which the name of God attempts to point, for it is their common bond with Moses' original experience that allows them to bring the Hebrew quest for wholeness to fulfillment. In this case, concrete reflection is the attempt to show how the name of God *mirrors* the content of Moses' experience, and how this name allows the reflective individual to enter the space where this experience occurs.

Reflective interpretation

One of the most familiar interpretations of the name of God received its classical expression in the thought of St. Thomas Aquinas. Of course, this interpretation begins with Moses' experience at the burning bush and with God's initial declaration, "I AM WHO I AM." However, from this point on, St. Thomas' account is guided by the fact that in the translation of the passage available to him, the original formulation of the name is contracted immediately into a substantival form. In the Vulgate edition of the Book of Exodus, the passage in question reads, "I AM WHO I AM. . . . Thou shalt say to the children of Israel: HE WHO IS hath sent me to you."[71] As has often been suggested, this translation leads St. Thomas to focus his attention on the substantival form of the name, and to conduct the discussion of its meaning entirely within the context of theoretical discourse. Apparently he assumes that the problem of interpretation to be encountered here is simply the problem of giving an adequate account of the formula into which the original sentential utterance has been contracted. As we shall soon discover, this way of proceeding is inadequate, for it takes us away from the concrete context in which the name of God acquired its original significance, without attempting to reconnect the experiential and the reflective levels. This is unfortunate, for the kind of interpretation we are now considering means nothing unless it serves to ground the human journey we have been attempting to understand. Yet before we attempt to remedy this defect, there is a great deal to be learned from the Thomistic approach to the nature of God. In fact, a central insight which any interpretation must include is expressed in the three significant elements upon which St. Thomas bases his interpretation. First, he claims that the phrase, "HE WHO IS," exhibits the fact that in God, essence and being are identical. If the nature of God is formulated adequately in the utterance, "I AM WHO I AM," Aquinas reasons that God's very nature is to be. In the case of other beings, essence is only contingently related to being; in the case of God, essence and existence are the same. In the second place, St. Thomas claims that if God is to be understood as HE WHO IS, the very universality of the name points to the mystery of God. Any other name would be less universal than being and would serve to make the nature of God determinate. By contrast, this name preserves the mystery of God as he is in himself by not restricting his nature to a determinate content. Finally, St. Thomas asserts that the claim that God is HE WHO IS serves to signify the primacy of the present in the nature of God. He implies that God is not like his creatures in being subject to time, and that this fact is represented in the name, the verbal element of which makes reference to time only in the guise of the eternal present.[72] Thus, St. Thomas not only claims that in God, essence and being are identical and that God as he is in himself is essentially mysterious, but also that God can be understood as the eternal present, standing both beyond and in the modes of time.

This kind of analysis employs a set of distinctions that are of crucial significance for understanding metaphysical and theological issues. Terms like essence, existence, being, time, and eternity are indispensable as ways of giving us reflective access to the issues in question. In addition, St. Thomas' account not only places it within a context that is accessible to systematic reflection, but also points to the mystery and the transcendence of God which our earlier description of Moses' experience presupposes. Despite the substantival form into which the name is contracted, St. Thomas is careful to emphasize the mystery and the indeterminacy which the name of God reveals. As we have observed already, it is this mystery and indeterminacy that grounds the freedom of God's self-disclosure and upon which his unexpected interjections are founded. Moreover, it is the mysterious dimension of God's nature that Moses first encountered at the burning bush and that was present throughout the interaction between Moses and God. However, the encounter between Moses and God also suggests that He is not to be understood simply in terms of mystery and indeterminacy, nor simply as the being in whom essence and existence are identical.

Due to the interaction between them, *the name of God must also be characterized in relational terms and must be understood within the context of utterance and interaction in which its significance was first expressed.* What, then, was the meaning of the name as it was understood within this experiential context, and how can the name be interpreted so that it can answer Moses' question about the nature of the one who had spoken to him?[73]

When the question is formulated in this way, we find that part of the answer is somewhat surprisingly contained in the question itself. One of the things which the name of God enabled Moses to conclude about his nature was simply that he had chosen to reveal himself. God revealed himself to Moses at the burning bush, and within this concrete setting, the *existential* formulation of his utterance can be rendered, I AM PRESENT. He then answered the anticipated question of the Hebrew people about his nature by declaring, "Thou shalt say unto the children of Israel, I AM PRESENT hath sent me unto you." Reference to God as the eternal present is thus only one of the ways in which we may attempt to characterize his nature. The etymology of the name also permits the existential and relational characterization in terms of which the eternal present is said to *manifest its presence.*[74] Now it is important to notice that the existential and relational characterization is not incompatible with the Thomistic account of the meaning of the name. In fact, both accounts can be understood as aspects of a more nearly adequate interpretation which attempts to preserve two distinguishable dimensions of the nature of God, while it also binds the divine and human realms together. The Thomistic interpretation points to the mystery and the indeterminacy of God as it is reflected in the notion of the eternal present, while the existential account indicates that the mystery of this eternal present is also to be understood as present to the people to whom God chose to address himself. In the final analysis, the two dimensions of the nature of God are intrinsically connected: the notion of the eternal *present,* which the philosophical and the theological traditions have attempted to articulate, manifests itself in the guise of an eternal *presence;* this presence, in turn, gives us access to the eternal present which it both embodies and reflects.

Some of the earlier names of God to be found within the Hebrew tradition are used almost exclusively to point to God's transcendence. For example, the name *El Shaddhi* characterizes God as a mysterious center of power,[75] while the name *Elohim* refers to the transcendent majesty of God, who lives beyond the world and who is separated from the human realm by a chasm that can never be obliterated.[76] Thus, if it is to reflect this earlier tradition, it is important that the name revealed at the burning bush have a transcendent dimension and that our attention be directed to the mystery and the indeterminacy of God that his transcendence always presupposes. In the Hebrew tradition, God transcends the world, and he can never be restricted to a place within a larger totality. For this reason, the Hebrew quest for wholeness always occurs against the background of mystery and forces us to acknowledge the fact that the Ground of existence can never be fully comprehended. However, the crucial point about Moses' experience at the burning bush is that the transcendent God reveals himself as fully present and that the mysterious source of power of the earlier tradition manifests itself as an immanent force within the temporal order. Moses overcomes his fragmentation within a mysterious context, but he is able to find wholeness for himself and for his people only when God reveals his presence in this context and promises to bind the past and the future together in the wholeness of a unified life. Abraham had been asked to leave his family in order to stand before the Ground of his existence and in order to become the founder of a new nation. But now that this nation has come into existence, God reappears in a richer form to Moses, demanding that this new nation be reestablished and that it be taken into the Promised Land as a free people. It is of course true that even after they had been liberated, the ancient Hebrews refused to utter the name that God revealed to Moses. However, they did this, not because God remains transcendent when he addresses Moses, but because he comes so near that the worshipper feels compelled to reassert the distinction between God and the world by refusing to utter his name. At the burning bush, the transcendence of the eternal present manifests its presence, and it is God's claim to be both transcendent and present that constitutes the meaning of his name for future generations.

Perhaps the account to be given of this duality within the nature of God can be enriched if we focus briefly upon two of the other well-known philological interpretations of the meaning of the name. We can then return to our earlier discussion and can gather up the results of our inquiry. The first of these alternative interpretations of the name renders the original Hebrew formulation in essentially causative terms. According to this account, the Hebrew phrase, "'ehyeh asher 'ehyeh," is not to be translated, I AM WHO I AM, or I AM PRESENT WHO AM PRESENT, but instead, I MAKE TO BE WHAT COMES TO BE.[77] Thus, the interpretation in question mobilizes the traditional Hebrew conception of God the creator and points to the originative dimension to be discerned within the nature of God. However, this interpretation also preserves the original duality to be discovered in the nature of God. On the one hand, the notion of creation points to an originative *relation* between creator and creature. If God creates the world, he must be related to it, and in fact, must be related to it more intimately than things within the world are related to each other. A created product is the termination of a creative act, and it always bears the stamp of its maker upon its nature and existence. On the other hand, the relation of creation is unique, for the creator of finite beings is not only related to them, but also transcends them infinitely. As creator, God must be regarded as an inherent duality, not only present to his creatures, but also transcendent of the products he brings into existence.[78] However, the present interpretation does not merely reiterate the previous account, but directs our attention to a dimension of the presence of God that enriches the original characterization. According to this interpretation, the nature of God has a bearing upon the present moment within the experience of Moses, and upon his attempt to recover his origins because it is also *the originative ground* upon which the existence of Moses and of other men is founded. The eternal present which manifests its presence to Moses is also said to be *present in the beginning,* and he is present there as the ONE WHO CREATES WHAT COMES TO BE. *In this way, the past and the present are connected at the primordial level, and Moses' attempt to recover his origins is given a metaphysical foundation.*

The final interpretation of the meaning of the name which has often been suggested serves to refocus the mysterious dimension of the presence of God; however, it also expands the previous account by emphasizing a futuristic aspect of the issue that is yet to be considered. According to this interpretation, the verb in the original formulation has a futuristic reference, and the sentence as a whole is to translated: I WILL BE WHO I WILL BE. This translation preserves the freedom and the mystery of God because the sentence can be read as an explicit refusal to convey a determinate characterization of the meaning of the name. In answer to the question, "What is thy name?" which might possibly be interpreted as an attempt to gain control over God by gaining access to his name, the reply is given, I WILL BE WHO I WILL BE. In other words, no determinate characterization of the name is given that would enable the worshipper to gain manipulative and controlling access to the object of worship.[79] On the other hand, the dynamic character of the verb emphasized in this account also suggests that God's action has a bearing on the future. The formulation in question not only points to the mystery of God, but also indicates that he is free to manifest himself in the future in a variety of ways.[80] God says, "I *WILL BE* WHO I *WILL BE*." Accordingly, the interpretation that denies the worshipper manipulative access to the object of worship also directs his attention outward toward the larger world and toward the future as the temporal context in which God's freedom of action can be exhibited.

All of these accounts of the name of God may of course be elaborated, for each of them points to an aspect of its meaning that requires more detailed analysis and articulation. However, it is also true that each of these interpretations is already a familiar part of the critical literature about the meaning of the name of God. What is needed at this point is not a further recapitulation of previous opinions. Instead, we must attempt to collect the variety of insights contained in the preceding accounts and indicate the ways in which they can be related to the concrete context of Moses' life. In this way, the abstract distinctions that separate these alternative interpretations can be held together, and perhaps our reflections can begin to approximate the concrete content reflected in the name itself. In attempting to understand this content in the richest possible fashion, let us first return to the formulation of the name with which we began, indicating the ways in which it can be transformed in order to unify the central insights of our earlier discussion. As I have suggested already, the initial formulation, I AM WHO I AM, embodies the notion of the eternal *present* and the notion of the divine *presence*. Let this duality of reference now be reflected by transforming the phrase, I AM WHO I AM, into the sentence, I AM PRESENT WHO AM PRESENT. In this transformation, the divine presence appears explicitly, while the notion of the eternal present is reflected in the phrase, I AM. Taken together, these two elements point to the duality always exhibited by the nature of God, but as the transformation now before us suggests, they are also held together in a larger unity. At this point in our earlier discussion, we turned to the causative dimension of the name and as a consequence, retranslated it in the phrase, I MAKE TO BE WHAT COMES TO BE. Instead, let the causative insight now be incorporated into our more comprehensive account by adding a dimension to both the form and the content of the translation, I AM PRESENT WHO AM PRESENT. Let this earlier translation now be rendered: I AM (*was, am*) PRESENT *IN POWER* WHO AM PRESENT. The reference to power now included reflects the notion of creation and incorporates the causative element of the verb into the meaning of the name, and the verbs in parentheses indicate the modes in which the eternal present can be related to time in terms of the notions of creativity and presence. God *was* present in power because he is the God of creation, and he *is* present because he reveals himself to Moses at the burning bush. Thus, the eternal present, who manifests his presence, also reveals himself in power, and his creative power is related both to the past and to the present as the power of being itself. Finally, we have suggested that the freedom of God's action can be understood in terms of his relation to the future, and that the inescapable mystery of God must also be preserved. Accordingly, let the phrase, I AM (was, am) PRESENT IN POWER WHO AM PRESENT, now be rendered: I AM (*was, am, will be*) PRESENT IN POWER, *AS WHO I AM,* AM I PRESENT. The verbs in parentheses point in two directions and span all the modes of time, calling our attention not only to the past and to the present, but also to the future. Moreover, the eternal present is reflected in the phrase, I AM, for the God who reveals himself in time nevertheless remains transcendent. Reference to the creativity and to the presence of God is also incorporated in the words, PRESENT IN POWER, and these notions are related to the past, the present, and the future. In this way, the eternal present is said to be present in power throughout all the modes of time. Finally, the mystery of God remains inescapable, and it reveals its presence in the phrase that separates the dual reference to power and presence: I AM (was, am, will be) PRESENT IN POWER, *AS WHO I AM,* AM I PRESENT. This phrase, AS WHO I AM, stands within the center of the name, and it points to a mystery that can never be fully articulated. However, we are given access to this mystery, both in the experience of Moses and in the experience of the people he led into the Promised Land, *by listening to the poetic echo that the name itself contains:* I AM (was, am, will be) PRESENT IN POWER, AS WHO I AM, AM I PRESENT. In this echo, the notions of time and eternity intersect; the two directionalities of our earlier analysis come together; and a space is generated that can bring wholeness to the human situation.

We have already described in some detail the ways in which Moses once stood within the sacred space reflected in the meaning of the name. Let us simply recall our earlier suggestion that the name serves to confirm the claim of God to be present throughout the modes of time. God was present to Moses at the burning bush; he told him that he was the God of his fathers; and he promised to be present in the future, both to Moses and his people. Of course, it should now be evident that the meaning of the name is the *ground* of this threefold unity, for God can be present to Moses and to his people on a variety of temporal occasions because *his very nature* spans the modes of time. Yet we have also suggested that the name of God has a bearing on the existential aspects of Moses' experience. The first dimension of God's presence enables communication to take place between Moses and God; the second dimension enables him to recover his past; and the third dimension allows him to confront the future with some measure of confidence and to lead his people to the boundary of the Promised Land. When Moses returns to his origins and undertakes the task to which he has been called, he does so by first returning to the ground of existence itself, and it is this ground that gathers up the modes of time into a unity and that allows Moses to gather up the temporal elements of his own experience as well. God first appeared to Abraham, Isaac, and Jacob in order to found a new community. He then promised Moses that he would be present in the past, the present, and the future and that he would hold these elements together in a community of temporal moments. Finally, he reveals his nature as spread out over time and as the foundation of both the Hebrew community and of the temporal elements that make this unity possible. It is finally by gathering up the modes of time into a unity that the name of God is the foundation for the wholeness of the Hebrew tradition and is the ultimate ground to which their return to origins must be related.

Concrete embodiment

When Moses returns to his people, he attempts to embody concretely the various dimensions of the relationship that had developed between himself and God. In this way, he gives a "practical" interpretation of the name of God that mirrors the content of our "theoretical" account. For example, in the course of the journey from Egypt to the Promised Land, Moses establishes a place of worship at the center of which he places what is called "the Holy of Holies." The moveable temple that he creates is accessible to the people and is always open to those who wish to encounter the presence of God. However, the Holy of Holies cannot be entered except by the High Priest, and even then only once a year, for it points to the mysterious aspect of the ultimate dimension of experience to be encountered there.[81] Just as the name of God contains a mysterious element at its center, reflecting the mystery of Moses' experience at the burning bush, the temple Moses builds contains a mysterious element as well. The accessibility of the temple mirrors the actuality of God's presence and reflects the dimension of presence revealed in the name, but the temple also depicts the mystery of the one who is present AS WHO HE IS. It is this dimension of mystery that stands at the center of Moses' original experience and that will always be an inescapable element in the experience of the Hebrew people as a whole. However, the fact that the temple can be moved also reflects the plurality of temporal modes in which God manifests his presence. Having been created, the temple moves with the people in the course of their journey, and like God himself, it acquires a history as it goes with them into the Promised Land. The temple Moses places at the center of the Hebrew community depicts the mystery, the presence, and the "temporality" of God. In doing so, it reflects in concrete terms the dimensions of the name of God revealed to Moses at the burning bush.

As the people journey toward the Promised Land with this concrete image of God's nature before them, they finally arrive at the place where Moses first encountered the presence of God, making their camp at the foot of the mountain, as God himself had promised. While they remain there, Moses tells them that he must climb the mountain to speak with God. However, on this occasion, a cloud of smoke surrounds the mountain, separating the people from God's presence, and it is into this surrounding smoke that Moses vanishes to speak with him.[82] As time passes and as they continue to be separated from their leader, the people become restive. Some of them conclude that he will not return, while others propose that a golden calf be fashioned from the rings and the bracelets that have been brought from Egypt and that it be placed in their midst as an object of worship. In this way, the Hebrew people recapitulate the theme of human disobedience, falling prey to the temptation to fall away from God in the moment in which he is hidden from them behind the clouds of smoke. Moses, the image of God, has vanished from their midst, and into the vacuum created by his absence, the people thrust a golden calf.[83] When Moses returns to see what his people have done, he exhibits the divine wrath that he himself had experienced when he had once considered the possibility of disobedience to God. Moses had come down from the mountain intending to give the people a table of laws that he had received from God. Instead, he dashes the tablet that contains the Ten Commandments against the rocks.[84] But then Moses returns to the mountain and comes back once more with a second tablet containing the laws which the Hebrews were required to obey, *in spite of their inevitable tendency toward disobedience.*[85] The Law that Moses brings this second time reflects the nature of the Covenant that had been established between Abraham and God. Though it directs our attention to the separation between the Hebrew people and God, it also mediates the contrast between them, refusing to allow the people to escape the demands that must be fulfilled if wholeness is to be achieved. In the context of Hebrew religion, the Law fulfills the Covenant, for it provides the final bond in terms of which both the transcendence and the presence of God are reflected.

With the tables of the Law in their possession, the Hebrews finally come to the boundary of Canaan. However, God tells Moses that he will not be permitted to lead his people into the Promised Land. In the course of the journey from Egypt, Moses had once disobeyed the voice of God. God had asked him to touch a rock with his staff in order to obtain water, but he had struck the rock instead. As a result, God tells him that he will not be permitted to cross the boundary of Canaan.[86] However, this prohibition is not merely negative, for God takes Moses up into a mountain and allows him to look out across the land that he had promised to give to Abraham's descendants. As he stands there, Moses is no doubt reminded of the fact that one day he had recovered his past by discovering that God spans all the modes of time, for as he now looks into the future that he will not be permitted to enter, he finds that the Land itself is a symbol of God's boundless presence. Because his vision of the past and the future is so clear, Moses' present inability to go into the Promised Land is not a loss of wholeness. In fact, his acceptance of his finitude is a crucial element in the wholeness he achieves. The limitation imposed upon him points to the fact that his place within the Hebrew community must be taken by another and that wholeness within the Hebrew tradition can only be achieved by a developing community of participants. This endless task is an image of the mystery and the openness of the concept of wholeness and a reflection of the mystery and the openness of God himself. The individuality of Moses also requires that he accept his limits, for it is only by accepting the fact that he cannot enter the new land that Moses lives and dies with his own space intact. Moses' existence within the larger community is defined in the face of limitations — limitations that allow him to bind the past and the future of his own life together in a finite unity. However, at this final moment, it must not be forgotten that Moses is not only a finite individual, but that he also stands before God and that he is buried with God's own hands.[87] At the end of his life, Moses returns to his origins at both the horizontal and the vertical levels, and it is in this respect that his quest for wholeness is finally brought to fulfillment.

3

The Conflict between Religion and Philosophy

In the previous chapters I have suggested that the quest for wholeness moves in two directions and that the human journey can be understood from two radically different perspectives. On the one hand, the quest often begins with fragmentation and attempts to move beyond it by seeking fulfillment in the larger world; on the other hand, it sometimes begins with a direct encounter with what is ultimate and attempts to develop the significance of this original experience. Those who adopt the first of these directions often acknowledge the alienation of the human condition, but in doing so, they sometimes affirm the fact that man participates in what is ultimate and that he must attempt to come to terms with his original condition. In fact, in Chapter 1 we found that Ahab, Queequeg, and Ishmael are all united in a common venture, and that in each case, the whaling voyage they undertake is intended to bring their participation to progressive fulfillment. By contrast, the Biblical tradition is oriented in a different direction and is grounded in a developing relationship between a particular individual and God. Abraham's journey is an attempt to recover the origins of human existence and to originate a new community, each member of which stands before God as a radical individual. We must not forget that Abraham, Isaac, Jacob, and Moses are bound together in a common tradition. However, their unity does not depend upon their participation in this larger context, but upon the part they play in originating a new world that reflects the intentions of the ground of their existence. There can be little doubt that the quest for wholeness moves outward toward a more inclusive unity, but it also moves backward to the origins from which it emerges. In both cases, it attempts to bring fulfillment to the human soul.

At the experiential level, it is possible to be engaged in the quest for wholeness without distinguishing the two directions in which it develops. In thrusting beyond our original condition, we are sometimes so preoccupied with the wider context in which we exist that we are only dimly aware of our origins; while in returning to our origins, we sometimes focus on them so exclusively that we lose sight of the end toward which our journey is directed. And even when both directions come together in the experience of a single individual, as they do when Ishmael's whaling venture culminates in the recovery of his family or when Abraham's return to his origins requires him to journey into an unknown land, the relationship between the two directionalities often remains a merely implicit element in the discussion. Melville's novel is dominated by an outward journey, while the Biblical tradition is concerned primarily with the recovery of origins. As a result, each of these contexts deals only derivatively with the directionality which is central for the other, almost unconsciously attempting to unify the quest for wholeness from only one direction. Yet having plunged into the quest for wholeness and having reflected on the significance of the human journey in these two separate contexts, we should now ask how two such different frameworks are to be related. At this stage of our discussion, we must not focus our attention on a single direction, but should make an explicit attempt to understand how the two directionalities are to be ordered and connected. In order to do this we must move beyond the context of immediate experience and must shift our attention from doing to knowing and from action to inquiry. However, this transition is not so radical as it might seem, for we have already discovered that reflection itself is an integral part of the human journey. When alternative conceptions of the quest for wholeness appear, reason demands that we move beyond them and that a framework be generated in which the contrast between them can be examined in reflective terms. In this chapter, we shall continue to depict the quest for wholeness as it unfolds within direct experience, but we shall also ask about the relationship between two kinds of journey, each of which is rich enough to bring fulfillment at the experiential level.

Of all the frameworks available to us, the philosophical dialogue is the most appropriate place to raise a question about the relationship between the two directionalities. In the first place, dialogues often begin with direct experience, and they often call our attention to places in experience where fragmentation is encountered and where the quest for wholeness is generated. As a result, the examination of a dialogue will allow us to preserve the experiential dimension of our inquiry, while it will permit us to move the discussion to a more explicitly reflective level. In the second place, the structure of a dialogue presupposes that alternative points of view are represented within a common context of reflection. In our own discussion, this means that the outward journey and the return to origins can be brought together and examined as alternative conceptions of the human quest for fulfillment. In fact, in the dialogue that we shall consider, two characters are to be found who represent the two conceptions of the quest for wholeness we have already distinguished, and the dialogue itself is devoted to a detailed examination of their relative priority. However, we should also notice that the characters in a dialogue can preserve their integrity only because they encounter one another from different perspectives and because the dual focus of their conversation reflects this original moment of difference. In the dialogue to be examined here, the two directionalities to be found within the quest for wholeness open out toward one another in a reflective quest for understanding, but they also remain in radical contrast. As a result, the spatial separation between the characters and the contrast between the two directions they represent can be preserved while they are brought together in dialogic interaction. Finally, the purpose of the dialogue to be considered in this chapter is to understand the meaning of wholeness through a process of philosophical reflection. Our discussion of the contrast between the two conceptions of the quest for wholeness at the experiential level will thus become the reflective attempt to understand their underlying structure and to assess the relative value of the two directionalities these conceptions presuppose.

Of the many philosophical dialogues that we could consider, the one which deals most incisively with the two directionalities is Plato's *Euthyphro*. In this dialogue, which has been placed by tradition at the beginning of the Platonic corpus,[1] a confrontation occurs between Euthyphro and Socrates about the nature of piety.[2] From an existential point of view, Socrates suggests that piety can be understood by undertaking an outward quest for unity, while Euthyphro claims that it is to be achieved only by returning to the origins of his individual existence. Thus, the dialogue can be read as an encounter between the two directionalities we have already considered and as an attempt to exhibit their differences within a common existential framework. However, the conversation between Euthyphro and Socrates is not merely existential, but also theoretical, for in discussing the nature of piety they become engaged in a reflective inquiry about the meaning of wholeness itself. In the course of the discussion, a number of definitions of wholeness are considered that both recapitulate and move beyond our previous reflections, finally forcing us to come to terms with the abstract dimension of our inquiry. In their quest for a definition of piety, Socrates transforms the quest for wholeness into a philosophical attempt to understand the Whole, while Euthyphro transforms the religious attempt to obey the will of the gods into the theological attempt to understand and to imitate their nature. Thus Euthyphro and Socrates stand in contrast with one another, not merely as individuals with different beliefs and opinions, but also as representatives of two radically different reflective orientations. The link between the two levels is to be found in the Socratic conviction that wholeness can be achieved only by understanding the world as a whole and man's place in it and in Euthyphro's belief that obedience to the will of the gods presupposes an accurate knowledge of their nature and intentions. But this suggests, in turn, that the reflective attempt to obtain knowledge is integral to the quest for wholeness as a human undertaking and that reflection itself may be understood as a way of bringing the quest for wholeness to fulfillment.

Plato's *Euthyphro* is an aesthetic unity, focused on the meaning of wholeness and demanding a reflective response to the two directions in which it develops. Rooted in direct experience, it begins with action and with the existential context from which the quest for wholeness always emerges. However, the dialogue also shifts our attention from action to reflection and to the contrast between philosophy and theology, allowing the quest for wholeness to unfold as a reflective undertaking. In the process, the logos of narrative discourse to be found in Melville's *Moby-Dick,* and the logos of the divine–human encounter to be found in the Hebrew religious tradition, become the structure of abstract theoretical discourse and the logos of dialogic interaction. The purpose of Plato's *Euthyphro* is to understand the meaning of wholeness and to discuss the relationship between the two directionalities in which the quest for wholeness develops. In this respect, the concrete circumstances with which both Euthyphro and Socrates begin are vehicles for achieving philosophical insight and for articulating the meaning of wholeness at the reflective level. However, we shall also discover that the dialogue raises more questions than it answers and that in the course of the discussion a definitive formulation of the meaning of wholeness is never achieved. Apparently, wholeness is to be found more in the dialogic process than in a final product and more in the middle ground between the two characters than in the goal toward which their conversation is directed. In the space in between Euthyphro and Socrates, Plato gives the two directionalities a place within the "whole" of dialogic interaction, and in the end it is the dialogue itself that binds them together.

The Family, the City, and the Task of Philosophy

At the beginning of the dialogue, Euthyphro and Socrates meet on the porch of a law court (2a), located at the center of the city of Athens.[3] In this fashion, Plato indicates that their conversation is rooted in the social and political life of Ancient Greece and is bounded by the cultural context represented by the walls that encircle the city. Within the larger framework of the natural order, the city is an island of cultural and political interaction, and it is within this more limited context that the conversation between Euthyphro and Socrates takes place. On the other hand, since the particular court where the conversation occurs is restricted to suits pertaining to the state religion,[4] Plato's reference to it suggests that the religious life of the city will also have a bearing on the ensuing discussion. In fact, we quickly discover that religion will be at the center of the dialogue, for Plato tells us that both Euthyphro and Socrates are soon to be involved in cases to be brought before the court itself (2a–b, 3e). Despite their differences, they share a common problem, and in each case the issue to be decided pertains to the concept of piety — a concept that is central for our understanding of Greek religion and for our conception of the social order that underlies the ancient city.[5] There is of course a great distance from the ocean of Melville's novel and from the desert of the Hebrew religious tradition to the center of the city of Athens. Yet in each case, the problem of fragmentation arises with equal seriousness, and the quest for wholeness occurs as a response to the discord to be found within the human situation. In Plato's *Euthyphro,* the problem of fragmentation results from a fear of religious pollution, and the quest for wholeness takes place as an attempt to overcome this fear through a reflective understanding of the meaning of piety. As a result, human wholeness becomes the subject-matter of reflection and the goal of a quest for wholeness at the reflective level.

Before this reflective undertaking begins, both Euthyphro and Socrates have stories to tell, and we must first turn to them if we are to understand the experiential situations from which their reflective problems emerge. Euthyphro tells us that his suit before the religious court in Athens stems from an event that had occurred sometime before at his home on the island of Naxos. One of the servants working on Euthyphro's farm had one day gotten angry with a house slave, and in a drunken stupor, killed him. As the head of the household, Euthyphro's father responded by binding the servant hand and foot and by throwing him into a ditch, sending a man to Athens to ask the religious advisor what he ought to do. In the meantime, he neglected the servant, thinking that he was a murderer and that it didn't matter even if he were to die. Euthyphro tells us that this is precisely what occurred, for the servant died of hunger and cold before the messenger returned. Death thus stands at the beginning of Euthyphro's story, and it is the concrete circumstances that produce it that lie behind his journey to the city of Athens. Euthyphro says that the other members of his family approved their father's act, possibly because they believed that the father's authority was absolute in matters of this kind or perhaps because they thought that the death of the servant atoned for the death of the slave. Yet because he felt responsible for his servant and because his father had allowed him to die, Euthyphro himself was convinced that his father was guilty of murder and that he must be brought to justice. As a result, he has come to the courtroom in Athens to prosecute his father for murder. But Euthyphro also tells us that he *feels compelled* to prosecute his father, for he says that if a murderer is allowed to go unpunished in the family, the stain of religious pollution will not only affect the murderer himself, but will also taint the other members of the household (4c–e). It is finally this fear of pollution, and of the fragmentation it brings to the unity of the family, that transforms a civil suit into a religious question and that brings Euthyphro to the religious court in Athens to pursue his indictment.[6] In our earlier chapters, Ishmael was ejected from his family and undertook a quest for wholeness in the larger context of an ocean venture, while Abraham was asked to turn away from his family and to journey into an unknown land where he would finally bring a new kind of community and a new conception of human wholeness into existence. By contrast, Euthyphro attempts to overcome the fragmentation that threatens his family by turning against his father and by purging the pollution that had occurred because of his father's act. In Euthyphro's case, the quest for wholeness is to be undertaken because of the stain of pollution, and wholeness itself is to be purchased at the price of violence against his origins. There is of course a very deep truth in this suggestion, for we often find that our origins must first be repudiated before they can be reinstated. In any case, this principle will certainly prove to be true in Euthyphro's experience.

Unlike Euthyphro, Socrates tells us that he is being indicted, rather than prosecuting another. However, in this case the concepts of fragmentation and pollution also play a crucial role. Socrates says that a young man named Meletus has brought an indictment against him for inventing new gods and for leading the youth astray. Meletus claims that Socrates wishes to replace the traditional gods of the city with new ones and that he is corrupting the youth by asking philosophical questions. In social and political terms, he is bringing an indictment for impiety against Socrates on behalf of custom and tradition. In fact, the charge that Socrates is corrupting the youth and inventing new gods is a single charge insofar as both of its prongs are grounded in the wish to preserve the customs and traditions of the city. The gods of the city are the guardians of the past, and attempts to raise philosophical questions about custom and tradition not only threaten the unity of the city, but also alienate the youth from the origins of the city to which these customs and traditions call our attention. Meletus apparently believes that the questions of Socrates fragment the city, and he attempts to overcome this fragmentation in the indictment that he brings against him. In Euthyphro's case, the problem of fragmentation is confined to an individual family, while in the case of Socrates, it is apparently present with reference to an entire city. However, there is a sense in which the city of Athens can also be regarded as a family. Socrates suggests that this is the case when he compares the city with a mother (2c), and Euthyphro suggests it when he claims that the charge of Meletus will strike a blow at the *hearthfire* of the state (3a). It is no accident that the language of corruption is the language in terms of which the indictment of Socrates is formulated: the analogy between the state and the family and the fear of pollution in both cases are the fundamental facts that bind these cases together.

Though Euthyphro and Socrates meet on the porch of the law court, and though they share a common problem, they meet outside the court itself (2a). This fact is significant, for it suggests that other contexts are relevant to the issues at hand than the merely legal framework that the city-state provides. These alternative frameworks may be loosely characterized as the contexts of religion and philosophy, and it is in these terms that the conversation between Euthyphro and Socrates develops. As we have discovered already, Socrates meets Euthyphro as a philosopher: his customary haunts are in the Lyceum,[7] where he often engages in philosophical inquiry. As a result, Euthyphro expresses surprise that he has abandoned his station to come to the court of the King Archon (2a). However, Socrates informs him that the problem that has forced him to appear at the courtroom has arisen as a result of his customary activities. In the course of nearly a lifetime of philosophical reflection, conflicts have developed between Socrates and the Athenians that have finally issued in a charge of impiety, and it is in response to this charge that Socrates has come to the religious court (3d–e). Yet in telling Euthyphro about the indictment outside the court itself, Socrates suggests that the issue at hand transcends the framework of custom and tradition that the courtroom presupposes. In fact, Socrates is committed to the view that the charge of impiety, which has arisen as a result of philosophy, must itself be subject to philosophical examination. It is for this reason that the conversation recorded here begins in the open space of the portico, rather than within the legal confines of the building itself.

Euthyphro also comes to the King Archon's court from a frame of reference that transcends the legal framework of the city. He lives with his family on the island of Naxos and is in a number of ways relatively uncomfortable with the city life of Athens. For example, he says that the other citizens laugh at him when he addresses the assembly and that they say he is mad when he speaks about divine matters and when he attempts to foretell the future (2c). These remarks have led several commentators to suggest that Euthyphro is certainly not an orthodox representative of traditional religion. Some have even claimed that he is an adherent of a Dionysian cult that flourished on the islands of the Aegean and that as a result, he stands outside the context of Olympian religion.[8] However this may be, it at least seems clear that a contrast emerges at the beginning of the dialogue between the city and the country and between Athens and the island upon which Euthyphro's problem originated. Yet Euthyphro's description of his problem also transcends the city-state in another way: his fear of religious pollution points beyond the city of Athens to his participation in the ancient family religion of Greece. It is the religious framework of the family and the mythology that develops from it which Euthyphro presupposes in his conversation with Socrates.

In the ancient family, the members of the household were united around a common hearthfire, and all of them worshipped their own ancestral gods. These gods had once been members of the family and were buried on the family's land.[9] As a result, worshipping them provided a way of establishing continuity between oneself and the past. It was the way in which the members of an ancient family were able to participate in a tradition that transcended their own particularity. The wholeness of the family was defined in terms of its unbroken continuity with the past, and the wholeness of the individual depended upon his participation in this larger context. As we discovered in our earlier discussion of Abraham, the individual member of an ancient family is who he is because of the role he plays within the family, and the individual himself is defined as a part of a larger totality. When a break in the continuity of the family occurs, as was the case in the death of the house slave, it becomes necessary to reestablish continuity through an act of purgation.[10] From the perspective of Euthyphro's family, the death of the slave creates discontinuity, and it issues in pollution because it generates a gap in the unity of the family. Moreover, each family member is threatened because the meaning of his existence is defined in terms of the family and because the family itself has lost the unity necessary to bring stability to its individual members. However, in this particular case, it is apparent that the family also believes that the death of the servant atones for the death of the slave and rids the family of the pollution that results from discontinuity. The chasm created in the family by the death of the slave is purged by the death of the servant, and as a result, the wholeness of the family, which depends upon unbroken continuity, is restored.

On the other hand, we have already indicated that Euthyphro is not an ordinary practitioner of traditional religion and that he disagrees with his family's evaluation of their father's act. Euthyphro claims that he is an expert about religious matters and that his knowledge of religion separates him from the multitude (3c). In fact, he implies that he is a theologian and that his superior wisdom enables him to transcend the traditional religion of his family and of the other citizens. Now it is important to remember that in ancient Greece, the religion of both the family and the city was primarily ritualistic.[11] Religious orthodoxy did not depend upon faith, or dogma, or correct religious opinions, but upon one's willingness to perform rites and rituals around the hearthfire in the prescribed manner. From a religious point of view, the wholeness of both the family and the city depended upon the participation of the citizens in ritualistic activity that bound them together. In both contexts, unity was grounded in action and had

nothing to do with assent to a set of beliefs or with the attempt to ac-
quire knowledge of the ground of human existence. Thus, it is especially instructive that Euthyphro claims that he is superior to others
because he possesses genuine religious insight. Though he presupposes the framework of the family in his conversation with Socrates
and though he often relies upon his own special interpretation of the
religion of the city, Euthyphro moves beyond these contexts to a reflective framework that is much more universal. In describing himself,
Euthyphro makes no reference to the religious rituals of his family or
of the citizens of Athens, but focuses instead upon his own claims to
superior wisdom. In doing so, he attempts to transcend these more
restricted frameworks, moving beyond religious practice to knowledge
of the foundations of religion itself.

What Euthyphro claims to know with special clarity are stories
about the Olympian deities — details about the gods that most other
people do not know (6b–c). And as we shall soon discover, it is his
"knowledge" of these stories that grounds Euthyphro's decision to
prosecute his father for murder and to turn away from the origins of
his family. Euthyphro has decided to indict his father because he fears
the pollution that will otherwise result, and he attempts to use his
superior wisdom to restore harmony to the family hearthfire. It
should of course be evident that the Olympian gods to whom Euthyphro turns are not simply the gods of his fathers on the island of
Naxos, but the gods of the city of Athens, and indeed, of the whole of
Greece. In the prosecution of his father, Euthyphro appeals to the
Olympian deities to justify his act, rather than to the need to preserve
the continuity of his own religious and family traditions. Yet in moving beyond the earth gods of his family to the sky gods of the city to
defend his actions, Euthyphro also moves beyond the worship of the
gods of Athens to claims of superior knowledge about their nature and
intentions. At the outset, Euthyphro does not deal with the problem of
pollution by returning to his origins and by recovering the religious
traditions of his family or by coming to the city of Athens to worship
the Olympian gods and to ask advice about what he ought to do.
Instead, he moves beyond the family and the city to knowledge of the
mythic foundations of religion, and on this basis, attempts to justify
his indictment. Of course, from the perspective of his origins, this
indictment fragments the unity of his family, and from the perspective of the city, it is at best an attempt to use the Olympian gods in a
silly and unconventional fashion. However, from Euthyphro's point of
view, knowledge of what the gods require forces him to turn away

from traditional religion and to move outward to the more universal context that knowledge itself presupposes.

This outward journey beyond the family and the city is reflected in the details of Euthyphro's story. As we should recall, it was a hired servant that Euthyphro's father threw into a ditch, while it was a house slave of Euthyphro's own family that this servant had killed. Now the slaves of a family were adopted members of the household in which they lived,[12] while servants were members of other families, and in the strict sense, not parts of the original family at all. When the servant kills the slave, the family regards him as an alien, and the father takes revenge upon him by allowing him to die. In this way, the unity of the family, partly defined in terms of the slave as an adopted member, is restored through an act of purgation. In addition, the humanity of the other members of the family is secured at the expense of an alien intruder, who even from the outset was not re-garded as fully human. We must not forget that to be a person in the ancient world was to have a place within one's own family, and that human wholeness was defined in terms of the continuity of this bounded family circle. When this continuity is broken by an external encroachment, it is the duty of the patriarch to take decisive action.[13] The other members of the family approve their father's act, telling Euthyphro that it would be absurd for a son to oppose his father and even more ridiculous for him to destroy the unity of his family by prosecuting him for murder (4d–e).[14] However, Euthyphro refuses to heed their warnings, for he apparently believes that the servant whom his father neglected is as fully human as his own brothers, even though he lives in another family whose unity is defined in terms of rites and rituals peculiar to themselves. Euthyphro acts against his father because he sees an *analogy* between the humanity of the ser-vant and the humanity of his own family and because he believes that a larger context can be found in which the harmony of them all can be achieved. Apparently, Euthyphro believes that this larger context is to be found in the Greek mythos and in his special theological insight into the foundations of Greek religion. According to Euthyphro, whole-ness is to be defined, not in terms of the family or the city, but with reference to the mythical origins of humanity itself. And since these origins range over both Euthyphro and his servant, and not simply over the members of his own family circle, he comes to Athens seeking justice for a stranger in more universal terms than the family or the city can provide.

This quest for universality becomes explicit in the initial interchange between Euthyphro and Socrates. When Euthyphro tells Socrates that he intends to prosecute his father for murder, Socrates is incredulous. He reminds Euthyphro of the traditional distinction between family and strangers and says that Euthyphro surely does not intend to prosecute his father on behalf of a stranger (4a–b). However, Euthyphro replies in a fashion that confirms his emancipation from this tradition and from the definition of human wholeness in terms of the family or the city:

> It is ridiculous, Socrates, that you think it matters whether the man who was killed was a stranger or a relative, and do not see that the only thing to consider is whether the action of the slayer was justified or not, and that if it was justified one ought to leave him alone, and if not, one ought to proceed against him, even if he share one's own hearth and eat at one's own table. For the pollution is the same if you associate knowingly with such a man and do not purify yourself by proceeding against him. [4b–c]

In the argument with his family, Euthyphro does not agree that it is impious for a son to prosecute his father for murder. Instead, he appeals to justice as a more universal standard than family participation in order to deal with the problem of pollution. Now even though Socrates is surprised when Euthyphro does this, he sees that Euthyphro's rejection of the distinction between family and strangers and his transition to the more universal context of justice have positive consequences. In fact, Euthyphro's claim to special insight about the nature of piety and his appeal to justice as a universal principle of action becomes the ground for the philosophical conversation between Euthyphro and Socrates. Both of these claims are sufficiently general to lend themselves to reflective inquiry, and as claims to knowledge, they are ideal places for philosophical reflection to begin. As a result, the transition from the family and the city to a universal demand for justice becomes a transition to reflective discourse.

The possibility of a conversation between Euthyphro and Socrates also depends upon the fact that Socrates claims to be ignorant of the meaning of piety, while Euthyphro claims that he understands it already. Thus Socrates says that he intends to discover the nature of piety by asking Euthyphro a series of questions about the knowledge he claims to possess (5a–c). In terms of our earlier distinctions, this means that two directionalities are built into the very fabric of the dialogue: on the one hand, Euthyphro claims to stand at the point from which Socrates' inquiry into the meaning of wholeness can originate and is prepared to articulate his knowledge of the foundations of religion in universal terms; by contrast, Socrates intends to begin with Euthyphro's stories about the origins of the gods and to uncover the significance of human wholeness as he undertakes an outward journey. The philosophical questions Socrates asks are intended to be a quest for wholeness in their own right. The asking of a philosophical question is a quest for what it lacks and is an attempt to replace the fragmentation of ignorance with the wholeness that comes from adequate understanding. As a result, the dialogue between Euthyphro and Socrates is not merely concerned to discuss the problem of wholeness, but is itself a quest for wholeness in philosophical form. Euthyphro's claim to theological insight into the foundations of religion and Socrates' claim to philosophical ignorance about these same issues constitute a constructive dichotomy with which their conversation begins. This conversation, in turn, opens out into a dialogue in which the quest for wholeness can be developed in reflective terms.

Initial Definitions of Piety

As they move into a reflective context, Socrates asks Euthyphro a crucial question about the meaning of piety: he asks him to explain the *nature* of piety, both in relation to murder and in relation to other things (5c–d). And in order to guide him toward the kind of definition he seeks, Socrates suggests that piety is a *univocal* concept and that it designates a *single characteristic quality* that is always the same in any context. It is for this reason that Socrates asks what piety and impiety *are,* not simply in the case that is of special interest to Euthyphro, but in every case to which these concepts are relevant. This quest for a universal definition is characteristic of philosophy, for philosophical reflection always attempts to move beyond the particular circumstances with which it begins toward a more general understanding of the issues involved in the particular case. As a result, Socrates does not ask Euthyphro what piety means in his own case, but what it means in every case in which the problem of piety arises as a special issue. Socrates turns away from nature and away from the gods in the attempt to understand the *essential nature of things,* and he seeks to consummate his quest for understanding in the logos of a universal definition. Moreover, his initial suggestion that the concept of piety has a single meaning is a way of pointing to the kind of unity or wholeness appropriate to the reflective consciousness. Socrates is convinced that if piety is a univocal conception, knowledge of it is the attempt to grasp a unity, which will in turn bring wholeness to the one who succeeds in understanding it. Socrates intends to transform the religious quest for wholeness into a philosophical quest for wisdom, but in the present context the first step in doing this is to transform the problem of pollution into the problem of ignorance about the concept now before us. In asking Euthyphro to give a definition of piety, Socrates implies that he does not know the answer to his own question and that he suffers from the "pollution" of ignorance. But in attempting to move beyond ignorance to knowledge, he seeks to replace the fragmentation that results from a lack of understanding with the unity that knowledge often brings. The series of definitions that will be given in response to Socrates' questions should be understood as stages in a reflective quest for wholeness and as an attempt to find the reflective satisfaction toward which the quest for knowledge is directed.

It is especially appropriate that Socrates ask Euthyphro a philosophical question about the nature of piety, for Euthyphro has abandoned his family to come to the wider context of the city to prosecute his father. It is reasonable to assume that Euthyphro would never have turned against his origins without a clear conception of his reasons for doing so and without some ground for repudiating the traditional requirements of piety toward one's ancestors.[15] Within the ancient family, the father was the last person that one would think a son would try to prosecute, for piety toward one's origins would seem to make such an action clearly inappropriate (4e). Thus Socrates asks what general conception of piety supports Euthyphro's actions and what justification undergirds his willingness to stand in such a radical contrast with tradition. Euthyphro claims that his rejection of his origins is warranted and that his transition from the family to the city is guided by an exact knowledge of the nature of piety. However, it is just this claim to knowledge that makes Socrates' question relevant to Euthyphro's situation and that allows him to move the discussion to a philosophical level. Scientific knowledge makes general definitions possible, and it is this kind of knowledge that Socrates' request for a general definition is intended to uncover. There is a sense in which Socrates' question is not only directed to Euthyphro, but also addressed to us all. Like Euthyphro, all of us move in two directions, looking backward toward the family, and facing outward toward the larger world. Standing at the intersection between these two directionalities, Socrates asks what piety and human wholeness mean, not only in the family from which we come, but also in the larger context in which our reflective development unfolds. It is this question, which springs from the inherent bi-directionality of the human situation, that drives us beyond immediate experience and that makes it necessary for us to engage in philosophical reflection.

Euthyphro accepts Socrates' suggestion that the concept of piety can be defined in general terms, and on this basis he attempts to provide a general characterization of its nature. Accordingly, he claims that

> I. Piety is doing what I am doing now, prosecuting the wrongdoer who commits murder or steals from the temples or does any such thing, whether he be your father or your mother or anyone else, and not prosecuting him is impious. [5d–e]

The most obvious fact about this definition is that it is formulated in terms of examples. Euthyphro says that murder and stealing from the temples are the kinds of act that should be prosecuted and that the one who prosecutes another on these grounds is behaving piously. Euthyphro answers Socrates' question about the nature of piety in terms of concrete illustrations that are intended to point to the correctness of his own behavior. Yet due to the particularity of these examples, Euthyphro's response to Socrates is not of the general kind that might have been expected. His definition does not provide a general characterization of piety as a common quality exemplified by every pious act. Instead, it simply indicates by enumeration the kind of act that should be prosecuted, apparently expecting us to infer the nature of piety from these particular instances. On the other hand, Euthyphro's initial definition does exhibit a certain kind of generality. He not only claims that murder and stealing from the temples warrant prosecution, but that any similar act also warrants it. Thus Euthyphro extends by analogy the range of cases to which prosecution for wrongdoing is relevant. In the previous chapter, Abraham was able to move beyond the particularity of his encounter with God to the universality of a larger community through the analogy that binds its members together. In the present instance, Euthyphro makes a similar transition from particular examples of piety to an indefinite series of examples, but in this case he uses analogy as *a principle of justification*. In the definition before us, Euthyphro makes an analogical transition from particular instances of piety to a general list of acts of indefinite extension. But we should also notice that Euthyphro's definition of piety is general in another sense. He claims that one must prosecute the wrongdoer who commits murder or sacrilege or any similar thing, "whether he be your father or your mother or anyone else...." As a result, his definition is neutral to the distinction between family and stranger and is *universal in its range of reference*. Unlike the Hebrew community that can include only those individuals who have stood before God, Euthyphro's definition applies to everyone unrestrictedly. The generality it exhibits in doing so is an essential element in Euthyphro's attempt to transcend the particularity of his own situation and in his attempt to formulate a definition that can answer the questions of Socrates.

On the other hand, this attempt to give a general definition does not force Euthyphro to lose touch with his particular situation or with the concrete circumstances from which his quest for a definition arises. Euthyphro suggests that his own decision to prosecute his father for murder is not only an example of piety, but also serves as a model in terms of which piety itself can be understood. "Piety," he says, "is *doing what I am doing now*, prosecuting the wrongdoer who commits murder or steals from the temples or does any such thing,...and not prosecuting him is impious." (Italics mine.) Despite its generality, Euthyphro's own action stands at the center of his definition, and he presumably expects other acts to be measured against his own, which should be taken as the standard of correct behavior. Spreading out quite generally over a wide range of cases, Euthyphro's definition comes to focus on Euthyphro himself and upon his tacit claim to be a model that other acts of piety should attempt to imitate. Yet Euthyphro attempts to justify his definition, not in terms of his own particularity, but by appealing to a *similarity* between himself and Zeus, the king of the gods. Euthyphro reminds Socrates that Zeus once put his father in chains for attempting to devour his children and that Cronus, Zeus' father, had castrated *his* father for similar reasons. Thus Euthyphro says that he cannot understand why men are incensed with him for prosecuting his father for murder, when this act is similar to an act performed by Zeus himself (5e–6a). Euthyphro's prosecution of his father is an image of Zeus' violent emergence from his origins, and the justification of his definition depends upon the fact that it reflects this divine, primordial act. Euthyphro is separated from his family by the death of the slave and by the death of his servant, and he comes to Athens to seek a new form of human wholeness that is not accessible within the confines of his family. Moreover, he finds this new conception by appealing to the fact that even Zeus could come to himself only by turning against his origins and by moving outward toward the larger world in which his individuality could be forged. Euthyphro's *universal* definition, which comes to focus on his own *particularity*, is grounded in an appeal to Zeus as an *ultimate* standard. And it is grounded there just insofar as Zeus' repudiation of his past is the prototype of Euthyphro's emergent conception of his own humanity.

In Hesiod's *Theogony*, we find a detailed account of the myths to which Euthyphro appeals in order to justify his definition of piety. A brief discussion of them will reveal the origins of Euthyphro's definition and will clarify the structure of his appeal to Zeus as a principle of justification. In the *Theogony*, Hesiod tells us that after Earth had come into being out of Chaos, she first produced Sky (Uranus), and that from the union of Earth and Sky, Time (Cronus) finally came into existence.[16] But then he says that when Uranus buried all his children in the bowels of the Earth, attempting to assure himself that they would never rival him for kingship, Cronus grew to hate his father.[17] It was in response to this attempt to prevent the future from challenging the past that Cronus, the youngest and the boldest child, castrated Uranus and set his brothers free. In Greek mythology, this is the first attempt of a son to displace his father, and it is represented graphically in the image of Cronus, understood as fleeting temporality. Cronus moves beyond his bondage to the past into the freedom of the future in which the essential nature of time as directional movement could first be established. Though Time first comes into existence through the union of Earth and Sky, it can come to itself and can reveal its essential nature only by negating its origins and by moving forward in an unending sequence of temporal stages. It is this drive toward the future which the radical rejection of origins is intended to make possible. Hesiod also tells us that Cronus would not be content with the destruction of the past, but that he attempted to devour his own children.[18] It would appear that Time not only turns against its origins but proves to be omnivorous, moving from the past to the future in a sequence of destructive acts designed to assure its hegemony. Time devours both the past and the future as it marches forward from moment to moment, realizing its own identity only at the price of radical destruction. But Hesiod also says that in his persistent attempt to overcome the threat of encroachment, Cronus did not succeed in devouring Zeus and that Zeus, with the aid of some of his ancestors, was able to bind Cronus and fling him down into Tartarus.[19] In this decisive act, Zeus became the king of the gods, overcoming the power of Time by making political alliances with his origins and by using the power of tradition to negate the effects of temporality upon both the past and the future. Hesiod suggests that Zeus brings Time to a standstill, and in doing so, allows both the past and the future to exist as a meaningful framework in which the quest for wholeness can be undertaken.

Having acknowledged the values of the past by seeking the aid of his ancestors, Zeus also acknowledges the claims of the future by refusing to destroy his progeny. It is this fact that distinguishes him most clearly from Cronus and Uranus, allowing the future to exist in its own right as an intelligible domain. However, Zeus also guarantees the loyalty of the future by generating one of his offspring from his own head. Athena, the goddess of the city to which Euthyphro had come to announce a new conception of human wholeness, emerged full-blown from the head of Zeus.[20] In more familiar terms, the city of Athens is Zeus' idea, and it is this offspring, who presides over the cultural space of the city, with which Zeus replaces time as the fundamental conception. The transition from time to the city leads to the development of a spatial framework that transcends the ancient family, and it is within this framework that human beings can find the stability that often results from organized political and cultural existence. Hesiod describes this transition in mythological terms by tracing the development of Greek religion from the Earth to the Sky through Time to the City. Yet in doing so, he also describes a pattern that leads from the earth gods of the ancient family to the larger horizon that includes other families, until a process of temporal development finally produces a city in which these many families can be organized into a larger community. Formulated in these terms, Hesiod's poem is not simply an account of the emergence of the Greek gods from chaos, but also the story of the development of Greek society and of the stages through which it moves from its origins toward the larger context that the city-state provides.[21] It is this outward development that Euthyphro retraces in leaving his family on the island of Naxos and in coming to the city to seek a more universal conception of justice than the family can provide. Euthyphro moves away from his origins and from the earth gods that originally sustained his existence toward a larger horizon, finally coming to the city as the place where his new conception of human wholeness can be expressed.

When Euthyphro's father binds the servant and flings him into a ditch, he is imitating the earlier behavior of Uranus in binding his children and in placing them in the bowels of the earth. In both cases, the ones who are bound pose a threat to their masters, attempting in the case of Uranus to depose him as a ruler, and in the case of Euthyphro's father, threatening to destroy the unity of his family by murdering one of the household slaves. When Euthyphro's father allows the servant to die, he is also imitating the behavior of Cronus, destroying his children by responding to the threat they pose through an act of radical negation. Of course, Euthyphro's father would claim that the servant was not his own child, but the offspring of another family, and that he did not kill him, but simply allowed the vicissitudes of nature to take their natural course. However, if Euthyphro's father is to be compared with Uranus, who in turn can be identified with the Sky, there is a sense in which every individual who falls within his horizon is his "child." Euthyphro's father is the head of the household, and everyone who works there falls within his jurisdiction. But Euthyphro's father can also be compared with Time, for he "devours" Euthyphro's servant, not by attending to him directly, but by turning away to other things so that he passes away from neglect and from "starvation." In systematic terms, the drive toward the future that neglects the past simply allows it to die, preferring newness to an attempt to preserve the offspring that have already come into existence. When the behavior of Euthyphro's father is understood in these terms, it is perhaps not so surprising that Euthyphro turns against him and that he rejects his origins to identify himself with Zeus. If the father is both Uranus and Cronus and if in both cases he has already transcended the family toward the larger horizon of humanity in an unrestricted sense, it is natural for Euthyphro to bring this transition to completion and to turn against his father in the name of the servant who has been bound up and devoured. Euthyphro attempts to stop the flow of time and to do justice to all of its offspring by finding a conception of human wholeness that can negate the effects of temporal development. He does this by identifying himself with Zeus and by coming to the city of Athens as the cultural center in which the erosion of tradition has been arrested, at least temporally.

If we pay close attention to Hesiod's account, we can also understand why Euthyphro not only comes to the city of Athens, but also claims to transcend the citizens of the city by possessing exact knowledge of the intentions of the gods. Euthyphro identifies himself with Zeus rather than with Athena, and thus with the *originative source* of the customs and traditions of the city in which his speech unfolds. He not only stands beyond the family and beyond Cronus and Uranus, but beyond the city as well. In the analogy between himself and Zeus, Euthyphro identifies himself with the primordial place where the transition from the family to the city occurs and with the superior standpoint from which both the past and the future can be grasped with absolute clarity. It is no accident that at the beginning of their discussion, Euthyphro tells Socrates that he is a prophet who has never failed to predict the future with perfect accuracy (3c). As identified with Zeus, he binds the past and the future together, claiming to comprehend them both with his superior wisdom. Euthyphro's first definition of piety, which comes to focus on himself and is justified with reference to the king of the gods, is an expression of a quest for wholeness that leads beyond the family, and beyond time and the city, to the powerful origins of the city itself. These origins are described in the myths and legends of Greek mythology, and it is through his grasp of the significance of these stories that Euthyphro stands beside Zeus at a point which lies beyond the city. In the previous chapter, we found that Moses once stood before God and was told that he could be an image of God himself to the people he was asked to lead. Now we discover that Euthyphro also stands in an imagistic relation to the king of the gods, but in this case he stands there because he claims to possess superior knowledge of the mythic origins of the city. It is this hybristic claim to wisdom that individuates him and that makes it possible for Socrates to engage in a philosophical discussion with him about the nature of piety.

In Euthyphro's transition from the family to the city and in his move beyond the city to the king of the gods, three conceptions of fragmentation and of human wholeness can be rather clearly distinguished. Within the family, fragmentation is understood as a break in the unity of the household, while wholeness is defined in terms of the continuity of family tradition and in terms of an unbroken series of family members that stretches back into the indefinite past. The family is the place where the living and the dead meet and where the past and the future are held together by the rites and rituals that are performed by the members of the family around a common hearthfire. It is this context that has been fragmented by the death of the house-slave and that Euthyphro's father attempts to preserve in his treatment of the servant Euthyphro defends. In the city, fragmentation is also understood as a break with the past, while wholeness is defined in terms of the prayers and sacrifices that are offered at the hearthfire of the city. Yet in this case it is not the earth gods of the family, but Athena, the guardian of the city, to whom these rituals are addressed. In the family, fragmentation and wholeness are understood in terms of the continuity of the family itself, while in the city, these phenomena are defined in terms of the larger unity which obedience to common customs and traditions makes possible. It is this larger unity that is threatened by Socrates' philosophical questions, and in the name of which Meletus has decided to bring Socrates to justice. Finally, in the case of Euthyphro, fragmentation occurs when one is separated from the gods, while wholeness is "achieved" in his claim to be *a perfect image* of Zeus himself. In this case, wholeness is not a relationship between an individual and the family of which he is a part, nor a relationship between a citizen and the city whose customs and traditions he is asked to obey. Instead, it invokes an imagistic relation between the divine and human realms in virtue of which Euthyphro claims to stand in perfect harmony with Zeus. Euthyphro's quest for wholeness comes to rest in his claim to stand before Zeus as an individual whose violent rejection of his past is a perfect image of the most decisive act of Zeus himself. Euthyphro suggests that Zeus has emerged from his origins to become the best and the most just of the gods, and he implies that since his own situation is similar, he is justified in regarding himself as a perfect model of correct behavior. Thus Euthyphro attempts to bring his quest for wholeness to completion by moving beyond the family and the city to the mythic framework upon which the city itself was founded.

Throughout our previous discussion, we have presupposed an intimate relationship between the religious concept of piety and the more general conception of the quest for wholeness. In order to make this relationship explicit, perhaps we should now indicate that piety can be understood as a means for making human wholeness accessible. In the family, the piety displayed by ritualistic activity is designed to unify the family, while in the city, the piety exhibited by paying careful attention to custom and tradition is a way of bringing wholeness to the city and its citizens. In both cases pious acts are performed in order to produce wholeness in the larger community in which they occur. In a similar fashion, Euthyphro's definition of piety in terms of harmony with Zeus has human wholeness as its intended consequence. In this case the wholeness in question is both individual and collective and is intended to secure the wholeness of Euthyphro and his family at the expense of their father. However, even here, piety is not of interest for its own sake, but because of the relation it bears to the quest for wholeness and to the definition of wholeness as humanly accessible. Within the Greek tradition, pious acts are always performed to avoid the pollution that results from fragmentation, and they are intended to replace the discord of fragmentation, either collective or personal, with the wholeness that results from correct behavior. Euthyphro obviously believes that his act of piety is an act of violence, but he also believes that violence toward his father will bring wholeness to himself. As a result, he turns away from his origins to the more fundamental framework represented by the Olympian deities. On the other hand, Euthyphro's preference for the Olympian gods also presupposes a bi-directional development, and this bi-directionality underlies the quest for wholeness he has decided to undertake. In turning away from his family toward the city and beyond it, Euthyphro moves forward into a larger and a more inclusive unity. But in turning back to the stories upon which the city of Athens is founded and to the originative act in terms of which Zeus became the king of the gods, he is also turning toward a conception of origins more fundamental than the family can provide. Euthyphro's outward development toward a larger world is a return to the origins that underlie the city of Athens, and it is from the standpoint of these origins that he attempts to answer the questions of Socrates about the nature of piety.

In response to Euthyphro's justification of his first definition, Socrates says that he finds stories about the gods hard to believe (6a–b). Of course, Socrates knows that at the very time his conversation with Euthyphro is taking place, the city of Athens is crumbling as a result of the Peloponnesian War. In addition, he apparently believes that the disruption of the city is reflected in the conflict of the gods, and that as a result, the mythological origins of the city are just as disrupted as the city itself. Thus it is not surprising that Socrates wishes to turn away from mythology to the quest for abstract understanding and that he wishes to transform the religious quest for wholeness into the philosophical quest for a universal definition. However, when Socrates asks whether Euthyphro himself really believes in mythology, he replies that he does, and that he not only believes the story he has just related, but even more wonderful things about the gods that most other people do not know (6b). And when Socrates asks whether he believes that there were wars, enmities, and battles among the gods as depicted by the artists and the poets, he again replies that he does and that he believes much more besides (6b–c). In this way Euthyphro makes it clear that he wishes to commit himself to a mythic frame of reference — a framework whose hidden depths are presumably rich enough to overcome the fragmentation of his family and to establish a more universal conception of justice than the family or the city can provide. As I have suggested already, the quest for wholeness often begins with a story, but in Euthyphro's case this is true in a double sense: Euthyphro's conversation with Socrates about the nature of piety not only presupposes the story of his relationship with his family, but is also *grounded* in the images that depict the emergence of Zeus as the king of the gods. It is the story of origins in this second sense that generates the mythological framework to which Euthyphro appeals.

Yet we have also discovered that Euthyphro is to be distinguished from his family and from the other citizens, not by the intensity of his commitment to Greek mythology, but in his claim to possess exact knowledge of the nature and intentions of the Olympian deities (5a). It is this claim to knowledge that has driven him beyond the family and the city to a way of thinking and to a conception of justice that are absolutely universal. However, this claim to knowledge also produces a decisive transition in the argument, for it enables Socrates to turn Euthyphro's attention away from the mythic *content* of his definition to the need to provide a definition that is scientific in *form*. Socrates reasons that if Euthyphro possesses exact knowledge of the nature of piety, he should be able to formulate a definition that not only mentions some examples of it, but that also gives a general account of the characteristic that all pious acts have in common. Scientific definitions are distinguished by their simplicity and generality, and Euthyphro's claim to possess "scientific knowledge" would seem to commit him to a definition of this kind. Socrates moves the discussion in a philosophical direction by asking for a definition that does not mention murder and stealing from the temples, but that gives instead an abstract account of the *structure* that every pious act exhibits.

We have already observed that Euthyphro's first definition is universal in two distinguishable senses: in the first place, it applies to everyone unrestrictedly; and in the second place, it ranges over an indefinite number of acts that are similar to the ones he mentions explicitly. The distinction between family and strangers is irrelevant to the definition he wishes to give, and murder and stealing from the temples are only two of many similar acts that should be prosecuted. In both cases the definition is universal because it applies quite generally to a wide range of particular instances. However, when Euthyphro claims to possess exact knowledge of the nature of piety, Socrates assumes that he is prepared to give a definition that is universal in another sense. Thus he asks for a definition that mentions the characteristic feature exemplified by every pious act. Socrates attempts to supplement the distributive universality of Euthyphro's first definition by seeking a quality that is universal in the sense that it is common to many instances. And he seeks an account of this kind, not simply because Euthyphro has claimed to possess the kind of knowledge that should give him access to it, but because he wants a definition that is stable in content. Socrates says that he wants to understand the universal feature common to many instances of piety because it will give him access to the *structure* of piety itself, which can then be used as a model in terms of which particular instances of piety can be assessed (6e). Euthyphro has moved from the family, to the city, and to knowledge of the Olympian deities in order to bring his quest for wholeness to fulfillment. But now Socrates asks him to move beyond the particularity of all these contexts, and beyond the stories to which he has appealed in order to justify his first definition, to the abstract structure of piety itself, a knowledge of which will bring wholeness and stability to the human soul. Within the family, the family itself is the ground of unity, and within the city, unity is to be found in the customs and traditions that bind the citizens of the city together. By contrast, Euthyphro has found wholeness in his own claim to be a perfect image of the king of gods and in his appeal to Zeus as a model in terms of which pious acts are to be measured. But since he also claims to possess exact knowledge of divine matters, Socrates uses this claim to point to the possibility of wholeness in a further sense: it is the wholeness that comes from an abstract understanding of the objective structure of the cosmos; that appeals to a unified conception of piety as a model of correct behavior; and that is to be reflected in the kind of general definition Socrates asks Euthyphro to give. Thus, a contrast begins to emerge between two distinguishable models in terms of which human action can be assessed: on the one hand, stories about the gods which serve as foundational images of the human community; and on the other hand, abstract structures which serve as the unchanging standards of philosophical reflection.

In order to give Socrates the kind of definition he requires, Euthyphro now characterizes the nature of piety in a very brief and general formula. He says, simply,

II. What is dear to the gods is pious, and what is not dear to them is impious. [6d–7a]

The first thing to notice about this definition is that it is universal in

Socrates' sense: it mentions the property of being dear to the gods as the common characteristic exemplified by every pious act. This new definition moves beyond the distributive generality of Euthyphro's earlier account to a single characteristic common to many instances. However, in this instance Euthyphro very cleverly combines generality of form with the mythic framework in which his first definition was formulated. The *content* of his new account makes direct reference to the Olympian deities, blending the mythos with which Euthyphro began with the logos that Socrates demands. Euthyphro combines reason and religion, not only by appealing to the gods to justify his conception of human wholeness, but also by embedding his reference to them in a definition that fulfills the formal requirements of Socrates. However, this second definition is general in a more fundamental sense: it no longer makes reference to Zeus as a model in terms of which pious acts are to be measured or to Euthyphro as Zeus' perfect image, but suggests instead that the gods are to serve collectively as the standard of correct behavior. Euthyphro generalizes his position in a more radical way than Socrates demanded, moving beyond the particularity of Zeus and the particularity of his own situation to a distributive plurality of gods taken collectively. Euthyphro could have complied with Socrates' request for a general definition by claiming that what is dear to Zeus is pious and what is not dear to him is impious. In this way he could have held onto the particularity of his earlier account and to the myth in terms of which it was justified, while still framing his account in general terms. However, we now find that he not only generalizes the form of his definition to conform to the standards of Socrates, but generalizes its content as well, taking up the distributive generality of his earlier definition into this revised account. Euthyphro now gives Socrates a definition that is *general in form* in that it mentions a quality common to many instances, but that is also *general in content*, referring collectively to the gods as the standard by which pious acts are to be assessed.

In Chapter 1, we spoke about the quest for wholeness as a journey that can begin anywhere, that must begin somewhere in particular, and that always begins nowhere. In more strictly philosophical terms, the quest is *distributively universal* in that it can begin with anyone; it is *absolutely particular* in that it must begin with the one who actually undertakes it; and it is *ultimate* in that it always begins with something that lies beyond the temporal dimension. In Chapter 2, we used these same categories to suggest that the quest sometimes begins with a decisive act of what is ultimate, breaking into the family in order to individuate one of its members and allowing this individual to stand beside others in order to constitute a new kind of human community. In this case, the intersection of ultimacy and individuality leads to a distributive collection of individuals, permitting a new community to emerge from a plurality of divine–human encounters. Finally, in this chapter we have seen how Euthyphro's first definition of piety is *particular* in that it makes reference to Euthyphro himself as a perfect exemplar of correct behavior; how it is *ultimate* in that it refers to Zeus as the king of the gods; and how it is *universal* in that it applies to everyone unrestrictedly and to every act that is analogous to the ones it mentions explicitly. Now in the second definition, Euthyphro retains the ultimacy of the gods by including them in the content of his revised account; he gives a definition that is universal in a new sense altogether, in that it refers to a content that is common to many instances; and he includes the distributive generality of our earlier discussion by referring to the gods as a distributive collection. But due to the fact that he is now moving in an increasingly philosophical direction, particularity finally falls away, leaving us with a definition that combines generality of form and generality of content in a unified attempt to characterize what is ultimate and man's relationship to it. From this point on, we will be tempted to turn away from the particularity of our earlier discussion to what is distinctive about the reflective quest for wholeness: its attempt to understand the nature of things and to bring wholeness to the human soul through knowledge of the objective structure of the cosmos. In the following pages, we shall not only trace out the stages of this philosophical journey, but will also assess the results of this exclusively reflective undertaking, and will attempt to work our way back to the particularity with which we began. As I shall emphasize in the concluding section of this chapter, particularity will always be an irreducible element of the human journey, even when it takes place in philosophical terms.

Socrates accepts the form in which Euthyphro's definition is now expressed and commends him for finally answering the question about the nature of piety in the way in which he had been asked to answer it. But before the definition is accepted, Socrates proposes further inquiry (7a). He reminds Euthyphro of his earlier admission that the gods often quarrel and disagree and that their dwelling places have often been the scene of open conflict and rebellion. Even on the surface, it would appear that such a chaotic context could scarcely serve as a standard for correct human behavior. But in order to establish this conclusion in detail and to make the discussion more directly relevant to the human situation, Socrates asks that they first consider cases in which disagreements might arise between themselves. Euthyphro and Socrates quickly conclude that they would not argue about number, but would settle such disagreements through arithmetic; that they would not disagree fundamentally about the relative size of two objects, but would put an end to the disagreement by measuring; and finally, that they would be able to come to terms about the weight of a certain object simply by weighing it (7b–c). But then Socrates asks,

> about what would a disagreement be, which we could not settle and which would cause us to be enemies and be angry with each other? Perhaps you cannot give an answer offhand; but let me suggest it. Is it not about right and wrong, and noble and disgraceful, and good and bad? Are not these the questions about which you and I and other people become enemies, when we do become enemies, because we differ about them and cannot come to any satisfactory agreement? [7c–d]

Euthyphro readily acknowledges that all of this is true and that it is the realm of right and wrong, good and bad, that is genuinely problematic. But when Socrates asks whether it is not also the case that the gods disagree about these questions, and when Euthyphro agrees again, Socrates suggests that *he has not in fact succeeded in defining the meaning of piety.* If the gods disagree about matters of value, some would love one thing and some would love another, and the same things would then be loved and hated by the gods. As a consequence, the definition does not define what is pious in contrast with what is impious, but what is both pious and impious at once (7e–8a). Socrates concludes that it would not be surprising that if in punishing his father, Euthyphro were "performing an act that is dear to Zeus, but hateful to Cronus and Uranus...." It would seem that the generalized context of the gods taken collectively is internally discordant and thus cannot provide the standard by which human acts are measured.

Socrates accepts Euthyphro's analogy between the divine and human realms: Euthyphro had compared himself with Zeus; Socrates compares the gods with men. But in accepting the analogy, Socrates *reverses its directionality:* he attempts to learn something about the gods by comparing them with men, rather than attempting to justify a human act by appealing to stories about the Olympian deities (8b–c). Socrates seems to be suggesting that men should be given priority in contrast with the gods and that the focus of the quest for wholeness should be the human realm, rather than the realm of the gods. The descending order of the examples which Socrates uses in discussing disagreements among men (number, measure, weight, value) might be taken to indicate that problems of value are to be found in the marketplace and that the gods stand alongside men in being perplexed by them. In fact, in comparing them with men, he might even be suggesting that the gods are human surrogates and that stories about them are merely human inventions. If so, the implication would be that they cannot serve as a standard for correct behavior, since in this case their internal discontinuity would simply be a reflection of human fragmentation. Socrates implies that if the gods are to serve as a standard, they must be stable enough to provide a model by which human acts are measured. However, quarrels on Mt. Olympus suggest that the gods are in need of a standard, just as are their human counterparts. The conflict among the gods reduces them to a status that is almost human and raises again the question of the standard by which pious acts are measured.

Conflict among the gods produces instability, and this instability, in turn, produces an unstable definition. Piety can scarcely be defined by referring to what is loved by the gods taken collectively if they cannot agree about the objects of their affection. However, the important point to notice is that the instability of the gods has existential consequences, pointing to an instability within Euthyphro's version of the mythic consciousness and within the individual who attempts to find guidance for his actions in polytheistic terms. What is pleasing to the gods taken collectively leads in incompatible directions, and the attempt to find wholeness by imitating them produces fragmentation. For example, Cronus and Zeus move in opposite directions, and it is utterly impossible to imitate them both without being torn apart in the process. Of course, this simply means that Euthyphro should have never universalized the content of his original definition to include a reference to the gods in general. Instead, he should have claimed that what is loved by Zeus is pious and that what is hated by him is impious. In this way, he could have avoided the objection that what is loved by one is hated by another, and that as a result, piety cannot be defined in mythological terms. If Euthyphro had insisted on the primacy of Zeus, he could have committed himself to a single god and in doing so could have escaped the contradiction involved in attempting to worship a plurality of deities. In the end, the return to origins must be a return to unity, so that the real question to be answered is this:

What kind of unity is to be preferred? — the kind that is to be traced to an originative ground or the kind that depends upon stable structure? And what is to be the fundamental conception? — the originative act upon which human existence is founded or the intelligible contents that guide the process of philosophical reflection? It is these questions to which we must turn in the following section.

However, at the present stage of the discussion, Euthyphro still clings to abstract generality, resisting Socrates' suggestion that a reference to many gods is not sufficient to produce an adequate definition. He replies to Socrates' claim that the gods cannot provide a standard by asserting that none of them disagree about the piety of his own act, and more generally, that none of them believe that he who kills anyone wrongfully ought not to be punished (8b). Euthyphro attempts to avoid the implication of his earlier admission that the gods quarrel among themselves by making his own act an instance of a general principle which no one will dispute. However, Socrates again refutes him with a question: "*to return to men,* did you ever hear anyone arguing that he who killed anyone *wrongfully,* or had done anything else *wrongfully,* ought not to pay the penalty?" (8b) (Italics mine.) To the contrary, Socrates claims that men argue about particular cases and circumstances; they argue about "who is a wrongdoer, and what he did, and when" (8d). Socrates concludes that if the gods do dispute, they also dispute about each separate act (8e). In this way, Socrates returns to the *particularity* of Euthyphro's own situation in order to indicate that his action cannot be justified merely by appealing to a general principle. Once more we find the suggestion that particularity is inescapable, but this time it comes from a surprising source: on this occasion it is the philosopher rather than the theologian who points to its presence as an irreducible element. On the other hand, Socrates obviously believes that particularity cannot serve as a standard for human action, but that it only defines the fragmented circumstances with which philosophical reflection begins. In Euthyphro's case, this means that the particularity of his own situation merely defines the subject-matter of a larger inquiry, which must itself be regulated by a universal standard that lies beyond it. According to Socrates, the only standard that can bring stability to the human soul is a stable structure that makes knowledge of human wholeness accessible. Again, what is needed is a definition that mentions a unified structure which all pious acts have in common, and an outward quest for wholeness that will allow us to articulate its reflective significance.

In order to encourage this outward development, Socrates himself suggests that the previous definition should be amended and that it should be transformed to read: "whatever all the gods hate is impious and what they all love is pious, and what some love and others hate is neither or both" (9d). Euthyphro, in turn, finally agrees to accept this revised account, and having done so, he asserts that

> III. What all the gods love is pious, and on the other hand, what they all hate is impious. [9e]

Reference to *all* the gods in this third definition is intended to heal the split that has arisen among them. Accordingly, its immediate purpose is to overcome the fragmentation of the previous definition and to bring wholeness to the mythic context from which Euthyphro's definition originates. If one agrees to define "piety" in terms of what is loved by all the gods, conflict can scarcely arise among them, for cases of conflict are simply excluded by the definition itself. However, the ultimate purpose of the definition is not to eliminate conflict, but to intensify the generalizing tendencies that Socrates is attempting to encourage in Euthyphro and that are necessary if we are to reach objective structure. In this new definition we have an account that is general in the sense that it mentions a quality said to be common to many instances, general in that it applies to everyone unrestrictedly, and also general in that the ultimate ground to which it appeals is itself universal — the ground provided by all the gods taken collectively. The reflective quest for wholeness, which begins with the particularity of Euthyphro's initial situation and moves to a distributive collection of Olympian deities, finally moves to a universal definition that only mentions cases in which the gods are in absolute agreement. On the other hand, there is an obvious difficulty about this new definition that makes it irrelevant to all the difficult and interesting cases. If we are to define the concept of piety in terms of what is loved by *all* the gods, all the controversial cases for which a standard is needed cannot be subsumed under the definition in question. Euthyphro's quest for wholeness, and the particular context from which he emerges in order to undertake it, are unique. And as Socrates has already pointed out, what one needs to know in this case is whether Euthyphro's decision to prosecute his father for murder is an instance of pious action. However, since this case is also controversial, one would certainly not expect all the gods to be in agreement about it. This is especially true of Zeus and Cronus, and of Cronus and Uranus, for we have already seen that these gods are in radical conflict about the proper relationship between fathers and children. Thus it is easy to see that the definition of piety in terms of what is loved by all the gods is unlikely to be relevant to Euthyphro's own situation and that another standard would seem to be required.

In the middle section of the *Euthyphro,* Socrates attempts to point to such a standard by criticizing Euthyphro's third definition. In doing so, he suggests that *Piety itself* is the standard in terms of which all pious acts are measured and that the gods must be replaced altogether as the foundation of correct behavior. Socrates claims that Piety is not identical with the behavior of Euthyphro or with the actions of Zeus and that it is not to be identified with what is loved by all the gods. Rather, he claims that the stable structure to which it points lies beyond the fragmentation of the family, the city, and the Olympian deities, and that it is the ultimate standard that brings wholeness to the human soul. This abstract standard is independent from men in a different sense from the way in which the gods are independent, and present in them in ways different from the ways in which the gods can manifest their presence in the human realm. However, Socrates suggests that its presence to consciousness will enable us to define a new conception of human wholeness that can be secured only by the autonomy of philosophical reflection. In the following section, we shall focus upon this new conception of wholeness and upon Socrates' attempt to establish the autonomy of philosophy by considering the distinction he draws between the nature of piety and the nature of the gods. In this discussion the mystery and the power of the gods will stand in radical contrast with an abstract logos, and the notion of formal structure will stand opposed to the concrete richness of the mythological tradition. However, this contrast will allow us to bring the confrontation between religion and philosophy to a decisive turning point and will finally permit us to come to terms with two distinguishable conceptions of the human quest for fulfillment.

The Linguistic Conflict between Theology and Philosophy

In the middle section of the dialogue, Socrates asks Euthyphro the central question about the nature of piety by asking him about the relationship between piety and what is loved by the gods. "Is something pious [adj.]," Socrates asks,

> because it is loved by [pass. vb.] the gods; or is it loved by [pass. vb.] the gods because it is pious [adj.]? [10a]

When Euthyphro is first confronted with this question, he does not understand it, forcing Socrates to clarify his intentions with a set of simple illustrations. Socrates first distinguishes between

[1] being carried [pass. part.] and carrying [act. part.],
[2] being led [pass. part.] and leading [act. part.],
[3] being seen [pass. part.] and seeing [act. part.], [10a]

and then he asks whether Euthyphro understands that in each case the two expressions differ in meaning, and if so, how they differ. When Euthyphro replies that he *thinks* he understands, Socrates then asks whether we do not also distinguish between

[4] a thing's being loved [pass. part.] and a thing's loving [act. inf.]; [10a]

and when Euthyphro agrees that we do, he attempts to reinforce the point he has in mind with three additional questions:

[5] Is a thing in a state of being carried [pass. part.] said to be carried [pass. part.] because it is carried [pass. vb.] or for some other reason?
[6] And a thing is in a state of being led [pass. part.] because it is led [pass. vb.]?
[7] And a thing is in a state of being seen [pass. part.] because it is seen [pass. vb.]? [10b]

In all three cases, Euthyphro replies affirmatively. Finally, with Euthyphro's agreement, and with these initial distinctions in mind, Socrates comes to the following conclusions:

[8] It is not the case that something is seen [pass. vb.] because it is a thing which is being seen [pass. part.], but it is a thing which is being seen [pass. part.] because it is seen [pass. vb.];
[9] It is not the case that something is led [pass. vb.] because it is a thing which is being led [pass. part.], but it is a thing which is being led [pass. part.] because it is led [pass. vb.];

and

[10] It is not the case that something is carried [pass. vb.] because it is a thing which is being carried [pass. part.], but it is a thing which is being carried [pass. part.] because it is carried [pass. vb.]. [10b]

Let us consider briefly some of the most significant features of the foregoing interchange and the relationship it bears to our larger discussion. In the first place, we should notice that the word "because" occurs twice in the original question Socrates addressed to Euthyphro:

> Is something pious *because* it is loved by the gods; or is it loved by the gods *because* it is pious?

The occurrence of this expression calls our attention to an asymmetry between piety and the gods, and by implication, points to the difference between the two directionalities in which the quest for wholeness develops. The question asks whether piety depends upon what is loved by the gods, in which case we must return to our origins, or whether what is loved by the gods depends upon piety, demanding that we undertake a reflective journey in order to understand its significance. In separating piety from what is loved by the gods and in asking which conception is more fundamental — the will of the gods or objective structure — Socrates is attempting to separate religion from philosophy and to call our attention to a source of wholeness that stands in contrast with the origins of the city. His question points to two distinguishable conceptions of a ground for human existence, and by implication, to two distinguishable conceptions of human wholeness: on the one hand, it refers to the gods as active and originative sources, represented in mythic stories of origination, and bringing wholeness just insofar as this originative dimension can be reflected in human action; on the other, it refers to Piety itself as an unchanging standard of action, embodied in a scientific definition, and bringing wholeness insofar as knowledge of objective structure brings stability to the human soul. For the immediate purposes of the dialogue, the significance of Socrates' question is to be found in the fact that it formulates these alternative conceptions so clearly and asks Euthyphro to choose between them. However, the original question is also of general interest, for it is one of the clearest places in the entire Western tradition where Will stands in contrast with Understanding and where we are confronted with a choice between the mystery and power of the gods and the intelligible structure of an objective standard for human action. The question confronts the reader with a radical opposition between piety and what is loved by the gods, and it asks us to make a choice between the two directionalities in which the quest for wholeness develops.

I have indicated already that when Euthyphro was first confronted with Socrates' question and with the choice it forced upon him, he did not understand it. But before we take this as a sign of his reflective incompetence and attempt to answer the question ourselves, we should notice that it is appropriate that he does not understand it. Socrates' question seeks to separate what Euthyphro had attempted to unite, holding apart the elements of the definition that Euthyphro had bound together. Euthyphro had claimed that piety *is* what is loved by the gods; not that piety *depends upon* love or that love *depends upon* piety. In introducing an asymmetry between these two conceptions and in distinguishing so clearly the two directionalities they reflect, Socrates attempts to sunder the unity to which Euthyphro had appealed. In Euthyphro's case, the two directionalities are held together in the identity of his third definition and in the primitive belief that two different things can be absolutely united in a oneness that transcends diversity. For the primitive mind, this kind of unity is rooted in the originative action of the gods and in their capacity to constitute a primordial identity that the human mind is asked to imitate. More specifically, Zeus brings the cultural space of the city of Athens into existence by a unifying act which expresses his own will, and it is this unifying act that Euthyphro's definitions are intended to reflect. By contrast, Socrates' question separates piety from what is loved by the gods and holds them apart for reflective consideration, attempting to replace the unity of Euthyphro's original definition with the difference required by abstract reflection. Reflective inquiry introduces diversity into the primitive mentality, and it is this moment of radical difference that Socrates attempts to establish in the course of the discussion.

Socrates indicates the kind of difference he has in mind by introducing a series of examples — examples which illustrate the contrast between piety and what is loved by the gods in terms of the linguistic distinction between active and passive voices. At a minimal level, the contrast between active and passive participles points to the general notion of asymmetry. It suggests that 'x because y' differs from 'y because x' in a way which parallels the verbal distinctions between carried and carrying, led and leading, seen and seeing. In all of these cases, an asymmetry obtains among the notions in question, but it is also tempting to assume that the active–passive distinction is to be taken more substantively. We are tempted to read the contrast between active and passive participles back into the original question about what is loved by the gods and to ask which is active and which passive, the gods or piety. Of course, if we do this, Socrates' question not only suggests a difference of directionality, but also implies that a choice must be made between active and passive sources of unity. In the one case, the *activity* of the gods which brings a unified city into existence is reflected in the active voice of the series of examples, while in the other case, the *passivity* of objective structure, which points to Piety itself as an unchanging standard, is represented by the passive forms of this same series.

There is no doubt something to be said for this way of understanding Socrates' intentions. The gods are clearly active, in some respects at least, and the objective standards to which Socrates points are in some sense passive. The linguistic way of understanding the distinction between the gods and the concept of piety also has the advantage of allowing us to acknowledge the crucial role of language in the interchange before us and the extent to which the issues to be decided here are mediated linguistically. There is not only a substantive conflict between Euthyphro and Socrates, but also a conflict at the distinctively linguistic level, and this dimension of the conversation is reflected in the tenses of the language used to formulate the issue here. The bi-directionality of the quest for wholeness is taken up into a linguistic medium, and in the process, the substantive conflict between Euthyphro and Socrates is transformed into a mediated opposition. However, Socrates' questions at this stage also point beyond language to the *ground of language* and thus to a sense of difference that is more fundamental than the syntactical distinctions of ordinary discourse. The additional questions Socrates asks focus our attention once again upon an asymmetry, but this time he moves beyond the active–passive distinction to a series of questions in which both verbs occur in the passive voice. Socrates asks Euthyphro whether a thing is "in a state of being carried [pass. part.] because it is carried [pass. vb.]"; whether it is "in a state of being led [pass. part.] because it is led [pass. vb.]"; and whether it is "in a state of being seen [pass. part.] because it is seen [pass. vb.]?" Presumably, the kind of asymmetry he intends to suggest is more fundamental than the merely verbal contrast between active and passive voices, requiring us to turn to a sense of difference that is grounded in the nature of the cosmos.[22]

The contrast to which Socrates points in these examples is the distinction between act and state with reference to things.[23] The question at issue is whether a thing is in a certain state because of an act which brings this state about or whether the act occurs because its object is in a certain state. This question is formulated in the passive voice, and the distinction it presupposes is ontological rather than verbal. It is a distinction formulated with reference to the realm of genesis — formulated with reference to the distinction between states and acts of *things*. Thus it should be clear that the contrast between the gods and piety is not merely linguistic, but ontological as well, and that the opposition between them is *the ground of the linguistic distinction* already displayed between active and passive senses of unity. However, it should also be clear that Socrates is not concerned primarily with the contrast between act and state *within* the realm of genesis, but with the relationship *between* the realms of things and persons and standards of action considered in themselves. If the contrast between active and passive voices suggests a distinction between the gods and objective structures and if the contrast between passive verb and passive participle indicates that this distinction is not merely verbal, the contrast between the gods and ideal standards is itself more fundamental still. It is this distinction to which Socrates now points in moving beyond language (active–passive voice) and beyond the realm of genesis (act–state) to the more genuinely metaphysical contrast between changing things and the ideal patterns to which they must conform.

Socrates suggests that he intends to move in this direction by the *order* of the verbal examples he has already given Euthyphro. He first distinguished *carried* from *carrying*, then *led* from *leading*, and finally *seen* from *seeing*. The order of these examples exhibits the pattern appropriate to philosophical reflection: we are first to be carried and then led out of the realm of genesis into a vision of objective structure. First, we move within the realm of *language;* then we are caught up within the realm of *genesis;* finally, our attention is directed to a set of *ideal standards* considered in themselves. Yet the order of these examples not only calls our attention to Piety itself as a standard for action, but also stands in contrast with the order of the earlier examples Socrates mentioned in discussing the quarrels that occur among the gods. At that earlier stage of his argument, Socrates claimed that the gods do not argue about number, measure, and weight, but rather about problems of value. The descending order of those examples suggested that the gods stand alongside men in their ethical disagreements and that they cannot provide a standard in terms of which these issues can be decided. By contrast, the ascending order of the illustrations now before us suggests that Piety *can* provide the standard in question and that we should direct our attention to the task of discovering its intrinsic nature. Once more, a radical reversal of directionality occurs, and we are asked to turn out attention away from stories about the gods to a more objective context in which the quest for wholeness can be transformed into a quest for understanding.

In attempting to explain the contrast between piety and the realm of genesis, Socrates suggests an account of the nature of ideal standards which many of his followers have been tempted to adopt. He asserts:

If anything becomes [deponent vb., pass. form, act. meaning] or undergoes [deponent vb., act. form, pass. meaning], it does not become [pass. vb., act. meaning] because it is in a state of becoming [pass. part., act. meaning], but it is in a state of becoming [pass. part., act. meaning], because it becomes [pass. vb., act. meaning], and it does not undergo [act. vb., pass. meaning] because it is undergoing [act. part., pass. meaning], but because it undergoes [act. vb., pass. meaning] it is undergoing [act. part., pass. meaning]. [10b–c]

Socrates' explanation exhibits the same levels of complexity that have been distinguished already. First, the verbs in the operative contrasts are identical in voice; we are no longer at the merely verbal level of the active–passive distinction. In the second place, the verbs can be related according to the familiar ontological pattern of the realm of genesis. In this explanation, a distinction obtains between the state of a thing and the act in virtue of which it comes to be in such a state. Finally, the verbs which occur in Socrates' explanation are the verbs for becoming and undergoing, and these verbs themselves point to the domain of changing things. However, what is most important about this explanation is the fact that it introduces an additional asymmetry between verbal form and meaning which might seem to be crucial in Socrates' attempt to exhibit a normative standard. In the case of becoming, the verb is *passive in form* and *active in meaning;* in the case of undergoing, it is *active in form* and *passive in meaning.* Could Socrates be suggesting a distinction between verbal form and meaning, where meanings are to be the standards by which utterances and other occurrences within the realm of genesis are to be measured? If so, understanding the meaning of language would be the key for grasping objective structure, and by implication, the ground for the wholeness that results from the quest for scientific understanding.

A number of philosophers within the Platonic tradition have been tempted to adopt this account of objective structure. In this tradition, meanings have been said to stand in contrast with the realm of genesis and to be the ideal patterns which things within that realm merely approximate.[24] Yet in the difference between the meaning of becoming and the meaning of undergoing, we find that one is active and the other passive, just as some verb forms are active and some passive. Presumably we should conclude that *both language and meaning are domains which include both activity and passivity.* But this suggests, in turn, that the realm of meaning cannot serve as a standard for language, since both domains reflect the instability to which the active–passive distinction calls our attention. This is not to say that a contrast does not obtain between the ideal and the actual, for it is this distinction that animates the Socratic quest for wholeness and that allows him to transform it into a reflective form. The quest for wholeness can become the quest for objective structure precisely because it is possible to draw a distinction between an ideal pattern and the realm of changing things that merely images or approximates it. However, the contrast between ideal and actual is *not* the contrast between language and meaning, since a distinction can be drawn between language as ideal and language as actual, just as this distinction can be drawn within the realm of meaning. But this fact alone suggests that meanings do not provide the standard we seek. If Socrates is to find a standard that transcends activity and passivity and that can bring stability to the human soul, he must move beyond language and meaning to the *ground of meaning,* finding there an ideal pattern to which the realm of changing things can be related.

The subsequent interchange between Euthyphro and Socrates confirms the fact that the realm of meanings cannot serve as an appropriate standard for human action. Socrates asks Euthyphro,

> Is not that which is in a state of being loved [pass. part.] a thing which is either becoming [pass. part., act. meaning] or undergoing [act. part., pass. meaning]? [10c]

And is this case like the former ones:

> It is not loved [pass. vb.] by those by whom it is loved [pass. vb.] because it is in a state of being loved [pass. part.], but it is in a state of being loved [pass. part.] because it is loved [pass. vb.]? [10c]

In both cases Euthyphro agrees. The first thing to notice about this interchange is that it accords with the earlier conclusion that the state of a thing depends upon the act which produces it and that the act does not depend upon the state. Socrates intends for Euthyphro to agree that a thing is in a state of being loved because it is loved and not that it is loved because it is in the corresponding state. However, Socrates' questions also imply that a thing which is in a certain state is either becoming or undergoing, and we are not told which is the case. If we adopt the linguistic perspective, becoming would be passive and undergoing active, and if we adopt the perspective of meaning, becoming would be active and undergoing passive. But whichever perspective we adopt, *a thing which is in a certain state falls within the realm of genesis.* Whether a thing which is in a state of being loved is either becoming or undergoing and whether we adopt a linguistic or a semantical interpretation of the distinction between these notions, the fact remains that a thing which is in a certain state is *subject to time.* The active–passive distinction reflects the realm of changing things, and the semantic context, like its linguistic counterpart, can be made to conform to the realm of genesis. As a result, Socrates is convinced that what is needed is an *external* standard which transcends language and meaning and which permits the realm of genesis to be assessed. He concludes that the *philosophical space* of a *realm of radical externality* must be distinguished from the realm of changing things and that the patterns to be discerned there can serve as the standard by which things in time are brought to focus.

In order to point to the kind of standard he has in mind, Socrates asks Euthyphro two final questions about the nature of piety, and on this basis, reaches a decisive conclusion. First, he asks whether Euthyphro is still convinced that what is pious is loved by all the gods (10c–d), and when Euthyphro says that he is (10d), he asks, in the second place, whether what is pious (adj.) is loved (pass. vb.) *because* it is pious (adj.) or for some other reason (10d). But when Euthyphro agrees again, Socrates quickly draws the conclusion that brings this stage of the reflective quest for wholeness to completion:

What is loved is loved [pass. vb.] *because* it is pious [adj.]; it is *not* pious [adj.] *because* it is loved [pass. vb.]. [10d]

If we are to understand the philosophical significance of this conclusion, we should notice that the adjective "pious" is introduced at this point in place of the passive participle "in a state of being loved." At the earlier stages of the dialogue, the distinction upon which the argument has depended has been the contrast between act and state within the realm of genesis. At this point, however, Socrates does not ask whether a thing is loved (pass. vb.) because it is in a state of being loved (pass. part.) or in a state of being loved (pass. part.) because it is loved (pass. vb.), but asks instead whether a thing is loved (pass. vb.) because it is *pious* (adj.). In this case, the introduction of the adjective points to the existence of a realm which transcends the distinction between activity and passivity. Its presence suggests that 'x because y' is not to be interpreted linguistically as a contrast between active and passive voice, nor to be interpreted ontologically in terms of the distinction between act and state, but to be understood as a normative contrast between an ideal pattern taken in itself and the items which make up the realm of changing things. The asymmetry in question is not merely verbal, nor a distinction between act and state, nor even the contrast which might be thought to obtain between language and meaning. Rather, it points to the contrast between normative standards considered in themselves and the items within the realm of genesis which are to be measured by them. It is this normative dimension upon which Euthyphro finally stumbles and to which Socrates has been attempting to lead him. His recognition of this dimension is the final step in Socrates' attempt to transcend the realm of genesis, to detach the concept of Piety as an independent standard, and to point to the philosophical space of objective structure as a more fundamental ground of unity than the realm of time to which both men and the gods are subjected.

Given this final asymmetry and Euthyphro's reluctant acknowledgment of it, it only remains for Socrates to draw out a contradiction now present in Euthyphro's position. First, Socrates says that they are agreed that

[1] What is pious [adj.] is to be loved [pass. inf.] because it is pious [adj.]; it is not the case that it is pious [adj.] because it is loved [pass. vb.]. [10e]

Then he reminds Euthyphro that he has already accepted the claim that

[2] What is dear to the gods [adj.] is dear to them [adj.] because it is loved [pass. vb.]; it is not to be loved [pass. inf.] because it is dear [adj.]. [10e]

Finally, he suggests that if what is dear to the gods (adj.) and what is pious (adj.) were identical, then by substitution in step (1):

[3] That which is dear to the gods [adj.] would be loved [pass. vb.] because it is dear to the gods [adj.]. [10e–11a]

And again by substitution in step (2):

[4] That which is pious [adj.] would be pious [adj.] because it is to be loved [pass. inf.]. [11a]

But Socrates points out that given his earlier admissions, Euthyphro should now see that *just the opposite is the case.* What is dear to the gods is not to be loved because it is dear to them (step (3)); rather, it is dear to them because it is loved (step (2)). And what is pious is not pious because it is loved (step (4)); it is to be loved because it is pious (step (1)) (11a). Socrates concludes that Euthyphro is mistaken in equating Piety with what is dear to the gods and that in giving his definition he has at best mentioned an accidental feature which characterizes all pious acts (11a–b). Though it might be true that all the gods love what is pious, the argument has shown that *this is not its defining characteristic.* As a result, he says that it is necessary to return to the beginning of the discussion and to raise the question of the nature of piety once again.

At this concluding stage of the argument, Socrates not only makes reference to piety in terms of an adjective, but also refers to the realm of the gods in adjectival terms. He does not speak about what is loved by the gods or about what is in a state of being loved, but rather about what is *dear to them.* This point is important because it suggests that we have transcended the active–passive distinction as the fundamental contrast of the argument and that the significant contrast is now the distinction between a set of objective standards and the gods considered in themselves. The two adjectives and the two realms to which they call our attention stand in radical contrast, and the question to be decided at this point is this: which realm provides the normative standard in terms of which the acts of men are to be appraised — the realm of ideal patterns considered in themselves or the realm of the gods understood as originative sources? Socrates has argued that the active–passive contrast is *internal to* the gods and their behavior and that it does not appear as the operative contrast *between* the realm of the gods and the realm of the forms. In this way, he attempts to indicate that the gods are bound to the realm of genesis and that they stand alongside men in contrast with the forms. But having made this conclusion the focal point of the discussion with

Euthyphro, he now introduces a term which refers to the gods as such. In doing so, Socrates suggests that the gods are to be subordinated to ideal standards, not because they are active or passive, but because their activity and passivity is an expression of the realm of genesis. He claims that this realm *as a whole* is subject to ideal patterns, which manifest themselves as the normative standards in terms of which both the activity and the passivity of the gods are to be measured. According to Socrates, two "wholes" are to be contrasted with one another, and two conceptions of human wholeness are to be distinguished: the one seeks wholeness in stories about the gods, while the other attempts to find it in a scientific definition. One seeks unity in a primordial act of Will, while the other seeks it in an act of Understanding. It is finally this opposition between power and logos that stands at the center of the dialogue and which Socrates attempts to resolve by forcing Euthyphro to embrace a contradiction.

The permanent problem involved in the opposition between the realm of genesis and the realm of ideal standards is reflected in the fact that the validity of the deduction Socrates formulates so carefully depends upon a systematic conflation of these separate domains. More specifically, the argument depends upon a conflation of the ontological conception of passivity with the normative conception of Piety considered in itself. In step (3) of Socrates' original deduction, the consequent of the conditional (that which is dear to the gods would be loved because it is dear to the gods) contradicts the second conjunct of step (2) (it is not to be loved because it is dear). And the consequent of the conditional in step (4) (that which is pious would be pious because it is to be loved) contradicts the second conjunct of step (1) (it is not the case that it is pious because it is loved). But since Euthyphro has already accepted steps (1) and (2) and since his claim that what is pious and what is dear to the gods are the same commits him to steps (3) and (4), Socrates concludes that Euthyphro is mistaken in holding that what is pious and what is dear to the gods are identical. However, what Socrates fails to mention is that the contradictions in fact occur only if the passive verb (be loved) in step (3) is tacitly equated with the passive infinitive (to be loved) in step (2) and only if the passive infinitive (to be loved) in step (4) is equated with the passive verb (be loved) in step (1). Yet to equate these two forms of expression is to ignore the distinction between passivity and the normative dimension, failing to note the difference between being loved and being the kind of thing that *ought to be loved*. Of course, this distinction can be ignored only if we are already convinced that ideal standards are required and that passivity can be used as a symbol for the structural stability of the normative dimension. In the deduction he formulates and in the conflation of genesis and ideality which it involves, Socrates points beyond the realm of genesis to the normative standards by which both men and gods are measured. It only remains for us to decide how far to follow him in this and how to appraise the opposition between Will and Understanding upon which his argument depends.

The Quest for Completeness and the Emergence of Identity-in-Difference

The conflict which has now arisen between Euthyphro and Socrates about the nature of piety can be expressed in a variety of ways. In the first place, we have found an opposition between the gods as the originative ground to which Euthyphro appeals and the abstract structures with which Socrates attempts to ground scientific knowledge. In the second place, a distinction has appeared between the power of the gods, which issues in the founding of the city of Athens, and the power of reflection, which attempts to transform the real ground of religion into the logical ground of objective knowledge. Finally, a contrast has emerged between two kinds of *language,* one of which appeals to stories about the gods, while the other attempts to express knowledge in scientific form. It is this final opposition that comes to focus in Socrates' question, "Is something pious because it is loved by the gods [as the stories of the gods suggest], or is it loved by the gods because it is pious [as must be the case if we are to understand the concept of piety in scientific terms]?" However, what is most important about this opposition is that it leads to a distinction between two conceptions of human wholeness. Socrates' quest for a definition of piety is a quest for wholeness because knowledge of objective structure brings stability to the human soul, while the return to one's origins and to the gods as prototypes of human behavior is an attempt to find wholeness by becoming an image of the gods' originative action. In the first case, wholeness comes through scientific knowledge of what is common to many, while in the second, it is achieved in the image—original relation that binds the finite individual to his creative ground.

In the course of the discussion Socrates was finally able to lead

Euthyphro into a contradiction and to secure his reluctant agreement that Piety itself is the ground of what the gods approve. As a result, it might appear that the linguistic version of the conflict has been resolved and that the mythic stories of the gods are to be subordinated to the quest for scientific understanding. However, the apparent victory of Socrates in this linguistic confrontation is not as clear as it might seem. Euthyphro would not have fallen into contradiction if he had simply refused to admit that piety is loved by the gods because it is pious, and had insisted instead that Piety depends upon the divine Will. The burden of his argument is certainly to suggest that he holds this view, and nothing that Socrates has yet said is sufficient to undermine it. In addition, we should remember that the contrast between piety and the gods cannot be dealt with adequately merely in terms of the active—passive distinction. In fact, an entirely different linguistic framework would seem to be demanded, since Socrates' earlier distinction falls altogether within the realm of genesis to which the gods are confined. But is there a mode of discourse that can relate the realm of genesis to the realm of abstract structure? And can we connect the domain of changing things with a realm of absolute stability without moving beyond language altogether? It is these problems which will finally lead Socrates into difficulties of his own and which we must now examine in detail.

Before these problems can be considered, we should notice that a break occurs at this point in the discussion. Interposed between the rigorous deduction of the contradiction inherent in Euthyphro's position and the discussion of a more nearly adequate way of speaking about the relationship between the gods and the forms, is a brief but humorous interchange between Euthyphro and Socrates which attempts to assign the blame for the apparent failure of the previous discussion (11b–e). Having noticed that his attempt to equate piety with what is loved by the gods has led to a contradiction, Euthyphro claims that he does not know how to say what he means and that whatever statements *we* advance move about and will not stay put (11b). However, Socrates replies that the statements are not his, but Euthyphro's, and that they are to be compared with the works of Socrates' ancestor, Daedalus (11c). In the heroic age of Greece, Daedalus was a sculptor who created statues whose eyes and limbs appeared to move.[25] In comparing Euthyphro's statements with the works of Daedalus, Socrates identifies them with artistic creations, attempting to call our attention to their merely human origins. Of course, the statues of Daedalus did not really move but merely seemed to: the statues he created were a combination of rest and motion and in this respect, radically ambiguous. But if we develop the original analogy between Daedalus and Euthyphro, Euthyphro's statements might also seem to be an interplay between these separate elements. Like the statues of Daedalus, the statements of Euthyphro might only appear to move, while at their foundation they might also be at rest. If this should prove to be the case, the contradiction into which Euthyphro has been led does not reveal the truth in his position. The questions of Socrates suggest the ways in which Euthyphro's statements are in motion, but they do not reveal the sense in which they remain at rest.

We should also notice that the reference to the works of Daedalus is intended to remind us of the life and death of Icarus. According to legend, Daedalus and his son Icarus were once imprisoned on an island in the Mediterranean Sea, far from the coast of Greece. In order to escape, Daedalus fashioned a pair of wings for both himself and his son, binding the feathers together with wax. Daedalus warned Icarus not to fly too close to the sun. Yet the story tells us that in the flight to the coast, Icarus soared too high into the sky. As a result, the wax in his wings began to melt, the wings collapsed, and Icarus dropped into the sea.[26] Now of course, Euthyphro wishes to deny that he is to be identified with the Daedalus who created "moving" statues. But in denying that he is Daedalus, is he to be identified by implication with Icarus? If so, his defect is not that his statements move about like the creations of Daedalus, but that he attempts to come so close to the gods that his speech about them dissolves into a contradiction. Perhaps Socrates should have said that Euthyphro's statements reminded him of the behavior of Icarus, rather than of the creations of Daedalus. However, if Euthyphro were to be identified with Icarus, Socrates would then appear to be the Daedalus. Is he the Daedalus who warned his son not to fly too close to the sun or the one who is the creator of statues that appear to move? Perhaps Socrates is to be identified with Daedalus in both of these senses. His warning not to fly too close to the sun is contained in the questions he raises about Euthyphro's claims to knowledge, while his artistic creations are the dialogues into which he attempts to lead his interlocutors — discussions which appear to move but which in fact are grounded by a transcendent reference to an ideal standard. The mythological tradition itself suggests this interpretation, for we are told that Daedalus was the architect of the labyrinth where the Cretian Minotaur was imprisoned.[27] As a result, he alone knew the path that leads beyond it, just as Socrates seems to know the way beyond fragmentation toward the wholeness of dialectical inquiry. Presumably, it is this path along which Socrates intends to lead his interlocutors in the quest for wisdom.

Yet if this should prove to be the final account of Socrates' intentions, what are we to say about the relationship between the ideal standards which are the goal of the quest for wisdom and the concrete contexts with which it begins? More specifically, since Euthyphro is a participant in the discussion with Socrates and since his statements about his concrete situation are both in motion and at rest, how can the truth in Euthyphro's position be revealed? In order to respond to this problem, Socrates says that he will attempt to aid Euthyphro in his effort to characterize the nature of piety (11e): for the first time he offers to participate actively in the attempt to reach the goal of the inquiry. However, Socrates suggests the positive point he has in mind by shifting the focus of the discussion. Somewhat unexpectedly, he asks Euthyphro about the relationship between Piety and Justice: "Is everything which is just also pious," Socrates asks, "or is everything that is pious, just, and not everything that is just, pious?" (12a). And when Euthyphro says that he does not understand, Socrates explains himself by saying that he disagrees with the poet who wrote: "'Zeus the creator, him who made all things, thou wilt not name; for where fear is, there also is reverence'" (12a). Though Socrates apparently believes that reverence produces fear, he does not agree that fear always produces reverence. Thus he wishes to claim that where reverence is, fear is also present, but to deny that where fear is, reverence is always to be found (12b–c). In the same way, Socrates apparently wishes to suggest that justice is a wider notion than piety. He wishes to claim that where piety is, justice is also present, but to deny that the concept of justice is included in the concept of piety (12c–d). The notion of inclusion in a larger unity thus appears for the first time as a crucial element in the discussion, and as we shall soon discover, it is this notion with which Socrates will attempt to bring the reflective quest for wholeness to completion.

The disagreement Socrates mentions between himself and the poet is important in its own right. The poet who claims that fear produces reverence refers to Zeus as the creator of all things. By contrast, Socrates wishes to subordinate the gods to a standard that is more fundamental than the gods themselves. He does this by suggesting that justice is a wider notion than piety and that piety itself must be subordinated to this larger context. We are reminded in this connection of the Biblical tradition in which Abraham and Moses stand before God the creator prepared to subordinate themselves to his intentions. Apparently Socrates intends to suggest that he disagrees with this solution of the problem of fragmentation, attempting to find wholeness instead within a larger context to which both gods and men can be subordinated. Thus he claims that he disagrees with the poet who places Zeus at the origin of all things rather than within the overarching context of justice understood as a cosmic totality. However, the disagreement between Socrates and the poet is important for another reason which Socrates himself fails to notice: the disagreement suggests that though fear may be more fundamental than reverence in the sense that it has a wider extension, reverence is more fundamental than fear in that it has a richer intensional significance. Fear has a wider range of reference, but reverence is intensionally richer, since it implies the presence of fear in all the contexts to which it applies. The implication might seem to be that though piety may be subordinated to the larger human context, the human realm is also partly dependent upon the religious dimension of experience for its ultimate significance. But how is this apparent consequence to be reconciled with Socrates' wish to subordinate the gods to the forms and to subordinate Piety to Justice as a larger, more inclusive framework?

The answer to these questions, and the key for understanding Socrates' approach to the problem of piety, can be found by focusing on the linguistic form of the definition Euthyphro now gives. In attempting to follow Socrates' suggestion that piety is to be subordinated to justice, Euthyphro now asserts that

IV. The part of justice which has to do with attention to the gods constitutes piety, and the remaining part of justice is that which has to do with the service of men. [12e]

The most important thing to notice about this definition is that it differs radically from all the definitions given previously. According to this new account, the concept of piety is no longer to be equated with what is loved by the gods, but is to be subordinated to justice as a larger context. In more general terms, it is not to be identified with a notion on the same logical level, but is to be understood as a *part* within a larger *whole*. At the earlier stages of the discussion, Euthyphro had formulated his definition of piety within a mythic frame of reference, and stories about the gods were central to the account he wished to develop. But now in this radically different context, the concept of justice is more fundamental than mythology, and Justice itself supplies the new standard in terms of which the concept of piety is to be articulated. It should be clear that the move to justice as the framework within which the notion of piety is to be understood consolidates the attempts of Socrates to demonstrate that normative standards are more fundamental than the gods. According to this new definition, part of justice pertains to the gods; another part pertains to men; and both men and gods are to be subordinated to this common standard. As a result, the gods no longer stand over against men as the normative standards in terms of which the acts of men are to be assessed, but instead both men and gods are to be given a place within a larger cosmic context.

In order to develop the implications of this new approach to the problem of piety, let us first ask how Socrates' claim that justice is the most inclusive context serves to explain the relationship among the forms, the gods, and men. In one of Plato's other dialogues, Socrates characterizes justice as a harmony of parts — a harmony of other virtues, though not a virtue itself in the same sense. All the other virtues mentioned in the *Republic* are correlated with particular dimensions of the human psyche. But justice is said to be that virtue which binds all the others together into a harmony and brings unity to the person taken as a whole.[28] At a later point in the discussion, Socrates also suggests that the concept of justice can be used as an analogical term for understanding the concept of Goodness itself. He claims that just as justice can be understood as a harmony of virtues, the Good may be understood as a harmony which obtains among all things — not simply things construed as forms or virtues, but things construed in the broadest possible sense.[29] It is finally this conception of justice as an analogical term which underlies Socrates' suggestion in the *Euthyphro* that justice may be understood as an inclusive concept, and which is crucial in his attempt to reconcile the forms with men and the gods. Justice is an inclusive concept because it stands in an analogical relationship with Goodness. And justice is the concept in terms of which the gods, the forms, and men are to be related because it mirrors the concept of Goodness Itself — the concept in terms of which all things are said to exist in perfect harmony. Of course, the harmony among these elements is not always immediately evident, and the attempt to make it visible often involves us in a painful reflective undertaking. However, Socrates suggests that philosophical inquiry is the process in terms of which this universal harmony can be revealed. More specifically, it is the process in which reflective wholeness can be achieved by doing justice to the divine, the human, and the normative elements always present in the human situation.

At earlier stages of the inquiry, disharmony has been a central element in the discussion. The opposition between Euthyphro and his family and the contrast between Socrates and his accusers provide the initial framework within which the dialogue unfolds. In addition, the conflict between Euthyphro and Socrates, the disagreements among the gods, and the contrast between the gods and the forms simply develop this initial discontinuity in ways that make its presence inescapable. After his revolt against his family, Euthyphro attempted to find wholeness by introducing the Olympian gods as a standard in terms of which to judge his father. However, this attempt to find unity in mythological stories was challenged by Socrates' insistence that objective structures are the fundamental standards by which even the actions of the gods are measured. The unity of mythological discourse thus becomes the unity of abstract scientific inquiry, and the original wholeness of richly human language is undermined by the suggestion that reflective wholeness can be found only by subordinating oneself to the quest for a scientific definition. Yet as the argument now begins to reach its culmination, Socrates finally suggests that justice must be done, both to scientific definition and to the original divine and human contexts with which the discussion began. As a result, he suggests that the concept of piety must be subordinated to the concept of justice and that we must move to a context in which the gods, the forms, and men can be bound together in a larger unity. Socrates asks Euthyphro to transform the quest for wholeness into the attempt to understand the *Whole,* and in doing so, to share the task of philosophical inquiry — the task in terms of which the harmony and the continuity of the Whole are to be revealed.

The definition Euthyphro now gives reflects the confidence of Socrates that the concept of justice can hold the forms, the gods, and men together, for Euthyphro claims at this point that piety is that part of justice which pertains to the gods and that the remaining part has to do with the service of men. Thus we can see that the move to justice is a move toward integration and is an attempt to bind up the fragments of the previous discussion into the harmony of the Whole which stands at the end of the reflective quest for wisdom. At earlier stages of the discussion we mentioned three kinds of wholeness and three kinds of standard — one appropriate to the forms, one appropriate to the gods, and one appropriate to the original family context. But now we see that insofar as the framework provided by the concept of justice incorporates the forms, the gods, and men, it also subsumes these three conceptions of wholeness and these three conceptions of a standard within a larger unity. In fact, the concept of justice can be understood as an analogical extension of the original conception of the family, understood as a harmonious and continuous whole. In this case, however, the members of the "family" are not the ancestors invoked around a common hearthfire, but the forms, the gods, and men, taken as the constituent elements of the cosmos as a whole. This new cosmic totality that is formally analogous to the family transcends the simple particularity of the family in which Euthyphro's fragmentation originated. Yet in moving toward it, Socrates not only calls Euthyphro's attention to the outward directionality of the quest for wholeness, but also points to the kind of unity with which Euthyphro began and to which we must attempt to do justice at this concluding stage of the argument. The larger context which Socrates introduces at this juncture suggests once more that the quest for wholeness moves in two directions, not only luring us outward toward the larger world, but also calling us back to the human context with which our journey begins.

The introduction of the concept of justice as a way of pointing to a larger whole presupposes the introduction of the genus–species form of definition. Justice is the genus under which piety is to be subsumed, just as the ancient family (*gens*) is the larger context in which family members are to be included. The language of genus and species thus replaces the subject–predicate logic of identity and appears as an alternative to the active–passive contrast between the forms and what is loved by the gods. At this point, the problem is no longer to find a definiens with which piety can be identified or to decide which is more fundamental, the gods or piety itself, but to find a context rich enough for both to have a place within it. In addition, Socrates intends to claim that the context of justice is rich enough for even Euthyphro to be included. Socrates believes that the opinions of Euthyphro are internally discordant, and he objects to Euthyphro's one-sided insistence upon the primacy of the gods. But the philosopher wishes to correct this defect by doing justice to Euthyphro, and he intends to do this by giving Euthyphro's claims their due within a larger context. Earlier, Socrates had claimed that nothing Euthyphro said would fall to the ground. Now he expresses his confidence in the existence of a framework within which the contradiction into which Euthyphro has fallen can finally be overcome. However, Socrates also suggests that this contradiction can only be overcome through philosophical reflection, and that philosophy is finally richer than mythology because it attempts to mirror the Whole. In the end, he believes that the concreteness of philosophy is a reflection of the concrete richness of its subject-matter, and that this concrete richness is to be identified with the larger Whole to which philosophical reflection is directed. When Euthyphro claims that justice is a larger whole of which piety is a part, it is not surprising that Socrates endorses this idea (12e). Formulated as it is in accord with Socrates' suggestion that piety is to be subordinated to justice, this definition signifies the completion *in principle* of the attempt to reconcile the forms with the gods and the completion of the attempt to save Euthyphro from contradiction by incorporating the human dimension within the larger context of philosophical inquiry.

Yet before this human dimension can be reincorporated, two final questions remain to be considered. Euthyphro has asserted that piety is that part of justice which has to do with attention to the gods. But what does "attention" mean in this special case? (13a) Presumably, it is not the kind of attention paid to ordinary things. Ordinary attention aims at benefitting the one to whom it is given, but Euthyphro and Socrates agree that the gods cannot be benefitted or brought to a greater degree of perfection by anything that men can do. As a result, another definition of attention seems to be required, and Euthyphro attempts to give it by claiming that the kind of attention he has in mind involves a certain kind of *service* to the gods. Attention to the gods, he claims, is to be understood by analogy with the master–servant relationship (13d), where attending to them is to commit oneself to a divine service. In order to determine what kind of service is involved, Socrates asks Euthyphro a final question: "What great work is to be accomplished by men for the gods?" "What is the task which men help the gods perform?" (13e). Euthyphro replies that many great and glorious works can be accomplished (13e), but when Socrates presses him for details, he finally makes the following assertion: When one knows how to do what is gratifying to the gods, in praying and sacrificing, that is piety, and such things *bring salvation to individual families and states;* but the opposite of what is gratifying to the gods is impious, and *that overturns everything* (14b). In response, Socrates replies as follows:

> You might, if you wished, Euthyphro, have answered much more briefly the chief part of my question. But it is plain that you do not care to instruct me. For now, when you were close upon it you turned aside; and if you had answered it, I should already have obtained from you all the instruction I need about piety. But, as things are, the questioner must follow the questioned wherever he leads. [14b–c]

Socrates had attempted to assist Euthyphro in framing a definition of piety by introducing the language of genus and species and by suggesting that justice is a larger whole of which piety is a constituent element. By asking a question about the great work that men help the gods perform, he now attempts to bind the elements of this larger context together in terms of a task that gives it a directional orientation. However, when Euthyphro responds by reintroducing the gods as the primary element in his characterization and when he appears to be more concerned with what gratifies the gods than with the common task that both men and gods are to perform, Socrates concludes that he has turned away from an adequate definition of piety. Thus it is almost in despair that Socrates says that the questioner must follow the one questioned wherever he leads.

In elaborating his earlier claim that piety consists in gratifying the gods through prayer and sacrifice, Euthyphro gives a final definition. "Piety," he now asserts,

> V. is a kind of science of sacrificing and praying, a science of giving and asking. [14c–d]

When Socrates objects somewhat ironically that it would not be scientific to give the gods something that they do not need (14e), Euthyphro replies that we give them "honor, praise, and gratitude" (15a). Moreover, he adds that this is precious most of all. But then Socrates concludes that the discussion has come full circle and that Euthyphro again appears to be committed to the view that piety is what is dear to the gods (15b). Of course, it is just this claim that issued in the original contradiction, and it is apparently impossible to return to it without contradicting oneself again. At this point, Socrates proposes that they begin again in the attempt to understand the meaning of piety (15c–d). He commits himself once more to the belief that reflection is ultimate and that wholeness can be found only through reflective inquiry. Even at the end of the dialogue, Socrates asks Euthyphro to reimmerse himself within the context of philosophical investigation. But Euthyphro now brings his own participation in the dialogue to an abrupt conclusion: "Some other time, Socrates. Now I am in a hurry and it is time for me to go."

Socrates claims that it is necessary to return to the beginning of the inquiry by asserting that Euthyphro's final definition is merely a repetition of his earlier claim that piety is to be defined as what is dear to the gods. Yet what is central to Euthyphro's final definition is the claim that piety involves the acts of prayer and sacrifice and that these acts issue in the *preservation* of families and states. Socrates fails to consider these suggestions in detail, simply claiming that Euthyphro has turned aside from a proper definition of piety. Earlier, Socrates had claimed that in defining piety as what is loved by the gods, Euthyphro had mentioned only an accidental feature of piety, and that Piety as it is in itself must be understood in different terms. However, now he fails to notice that what is essential to Euthyphro's final definition are acts of prayer and sacrifice and that acts of this kind bring *wholeness* to the families and cities in which they are performed. These acts are pleasing to the gods because they unify families and cities, and the fact that they are gratified is only an accidental result of the unity these acts produce. Thus Socrates is mistaken in claiming that Euthyphro has simply returned to his earlier definition which led him to a contradiction. Instead, he has now relegated what is pleasing to the gods to the accidental status which Socrates had suggested, replacing it with an essential characterization of piety in quite different terms. Euthyphro's suggestion that piety involves prayer and sacrifice and that it brings wholeness to families and states also indicates a connection between the Olympian gods and the gods of the family within which Euthyphro's own fragmentation originated. In this way, Euthyphro binds the earth and the sky gods together, suggesting that the framework of the Olympian deities can be understood as a development of the earlier, more primitive family context. Euthyphro moves from the family to the city in order to find wholeness, just as Zeus had moved beyond his family by a decisive act that had transformed him into the king of the gods. Moreover, just as Zeus had brought the city of Athens into existence through a synthetic act of his own, Euthyphro now intends to imitate him by unifying the family and the city through the act of prayer and sacrifice. This derivative act is a mirror image of the original act of unity in terms of which the city came into existence, and it is the performance of this act that constitutes the essence of Euthyphro's final definition.

However, what is most important about this final definition is Socrates' reaction to it and the fact that with reference to it, the conflict between Euthyphro and Socrates finally surfaces in its most radical form. In making reference to prayer and sacrifice as necessary for the salvation of families and cities, Euthyphro points to *custom and tradition* as a principle of unity, while in claiming that Euthyphro turns away from a proper definition of piety, Socrates points to *the goal of philosophical inquiry* as the unifying principle. In the final analysis, Euthyphro and Socrates disagree in the most radical terms about what is essential for a proper definition of piety and for an adequate conception of human wholeness: on the one hand, tradition, rite, and ritual; on the other, philosophical reflection that is directed primarily toward the future. It is the tension between these radically different directional orientations which finally accounts for the opposition between Euthyphro and Socrates and which pervades the dialogue from the beginning. In turning back toward the past, Euthyphro focuses on the family as a *real whole* and upon the gods as *a real ground,* while Socrates moves toward abstract structure as the *logical ground* of intelligibility and toward the cosmos as the *logical whole* in which both men and gods are to be included. In Socrates' case, the process of philosophical reflection ties the human predicament, the forms, and the gods together, issuing in a dialectical conception of piety, while for Euthyphro, the act of prayer and sacrifice preserves both families and cities and in this way binds both ground and whole together.

As Socrates understands the concept of piety, it is not related primarily to the preservation of the past, but connected instead with the process of breaking apart premature definitions. The reference in the *Cratylus* to Socrates' need for purgation by a rhetorician after talking with Euthyphro suggests this interpretation.[30] For Socrates, philosophical discourse is the means by which pollution is to be dealt with and is the process in terms of which the divine realm of the forms is to be related to the realm of genesis. Formulated in a somewhat different way, Socrates apparently believes that discourse is the purgation needed for pollution. As a consequence, new conceptions of pollution, purgation, and piety emerge. For Socrates, pollution does not result from a break in the continuity of the family, nor does it consist in a discontinuity between the realm of the gods and the realm of men.

Rather, the pollution most to be feared is an inherent condition of the human soul and is the state in virtue of which one finds oneself alienated from truth. Thus, purgation consists in the process of dialectical reflection — the process in terms of which one is brought from the discontinuity of mere opinion to the continuity of knowledge. In the hands of Socrates the meaning of piety is transformed. It becomes the peculiar virtue of the philosopher, the servant of Apollo, and is directed toward the future and toward a permanent *noesis* which requires the destruction of all merely apparent stability. From the standpoint of Socrates, the discussion with Euthyphro illustrates this drive toward perfect harmony. Socrates suggests that justice is the larger whole in terms of which the differences between himself and Euthyphro can be transcended: their conversation begins with pollution; the conversation itself is intended to bring purgation; and piety consists in the destruction of premature attempts to find stability — attempts which must finally be interpreted as stages in the appropriation of Truth itself.

Euthyphro obviously does not believe that pollution can be dealt with adequately by philosophical inquiry. Though he is unable to answer all of Socrates' questions and though he is much too confident in his own capacity to imitate the gods, Euthyphro knows that piety cannot be attained by reflection alone. Thus, he points to the necessity for reestablishing his lost participation in the continuity of the past. It is true that in the discussion with Socrates, the progression of Euthyphro's definitions becomes increasingly universal and depersonalized. But in making the suggestion that piety involves prayer and sacrifice, Euthyphro returns to human acts as central to the definition of piety. In his final definition, he reestablishes the original relationship between himself and his family. As a result, his departure and refusal to be incorporated within the larger whole to which Socrates calls his attention is not the result of stubbornness or stupidity. To the contrary, it points to Euthyphro's need to return to the human origins of his existence. In the course of the inquiry, Socrates does not take these origins into account with sufficient adequacy, and in the end he deals with them only as subject-matter for dialectical reflection and not as a framework that warrants the active and positive participation of its members. By contrast, Euthyphro himself turns back from the philosophical quest for a definition of piety within the larger context of justice to the hearthfire from which he came and to the hearthfire of the city toward which his quest for wholeness had developed. Turning his back on further reflection, he returns to the

rituals, customs, and traditions which gave rise to his original definition of piety and which can bring stability to the family and the city
from which he emerges.

Before we bring our discussion of Plato's *Euthyphro* to a conclusion,
we should ask how we are to reconcile the two conceptions of piety
present at the end of the dialogue: the one which points toward the
past and the one that points toward the future; the one which demands prayer and sacrifice and the one that requires philosophical
reflection. Justice is finally too abstract a notion to hold these two
orientations together. Both Euthyphro and Socrates could affirm the
abstract demand for harmony that the concept of justice presupposes.
But a question still remains about whether this harmony is to be
effected in terms of the past or in terms of the future; in terms of
man's participation in custom and tradition or in terms of his participation in philosophical inquiry. Socrates' apparent orientation toward the future is really an orientation toward what is eternal and
unchanging, and his "temporal" quest for wholeness is oriented toward
the truth and toward the Whole in terms of which the truth is to be
articulated. Despite the fact that the truth will always remain partly
inaccessible, Socrates' desire to return to the beginning of the dialogue and to reexamine the meaning of piety points to the circularity
of the Whole and to the corresponding circularity of philosophical
reflection. And in the face of Euthyphro's resistance to the philosophical quest for completeness, he continues to call our attention to the
permanent noesis toward which philosophical inquiry is directed. On
the other hand, it is also a mistake to interpret Euthyphro's orientation toward the past in merely temporal terms. Rather, his "temporal"
orientation is to be understood as an attempt to recover his origins
and to return to the ground of his existence. In Euthyphro's case, as in
the case of Socrates, the temporal language of a journey must be
stretched beyond its ordinary meaning, forcing us to understand the
conflict between Euthyphro and Socrates on a more fundamental
level. The problem to be resolved in this case is not the problem of
theory and practice, custom and innovation, tradition and reflection,
but the problem of two kinds of language which point beyond the
temporal order. One mode of speech points toward the stability of the
Whole, the other to the originative Ground of human existence; and it
is the conflict between these two directionalities with which the dialogue concludes.

However, there is also a unity to be found in the discussion which
lies beyond the abstract unity of the Whole and which brings whole-

ness to the themes that have been considered in the dialogue itself. In the first place, Plato himself stands at the center of the dialogue, binding the two characters together in an aesthetic unity. The richness of Plato's language, and the subtle interconnections between the concrete circumstances of the characters and the abstract dimensions of their discussion, provide the foundation that holds the dialogue together. In addition, this initial aesthetic unity reverberates in Socrates' invitation to us to return to the beginning of the discussion, for the very inconclusiveness of the inquiry brings us back to the question of piety again and again. To ask, "What is piety?" and to ask the corresponding question "What is the meaning of wholeness?" is to face a problem that must be confronted on countless occasions, and it is the special merit of Plato's discussion that he makes both the urgency and the difficulty of this problem absolutely clear. But the unity of the dialogue is not only to be found in aesthetic terms or in the focus that comes from being confronted with an inescapable question, but also in the analogies that draw the characters of the dialogue together. Socrates and Euthyphro are mirror images of one another, for while Euthyphro moves from the *tribal whole* of his family toward the *particularity* of Zeus and back again to the *unity* of the family and the city, Socrates moves from the *particularity* of abstract structures to the *unity* of the cosmic Whole and then back to the *fragmented particularity* with which the dialogue began. In the end, it is the mirroring relationship displayed in this double movement that permits the dialogue to be held together, even though the characters in the discussion remain in fundamental opposition. Formulated in somewhat different terms, Euthyphro and Socrates are both together and apart, for there is a structural similarity in their development, while there is a difference of order in the pattern to be found within the development itself. Where Euthyphro moves from unity to particularity to unity again, Socrates moves from particularity to unity back to the particularity of the original discussion. This *identity-in-difference* is the analogical ground of unity that prevades the dialogue at the structural level and that constitutes the philosophical structure of the aesthetic unity to be found within the discussion.

Finally, we must notice that in addition to their common preoccupation with the problem of unity, both Euthyphro and Socrates are equally concerned with the problem of origins. Soon after this dialogue comes to a conclusion, Socrates will die a martyr's death, and his death will help to constitute the origins of the subsequent philosophical tradition. The death of Socrates as recorded in the *Phaedo* is a philosophical myth that sustains subsequent philosophical reflection, originating the repeated attempts of the philosopher to ask philosophical questions and to attempt to understand the larger Whole in which they are to be resolved.[31] In the end, both Euthyphro and Socrates return to their origins, but with this essential difference: the act of prayer and sacrifice that Ethyphro embraces sustains the unity of the family and the city and celebrates the origins of the city by attempting to recapitulate its original unity. By contrast, the acceptance of his own death is the act by which Socrates attempts to establish a new world that lies beyond the unity of the family and the city and that attempts to bring unity to the soul by keeping alive the quest for absolute comprehension. A common concern with the Ground and with the Whole is the dimension of the discussion that brings unity out of difference, while the directional difference displayed throughout the inquiry is the irreducible dimension of difference that allows each of Plato's characters to maintain his own integrity.

4

Art, Religion, and the
Absolute Standpoint

In the earlier discussion I have attempted to show how human fragmentation can be overcome when the two directionalities present in the quest for wholeness are held together in a meaningful fashion. For example, we found in Chapter 1 that even though Ishmael's quest is dominated by a single direction, both the origins and the goal of his journey are unified in the narrative discourse in which he tells his story. His outward thrust into the ocean is balanced by a counter-thrust from the ocean itself, which allows him to recover his origins and to formulate his story as the account of a unified life. At the end of his journey, Ishmael finds wholeness on the coffin that emerges from the depths of the ocean, and it is by standing there that he locates the point of intersection between the ocean as a whole and the ground that sustains human existence. In Chapter 2 we discovered that Moses also stands in between the ground of existence and the world as a whole, but unlike Ishmael, he first returns to his origins and only then moves outward toward a larger world. The fragments of Moses' life are gathered up into a unity when he listens to the voice of God, and it is by returning to it that he is able to lead his people on a journey from bondage to freedom. Finally, in Chapter 3 we found that the two directionalities of our earlier discussion are connected in the analogical unity that binds Euthyphro and Socrates together and in the aesthetic space in which the meaning of wholeness must be sought again and again. Though their conversation does not reach an unambiguous conclusion, we learn something about the meaning of wholeness by standing between the two characters and by observing the imagistic relation that binds them together and holds them apart. In fact, in all of these cases, existential and reflective unity are achieved, not at the end of the human journey, but at a point in between fragmentation and completion. It is by seeking the midpoint between these two extremes, and by preserving the dimension of difference to be encountered there, that we have pursued the quest for wholeness in these pages.

On the other hand, the contrasting elements to be found within the quest for wholeness not only call our attention to an irreducible moment of difference, but also point to the possibility of radical opposition. In fact, in Plato's dialogue an opposition between the two directionalities is visible on at least three distinguishable levels. In the first place, a conflict occurs at the level of direct experience between Socrates' outward journey and Euthyphro's attempt to return to his origins. Socrates moves beyond the family and the city toward a larger world, while Euthyphro seeks the origins of the human realm in stories about the Olympian deities. As a result, the dialogue contains an existential opposition between the two directionalities that can never be resolved in merely theoretical terms. However, as the discussion unfolds, we also find that this existential conflict is transformed into reflective language. At the center of the dialogue a radical contrast emerges between Socrates' attempt to give a definition of wholeness in terms of an abstract logos and Euthyphro's attempt to define it in terms of the will of the gods. At this level, the existential opposition between forward and backward directions becomes a theoretical conflict between two definitions, each of which reflects the experiential direction from which it derives. Finally, in the radical disagreement between Euthyphro and Socrates to be found at the end of the dialogue, a cross-level conflict arises between concrete participation in religious customs and traditions and reflective participation in theoretical inquiry. Socrates transforms the quest for wholeness into the attempt to understand the Whole, while Euthyphro transforms his interest in mythology into the attempt to return to his origins and to understand the meaning of wholeness in human terms. At this juncture, the impulse to participate concretely in direct experience stands opposed to the attempt to articulate the meaning of this antecedent mode of participation, and in the end, it is this opposition that prevents the dialogue from reaching a satisfactory theoretical conclusion.

The conflict between the two directionalities that occurs on all these levels of interpretation is inescapable, for nothing can prevent us from concluding that a single directionality gives us exclusive access to what is ultimate. A mode of experience that makes the ultimate

dimension of human existence accessible is easily understood as ultimate in itself, thus making it possible for the advocate of a single
directionality to make exclusive claims to absoluteness. When this
occurs, the defenders of the two directionalities either move in incompatible directions or come together in discord and conflict. In either
case it would appear that the unification of two such different orientations could never be achieved. Of course, it is the very existence of
such exclusive claims that led us to the philosophical dialogue as a
way of dealing with them. Though a dialogue holds its participants
together, it also holds them apart, emphasizing the differences between them and the need to take these differences into account in the
course of the discussion. The unity of a philosophical dialogue is an
identity-in-*difference,* and it is the acknowledgment of difference as
ultimate that allows the dialogue to deal with the problem of radical
opposition. In more concrete terms, Euthyphro and Socrates stand
together because they first stand apart, and they are finally able to
be separated because the unity in which they stand has taken the
moment of difference into account from the beginning. The aesthetic
and the analogical unity of the dialogue is a unity that presupposes
difference, and it is the acceptance of this dimension of difference that
allows Plato to come to terms with his characters and to deal with the
corresponding conflicts that arise between the two directionalities.

Yet we must not forget that the history of philosophy also calls our
attention to at least one place where the philosopher refuses to rest
content with dialogue and with the dominance of difference, attempting instead to transform even the most radical oppositions into a
larger unity. In the thought of Hegel we find the claim that philosophy
is comprehensive enough to encompass both directionalities and that
it is sufficiently rich to overcome the conflicts between origins and
form, Ground and Whole, participation and reflection. Hegel moves
beyond the dialogue context in which opposition prevails to a philosophical system in which oppositions are given a place within a larger
unity. In doing so, he attempts to speak for the philosophical consciousness by rejecting difference as ultimate and by claiming that
the oppositions we have been considering can be held together in a
completed system. Formulated in somewhat different terms, Hegel
attempts to overcome fragmentation by building a system that includes radical oppositions within it,[1] and he suggests that this can be
done by entering into and appropriating the concrete richness of direct
experience.[2] Thus he embraces the view that concrete reflection is not
to be found in dialogic interaction, nor in the aesthetic and analogical

unity that makes it possible, but in a system that circumscribes the Whole and that allows us to understand the relationship among its conflicting elements in holistic terms.[3] Standing in between the two directionalities, or moving back and forth between them, is not sufficient from a systematic point of view. What Hegel seeks instead is a way of thinking that binds the two directionalities together and that brings the quest for wholeness to completion in systematic terms.

Hegel's quest for unity and his corresponding demand for absolute comprehension clearly pose a challenge to the mode of procedure adopted in this book. From the outset, we have attempted to distinguish wholeness from completeness and have suggested that the quest for wholeness stands in between the fragmentation with which it begins and the completeness it might be tempted to affirm. Wholeness always displays a dimension of mystery and power that can never be included in a larger unity, but must simply be placed alongside the demand for intelligibility as an irreducible element. The experience of all the characters in the previous chapters confirms the fact that mystery, power, and structure are equally fundamental, and that none of them can be subordinated to the others without a degeneration of the quest for wholeness into a fragmented form. In our earlier discussion, philosophical reflection has been intertwined with stories and has exhibited an aesthetic and a religious dimension precisely because of the conviction that mystery and power must be acknowledged as irreducible dimensions of the human journey. The richness of art and the power of religion must be connected with the intelligibility of philosophy if concrete reflection is to take place in the richest possible fashion. In the previous chapters, our own way of engaging in concrete reflection has been to develop a series of richly imagistic descriptions of the quest for wholeness that are intended to capture its mystery and power, as well as its intelligible structure. Part of our task in this final chapter must therefore be an evaluation of Hegel's contention that philosophy can move beyond art and religion and that it can comprehend the pictorial language of our earlier discussion in systematic terms. This can scarcely be the case unless our entire approach to the task of concrete reflection has been radically mistaken. However, having discussed Hegel's comprehensive quest for unity, we shall not object to it from an external point of view, but will attempt to show that his thought can be exploded from within and that the openness and otherness of art and religion can reassert themselves as autonomous dimensions of his own system. When this occurs, the single system that Hegel elaborates will split apart into a series of worlds, all of which are equally fundamental, and none of which can be subordinated to the others as constituent elements. These autonomous worlds can then be identified with the chapters of this book, which are to be related to one another, not as parts within a larger whole, but as a community of images bound together as an open-ended totality. It is finally this more fundamental conception of unity that this book attempts to embody, and within which Hegel's own system can be given a positive place.

The Conquest of External Opposition

The first step in Hegel's quest for absolute comprehension is to generalize the context in which the religious quest for wholeness is to be located. In fact, he suggests that art and religion are only stages of a larger quest for unity and that the two directionalities of our earlier discussion are to be found even in our ordinary conceptions of experience and cognition. In the traditional conception of experience as a cognitive activity, a subject stands in contrast with an object and actively attempts to understand it in terms of a set of images or general features that can be imprinted on the subject.[4] Through an act of simple apprehension, the subject strives to know an object that lies beyond itself, while the object, in turn, "reveals itself" to the subject as an independently existing entity.[5] In this way, the bi-directionality of religion appears within the ordinary conception of experience itself, allowing us to understand it merely as a special case of this more generalized phenomenon. However, Hegel also suggests that there is a difficulty with this conception of experience that constitutes a barrier to the reflective quest for unity. If in the act of cognition we begin with the experiencing subject, the contrast between subject and object is never transcended completely, and if we begin with an object that gives itself to the subject only externally and partially, again the subject–object contrast reflects a merely external relationship. In fact, the traditional conception of experience assumes that the externality between subject and object is irreducible and that one can know an object only externally and partially through the images and abstract concepts that enable us to characterize its nature.[6] However, this means that a lack of wholeness pervades the underlying structure of the ordinary conception of experience and that fragmentation is not to be confined to the artistic and religious dimensions of the human journey. If the relationship between subject and object is merely external, fragmentation can be understood as a radical separation between subject and object, which demands, in turn, that a quest for wholeness be undertaken throughout the whole range of human existence.

The basic task of Hegel's first great book is to overcome the fragmentation implicit in the traditional view of experience as a merely external relationship between subject and object. In his own discussion of the nature of experience, Hegel rejects at once the usual conception of the subject–object relationship and suggests that in the strict sense, one does not experience an object merely by standing in contrast with it and by attempting to understand it from an external point of view.[7] To the contrary, he claims that experience is a dynamic process in which objects are first represented but are then taken up into the subject, understood in their essential nature, and moved beyond so that a new object appears in their place as a content of consciousness. In this process, the original object is given a place within a larger context of interpretation, while this larger context itself becomes the new object which must be taken up in turn.[8] The whole process of interaction between subject and object in which a new object emerges from our encounter with the first is what Hegel means by experience,[9] and it is this complex encounter with what lies beyond that can be understood as a quest for wholeness in its own right. Hegel admits that in the initial stages of experience, a subject stands in contrast with an object and attempts to represent it from an external point of view. However, he insists that this merely fragmentary relationship is only the first stage in the process of experience taken as a whole, and that for experience in the richest sense to occur, fragmentation must be overcome by placing the original object within a larger context of interpretation. In this way the process of experience which occurs in the middle ground between subject and object becomes a quest for wholeness at the cognitive level, unfolding as the cosmic story of the development of experience as such.

One of the most important consequences of Hegel's new conception of experience is that it involves a typically philosophical transformation of the otherness of the object into cognitive terms. In our earlier discussion of Plato's dialogue, we have already considered an example of this method of procedure. From the outset, Socrates attempts to transform the problem of pollution into the problem of ignorance, thus making the fragmentation implicit in his conversation with Euthyphro accessible to the reflective consciousness. In this way, Socrates moves from fragmentation as an external religious problem to ignorance as a problem that is internal to the human soul. Once this has been done, he then proceeds to deal with the problem of pollution as if the reflective quest for understanding were the solution to Euthyphro's predicament. In a similar fashion, Hegel suggests that the objects of cognition do not simply stand in contrast with the subject, but rather fall within consciousness as objects of knowledge. Of course, the experiencing subject begins by assuming that the object of experience stand over against him, just as Euthyphro assumed that his own fragmentation was the result of the action of his father. However, Hegel presupposes the Socratic transformation and suggests that just as fragmentation is a reflection of one's own condition, so the objects of experience are related essentially to the subject that experiences them as contents of consciousness. Hegel insists that the objects of cognition are internal to the cognitive process and that in this respect, they parallel the fragmentation of the one who undertakes the quest for unity. As he formulates the point himself in describing his revised conception of experience: "it comes to pass for consciousness that what it previously took to be the *in-itself* is not *in-itself*, or that it is only in-itself for *consciousness*."[10] In this fashion, Hegel makes the transition from an external object that stands opposed to us to an object of experience that can become accessible to philosophical reflection.

Perhaps a more fundamental way to make this point is to indicate that according to this new conception of experience, both knowledge and the objects of knowledge fall within consciousness and that consciousness itself is the third term that binds them together.[11] Though Hegel begins with the contrast between subject and object as these terms are understood traditionally, he quickly makes the transition from subject and object to knower and known, claiming that consciousness is the context in which these two terms are to be compared.[12] He tells us that

consciousness is, on the one hand, consciousness of the object, and on the other, consciousness of itself; consciousness of what for it is the True, and consciousness of its knowledge of the truth. Since both are *for* the same consciousness, this consciousness is itself their comparison....[13]

Now of course, if consciousness is itself the comparison between knowledge and its object, consciousness becomes aware of itself in the act of comparison, and it is here that the new object emerges for consciousness in the course of experience. This new object is *conscious-*

ness itself in its various forms, which constitutes a series of interpretive frameworks that can be understood as modes of access to increasingly richer kinds of experience. In the course of experience, the first external object gives way to a consciousness of this initial object, which in turn is conscious of itself as a whole sequence of forms, each of which is richer and more complex than the ones that precede it. In this way the religious quest for wholeness and the context of dialogic interaction are taken to a higher cognitive level where the various forms of consciousness appear as characters in the unfolding drama of experience itself. These modes of consciousness are products of the dynamic interaction between subject and object, and they arise as elements of a philosophical quest for wholeness that occurs in the middle ground between the knower and the known.

Hegel's redefinition of the concept of experience as a dynamic process of development calls our attention to two conceptions of the subject–object relationship which it is important to distinguish. According to the traditional account, the experiencing subject encounters the object from an external point of view, and as it apprehends the nature of what stands in contrast with it, the two terms in the experiential relationship remain substantially distinct. On this view both subject and object exist in their own right, while the very notion of existence points in each case to their substantial independence. By contrast, Hegel suggests that the subject always approaches the object as a content that can be comprehended and hence as an object that can be included as an element in its own cognitive activity. As a result, the existence of both subject and object is no longer identified with substantial independence, but is connected instead with the original meaning of existence as a process in which one stands outside oneself.[14] According to this account, the subject moves beyond itself in the activity of knowing, developing itself with increasing richness and complexity as it comes to terms with the objects it encounters. Correspondingly, the object of experience no longer appears as a content that remains external, but simply as a content of consciousness that can be included in a larger unity.[15] According to Hegel, wholeness is achieved by transforming the externality of the objects of consciousness into the internal differences among a series of experiential stages, each of which can be regarded as a moment in the quest for absolute comprehension. The dialogue between two centers of consciousness which we considered in the previous chapter is an element of this quest for absolute comprehension, and it appears within Hegel's account as the stage of self-conscious, dialogic interaction.[16] However, the goal of his quest for completeness is to move beyond the dialogue where difference is more fundamental than identity, to a systematic context in which differences are included in an overarching unity. If Plato's dialogue is an identity-in-difference, Hegel's system is a set of differences in a larger unity, and it is this larger unity which is the task of philosophical reflection to comprehend.

In elaborating his conception of the quest for wholeness, Hegel claims explicitly that the goal of experience is systematic completeness and that truth is to be identified with the entire sequence of experiental stages, connected as a necessary sequence. He tells us that each stage of the process he describes leads to the next, and that when the final stage appears, truth can be identified with the whole series of stages, understood as a dynamically developing totality.[17] Thus Hegel believes that the quest for wholeness must not only be transformed into cognitive terms, as was the case in Plato's *Euthyphro*, but must also transcend the tentativeness of the dialogue and must be brought to completion at the point where the desire for knowledge finally becomes knowledge itself.[18] Hegel assumes that absolute knowing is the end toward which the quest for wholeness is directed, and it is this end which he attempts to make accessible by developing his dynamic account of human experience. As he says himself in characterizing the philosophical quest for completeness:

> The necessary progression and interconnection of the forms of...consciousness will by itself bring to pass the completion of the series.[19]

Moreover,

> the *goal* is as necessarily fixed for knowledge as the serial progression; it is the point where knowledge no longer needs to go beyond itself, where knowledge finds itself, where Concept corresponds to object and object to Concept.[20]

Apparently, Hegel intends for us to conclude that wholeness is not to be found in a religious journey, nor in a dialogue in which the meaning of wholeness is examined again and again, but only at the end of a torturous process of philosophical development. It is this torturous process which constitutes Hegel's philosophical quest for completeness and his transformation of the quest for wholeness into systematic terms.

Hegel suggests that his revised conception of experience as a quest for completeness is superior to the traditional account because of the way it allows us to deal with the problem of death. He says that an object that exists merely as an independent entity is unable to transcend itself by breaking beyond the limits of its own natural existence. Instead, it is at some point driven beyond those limits by something other than itself. When this occurs, death comes to the object as a moment of annihilation, thrust upon it by something external over which it exercises no control. By contrast, Hegel claims that the conscious subject exists by moving beyond itself and deals with moments of resistance by taking them up into itself as contents of cognition. But this means that the death of the subject is not inflicted upon it by something external to it, but that it inflicts death upon itself as it moves through the stages of its own cognitive development. In this process, the external object is transformed into an object of consciousness, and the object of consciousness is developed, in turn, in increasingly rich and more complex ways. At each of these stages, the experiencing subject "dies" as the subject of an earlier stage, only to be reborn as the new subject of a richer content of cognition. In this way, death itself becomes an element within a larger context and is subordinated to the existence of the subject as a living center of activity.[21] In our earlier chapters, we have examined the problem of death and have discussed in particular the deaths of a number of characters within the larger cosmic drama we have attempted to describe. In Hegelian terms, it is now possible to say that in all of these cases, death was not simply a natural occurrence, but was mediated by a third term that gives it lasting significance. In the case of Ahab, death was understood in terms of the concept of power; in Queequeg's case, it was mediated by the concept of mystery; while in the cases of Ishmael, Moses, and Socrates, it was finally overcome by telling a story, by returning to one's origins, and by founding a philosophical tradition that would make it possible for philosophical reflection to develop toward completion. However, in Hegel's system, we find that death is not simply an external threat of annihilation, nor the Socratic ground out of which philosophy arises, but also the developing process that leads us from stage to stage in the philosophical quest for absolute comprehension. As Hegel understands the term, death is a determinate negation.[22] That is to say, it is the negation of the independently existing object and the transformation of it into a determinate object of consciousness, which is then negated repeatedly until this object is comprehended completely in the process of absolute knowing.

The stages through which the experiencing subject moves in the course of its own self-development may all be regarded as moments of a life-story.[23] And in the end, it is this fact which forces Hegel to tell a story of his own, thus allowing his thought to be assimiliated to the mode of procedure adopted in this book. The concrete reflection in which we have been engaged need not be restricted to a novel or to a religious text, nor is it to be confined to the dramatic interaction displayed in Plato's dialogues. To the contrary, the cosmic process of development which Hegel's system describes is also an expression of the quest for wholeness at the cognitive level, and it is this process which must be understood concretely if we are to grasp the distinctive form of the quest for wholeness in systematic terms. Of course, the story Hegel tells is not the story of an individual life, nor is it the account of the dialogic interaction between two centers of consciousness, each of which is moving in a different existential direction. Rather, it is the philosophical story of the development of consciousness itself as it moves from stage to stage in the quest for absolute comprehension.[24] However, Hegel claims that a connection is to be found between the two levels in the fact that the individual human subject can retrace the development of consciousness, and by doing so, can come to understand the stages of this process as a necessary sequence. When this occurs, he says that wholeness is achieved at the human level, for to think through the stages in the development of consciousness as a completed sequence is to have these stages reflected completely in one's own self-development.[25] The development of consciousness is a concrete process, for nothing in principle stands outside it; and the account to be given of it is a cosmic story, for no other mode of discourse can give us access to its concrete richness. As a result, Hegel suggests that concrete reflection is to be identified with the cognitive process as a whole, and that the world-story in which it is described is the vehicle for bringing the quest for wholeness to completion in systematic terms.

The world-story Hegel tells us moves through a series of stages in which the two directionalities of our earlier discussion are always present as essential elements. At each stage, the subject reaches out to the object and the object reveals itself to the subject, seeking in each case to overcome the radical differences that hold them apart. From the outset, Hegel attempts to establish the thesis that the subject and the object belong together, and he does this by showing that the radical opposition of external negation can be overcome in the course of experience itself. However, he also tells us that the unity he seeks is not achieved for the first time until we reach the standpoint of religion, which he regards as the penultimate stage of the experiential journey he describes. Hegel claims that at all the other stages of experience, externality is much more fundamental than unity, and that unity begins to emerge in some measure of fullness only in the concrete development of the religious consciousness. For example, at the earlier stage of perceptual consciousness, experience involves an external relationship between the experiencing subject and finite, unself-conscious objects of perception;[26] and at the level of self-conscious interaction, it involves a relationship with another self-consciousness in active opposition to us.[27] When we reach the level of Reason, the immediate "object" of cognition is an abstract structure with which the self-conscious individual stands in a merely external relationship;[28] while at the level of Spirit, the object of consciousness becomes a set of objective moral principles that remain in contrast with us, demanding that we bring our actions into accord with an external standard.[29] However, when we move beyond these stages to the standpoint of religion, the moment of externality is transcended, and we finally catch a glimpse of the kind of unity to which the quest for wholeness is directed. Hegel suggests that the two directionalities of our earlier discussion are unified within the context of religion and that this unity is accessible to us in the figurative language of the religious tradition. In at least one well-known passage, he even claims that religion is

> that region in which all the enigmas of the world are solved, all the contradictions of deeper-reaching thought have their meaning unveiled, and where the voice of the heart's pain is silenced — the region of eternal truth, of eternal rest, of eternal peace.[30]

On the other hand, Hegel also knows that not every religion succeeds in giving us access to the region to which it points, and he claims that in the end, religion can bring unity to the human soul only in terms of the events, the language, and the cultic celebration of the Christian tradition.[31] Of course, this means that Hegel regards Christianity as the highest expression of the religious consciousness and that other religions must be subordinated to it in his treatment of the nature of religion. However, he also defends the familiar view that Judaism and Greek religion are crucial elements in the emergence of Christianity and necessary components in the construction of a framework that can bring the two directionalities together.[32] Formulated in terms of our earlier discussion, Hegel claims that Judaism points to the dimension of revelation and to the radical externality between man and God that demands mediation; that Greek religion reverses the directionality of revelation and exhibits man's outward quest for unity; and that Christianity, in speaking about the death and the resurrection of Christ, succeeds for the first time in binding these two directionalities together. According to this account, Christ's descent into the tomb is the culmination of the process of revelation, while our celebration of his resurrection is the beginning of the process in which man is raised to unity with God. In a somewhat more extended formulation, Hegel tells us that the chasm that separates man from God can be overcome only if God abandons his external relations with his creatures, enters the world to stand alongside us in our pain and suffering, and finally takes us back up into himself to share the power of his resurrection.[33] Within this pictorial context, the downward direction is balanced by an upward thrust, and both directionalities come together in the concrete unification of creation, death, and resurrection. According to Hegel, the incarnation, the death, and the resurrection of Christ are the means by which radical externality is overcome and the only way in which the fragmented individual can find the kind of wholeness that comes from union with God.

The status of religion within the experiential story Hegel tells us is unique, for the development of the religious consciousness involves a story of its own, which displays its own distinctive structure. In fact, in the earlier chapters of this book, we have already considered certain crucial aspects of this story, beginning with the natural religion of Melville's novel and developing the discussion both with reference to the Hebrew religious tradition and in terms of the two prongs of Greek religion that were expressed in Plato's *Euthyphro*. In all of these cases, wholeness is achieved when the two directionalities of the quest for unity are held together and when the ultimate dimension of experience becomes accessible to the fragmented individual as a sustaining source of power and meaning. However, concerned as he is with the philosophical quest for completeness, Hegel himself focuses only upon the external elements of our earlier discussion, first suggesting that natural religion involves a subject–object relationship in which the object is the dominant element and the subject is subordinated to it.[34] In this case, the externality of the religious object remains an irreducible element, constituting a barrier to the quest for absolute comprehension. Hegel then develops this theme by claiming that Hebrew religion accentuates the opposition between the human subject and God, and that God reveals himself within this tradition only in a series of merely external relations. In the Hebrew tradition, God first expresses himself as the power of creation; then as the absolute Lord and Master; and finally as the arbitrary will that chooses a particular nation as his own and signifies this choice through the simply externality of a merely contractual agreement. Hegel concludes from this that God remains external to his own people, and that the abysmal mystery of God is not fully disclosed, even to the patriarchs with whom he chose to speak.[35] Finally, Hegel tells us that though Greek religion reverses the directionality of the subject–object relationship and attempts to move beyond fragmentation toward a larger unity, it is faced at once with a radical externality of its own: first, the resistance of Nature; then the recalcitrance of Fate; and finally, the externality of the gods — each of which constitutes an obstacle to the human quest for fulfillment.

The Greeks attempted to deal with these obstacles in a three-fold form, struggling in each case to bring the quest for wholeness to completion. In the first place, they regarded the natural order as a recalcitrant other that must first be overcome if the opposition between man and what is ultimate was to be transcended. Within this context, man stands in contrast with Nature as a surrogate for the infinite beyond; he confronts his own limitations as measured by the vastness of the cosmos; but instead of waiting to be addressed by the ground of his existence, he attempts to transform the natural order into spiritual terms through an effort of his own. According to Hegel, the development of Greek religion is a process of self-realization, for man becomes a spiritual being in the course of his struggles with what is formless and alien.[36] However, in the midst of this developmental process, the Greeks discovered that Fate often resisted their attempted transformation of Nature and that it appeared as an even more radical principle of externality that was impossible to transcend. In spite of their hybristic attempts to overcome the resistance of Nature, the Greeks always experienced the counter-thrust of Fate, and it was this encounter with what will always remain beyond that prevented them from bringing the quest for wholeness to completion. Yet Hegel also emphasizes the fact that the work of Fate makes possible a positive human response and that this response is displayed most clearly in the Greek attitude of resignation. In the act of resignation, the individual who has attempted to conquer Nature accepts the dictates of Necessity by saying simply, "It is so." Thus, the act of resignation may also be regarded as an act of reconciliation, for it is a way in which man can be reconciled to a life and death of self-acceptance within the finite order.[37] Finally, Hegel tells us that the Greeks attempted to deal with the externality of the gods by emphasizing the fact that they are works of art in human form, and that at the most fundamental level, they are to be understood as spiritual creations. Hegel also reminds us that these spiritual creations are not incomprehensible, as is the God of Hebrew religion. To the contrary, the Greek artist understands his gods as they are in themselves, for they are fully present in the mythical stories and artistic creations through which they come into existence. Thus, the Greeks attempted to overcome the externality of the gods by seeing them as reflections of their own nature and as products of their own creative activity.[38]

However, if we remain within the context of Greek religion, it soon becomes evident that neither resignation nor creation can bring the quest for wholeness to completion, for both these principles must finally be understood as merely human acts which point beyond the finite realm. Resignation stands in contrast with Fate and accepts it as an external principle, while human acts of creation are simply elements in an unending series of acts, the potential infinity of which suggests a contrast between the finite and the infinite. In both cases, the finite realm remains detached from the region to which it points, and as a result, a context is not available which bounds them both or holds them both together in a larger unity. If resignation and creation are to be brought together, Hegel suggests that a common principle must be found that can include their differences. But if both these attitudes merely fall on the side of the finite order, and if each of them remains detached from the ultimate dimension upon which it depends, no overarching framework can be found that includes them both within a bounded totality. In both instances, reference to what lies beyond constitutes a barrier to unification, preventing the Greek religious tradition from bringing its own principles together in a larger unity. In fact, even the analogical connection that unified the earlier conflict between Euthyphro and Socrates now seems insufficient to bring about the unity we seek. In the case of both resignation and creation, the infinite term to which they are related remains opaque, and it cannot be included as an element in any attempt to unify the two directionalities. But at this point it is precisely the unity of these two directionalities as they involve an ultimate dimension that seems to be demanded. Thus we must conclude once more that the Greek tradition is unable to bring the quest for wholeness to completion or to unify the principles which appear as crucial elements in its own version of the human quest for fulfillment.

It is finally because of the problem of religious externality that Hegel moves beyond Judaism and Greek religion to Christianity, claiming that the opposition between the finite and the infinite has been transcended in the Christian tradition. Within this new pictorial context, resignation is not simply the act of a finite individual in contrast with a divine ground, but the primordial act in which God resigns himself to death within the finite order. In this way, resignation no longer stands in contrast with an external demand, but is finally taken up into the life of God himself as an internal principle. But we must also notice that the transmutation of the act of resignation into the infinite domain unites the principles of creation and resignation: the second person of the Trinity, who is the divine logos in terms of which the world is created, is also the one who resigns himself to death and comes into the world to undergo the pain and the rejection of the cross. On the Christian account, God not only creates the world in contrast with himself, but also enters into it to share the pain and suffering of those within the world who would otherwise remain cut off from him. In this way, he reveals himself as more than the absolute Lord and Master of the Hebrew tradition and appears instead as the suffering servant, whom the prophet Isaiah had said would one day come to bear our griefs and carry our sorrows.[39] In the death of Christ, the infinite domain reaches down to the extreme limits of the finite order, sharing the fate to which everything finite must finally be subjected. However, Hegel also tells us that the appearance of Christ within the world finally culminates in a positive act that brings the religious quest for wholeness to completion. Christ not only dies, but is also resurrected, and it is his resurrection that finally overcomes the moment of radical externality represented most clearly in the threat of death. In the resurrection Christ combines creation and resignation with reconciliation, for the one who creates, and the one who dies, finally returns to his ground to complete the cycle of redemption. But Hegel also indicates that this moment of redemption is not confined to Christ himself, but is accessible to others in their pictorial participation in the original events. In the rites and rituals of the Christian tradition, the death and the resurrection of Christ are celebrated and reenacted, and it is in this celebration that the human subject is allowed to participate in the unity of God himself.[40] In fact, Hegel claims that by reexperiencing the birth, the death, and the resurrection of Christ, the Christian also conquers death and binds the beginning and the end of his own life together in a pictorial unity. It is because of this moment of completeness and because sin and death are conquered in our celebration of the resurrection, that the two directionalities are held together, and the Christian can say, "O death, where is thy sting? O grave, where is thy victory? As it stands written, Death is swallowed up in victory."[41]

From a religious point of view, it is perhaps difficult to understand how this expression of victory could be regarded as merely the penultimate stage of a larger quest for completeness. What could be richer than Hegel's own suggestion that in the pictorial language of the Christian tradition, the two directionalities of our earlier discussion are unified, and that the opposition between the finite and the infinite is finally overcome by the appearance of God himself within the finite order? In the earlier chapters, wholeness was achieved by standing in contrast with what is ultimate and by speaking about it in a fashion that always preserved its mystery and power. By contrast, the Christian tradition insists that the mystery and the power of God are made fully accessible in an incarnated logos, and that the Christian celebration of the incarnation, death, and resurrection of Christ is the concrete process in which fragmentation is overcome and the two directionalities of our earlier discussion come together in a concrete unity. Thus Hegel claims that wholeness finally gives way to completeness, and that this moment of completeness is expressed for the first time in the richly metaphorical and analogical language of the Christian tradition. However, Hegel also claims that a final problem arises which requires us to move beyond the pictorial language of religion and to comprehend the standpoint of Christianity in systematic terms. He maintains that though Christianity bridges the chasm between the finite and the infinite, it does so in a language that depicts these spheres as external to one another, even in the moment in which they are united. The events which the language of Christianity represents are separated in time from the moments in which these representations themselves take place, for the death and the resurrection of Christ are depicted as occurrences that are temporally removed from the present.[42] However, the real problem that concerns Hegel at this point is the externality of the language in which these pictorial representations are always embodied. Even if we abstract from the objective externality of the events in question, pictorial language is itself external in that it purports to depict a set of occurrences that lie outside itself. It is for this reason that Hegel claims that pictorial language is inadequate to bring unity to the human soul and that religious language raises a final problem of radical externality for the reflective consciousness.[43] What is required, according to Hegel, is another way of speaking that transforms the imagistic language of religion into nonpictorial terms. What is needed is a mode of discourse in which the incarnation, the death, and the resurrection of Christ are not simply depicted as external events, but are embodied concretely in the very act of speaking.

Hegel attempts to move beyond the standpoint of religion by suggesting that the Christian process of redemption is merely an external reflection of his revised conception of experience and by claiming that the stages of the Christian mediation are embodied concretely in the act of philosophical reflection. In the course of experience, an object is represented as it is in itself, just as in the incarnation, the second person of the Trinity is the initial term in the redemptive process. This term is then internalized as a content of consciousness and loses its substantial independence, just as the incarnated Christ must suffer the pain and the death reflected in the crucifixion. Finally, through the power of systematic thought, this term is given a "resurrected" place within a larger context and becomes the new object upon which the next stage of the experiential process is founded.[44] The resurrection of Christ and the transformation of objects of experience from death to life are thus analogous attempts to bring unity to what would otherwise have been a fragmented situation. The analogy between religion and philosophy in fact leads Hegel to suggest that these two separate regions are identical in content: the three-fold mediation of Christianity and the triadic structure of Hegel's system are mutual reflections of one another, and in both cases the quest for unity is directed against the belief that any aspect of experience can be cut off from the others by a merely external relation. However, Hegel also maintains that a crucial difference exists between Christianity and his philosophical system, for though he claims that they are identical in content, they are not identical in form.[45] Christianity depicts the process of redemption as a series of events, and it does so in a language that presupposes the objective externality of its contents. By contrast, philosophical reflection transforms this series of events, and the pictorial language in which they are reflected, into stages of the process of reflection itself. In doing this, it allows us to recollect the form of the experiential process which culminates in the conquest of objective externality.[46] According to Hegel, the process of death and resurrection occurs repeatedly in the course of experience, and it is not to be confined to a set of externally represented religious occurrences. Thus Hegel claims that philosophical reflection is the completion of Christianity, since it transforms a content which might otherwise remain a pictorial story into a process that is at work here and now. This transformation of religion into philosophy is the final conquest of radical externality, for it transposes the external stages of the Christian mediation into the internal moments of the process of philosophical reflection.

The most obvious virtue of Hegel's treatment of the language of religion is that it frees the religious consciousness from an infinite expectation that never seems to be fulfilled. Hegel suggests that the beginning and the end of things is not to be found in the past nor in the future, but in a developmental process that can be comprehended in the present moment. From the standpoint of religion, the eternal logos splits apart into a series of historical events, the unity of which can only be depicted in pictorial language. But from the standpoint of philosophical reflection, this same logos is a dialectical unity which includes all of its moments as circumscribed elements. As a result, the unity of philosophical experience gives us reflective access to the Whole, which is itself understood as a dynamic totality. Since a dynamic and spiritual dimension is at work in the systematic language that comprehends the standpoint of religion, the present becomes the place where we can enter the Absolute Process, which might otherwise remain an infinite project. Of course, in giving us reflective access to this process, Hegel transforms certain crucial aspects of religion into philosophical terms, and in the end, it is these transformations which lie at the foundation of his quest for complete comprehension. For example, he first transforms the infinite power of God into the power of reflection, and on this basis translates the logos of this power into the structural stages of reflection itself. Of course, mystery also appears within this transformed context as an irreducibly negative moment, for the power of reflection always orients itself toward an object which is external and recalcitrant and which presents itself as a barrier that must finally be overcome. However, what is most distinctive about Hegel's position is his belief that this obstacle can be transcended and that the quest for wholeness can be brought to completion as a fully articulated totality. As he says himself on more than one occasion, the Truth is the Whole, and the Whole is to be identified with the structured process of its own articulation.[47] In terms of our earlier categories, this simply means that mystery, power, and structure are unified in a dynamically ordered totality and that the articulation of this unity is Hegel's philosophical response to the human quest for fulfillment.

Perhaps this point can be elaborated most clearly by comparing Hegel's intentions with the pattern of reflection traced out in the previous chapter. In Plato's *Euthyphro*, the two directionalities which are always present in the quest for wholeness appear as irreducible elements, and they are embodied concretely in Socrates' outward journey and in Euthyphro's attempt to return to the sustaining ground of his existence. Socrates then transforms the religious quest for wholeness into the philosopical attempt to understand the Whole, while Euthyphro transforms the quest for origins into the quest for an originative principle that will bring unity to human existence. Finally, Socrates attempts to unify these two directionalities by binding their mystery, their power, and their structure together in a larger whole. However, at the end of the dialogue, Euthyphro and Socrates, the gods and the forms, power and logos split apart; for Socrates does not succeed in giving them all a place within a philosophical context. The Socratic Whole is an abstract totality which remains a mere ideal, and as a result, the opposing elements of the dialogue split apart within the abstract horizon that Socrates vainly attempts to articulate. It is of course true that Plato accomplishes what Socrates cannot, for he succeeds in bringing his characters together in the aesthetic and the analogical unity of dialogic interaction. However, even here unity is dominated by difference, so that Plato's dialogue brings us much closer to the moment of irreducible difference than it does to the moment of unity. It was for this reason that we turned to Hegel's system in an attempt to bring the moment of unity to a more explicit focus.

By contrast with Plato's dialogue, the Ground to which Euthyphro returns and the Whole to which Socrates attempts to point are brought together in Hegel's systematic articulation of the absolute standpoint. In Hegel's system, the Whole ceases to be a merely abstract totality and is identified instead with the process of articulation that occurs in the process of philosophical reflection. In this way, the goal of the Socratic quest for wisdom is made accessible in a cognitive process that unfolds in the present moment. In addition, the real ground of our earlier discussion ceases to be a primordial beginning to which we can return only in terms of religious ritual and religious celebration. In Hegel's systematic account of the development of experience, the ground first appears as an external object which stands in contrast with the experiencing subject. As I have suggested already,

Hegel always begins with our encounter with what lies beyond and with its real resistance to our cognitive encroachments.[48] However, in the course of philosophical reflection, the real ground of cognition is transformed into the cognitive content of the original object, which becomes in turn the logical ground which enables us to distinguish one object from another in the course of experience.[49] Yet the most important point to notice about Hegel's account of the nature of experience is that the notion of ground in both senses is taken up within a larger Whole. The original external object is transformed into an object of cognition, and the cognitive content of this same object becomes merely an aspect of experience itself as a dynamic process of development. As the point might be formulated in a different way, Hegel shifts his attention from the abstract logos of Socratic form to the dynamic structure of the process of reflection. As a result, he attempts to bring the quest for wholeness to completion on the cognitive level by subordinating the object as real ground, and the form of the object as logical ground, to the dialectical process as the holistic Ground within which both can be contained.[50] In this way, Hegel attempts to avoid the conflict between logos and power reflected in the conversation between Euthyphro and Socrates and attempts to overcome the moment of difference present throughout our earlier discussion. In summary form, he does this by developing a dynamic account of human experience that gives both power and structure a place within a larger systematic context.

Hegel's account of philosophical reflection, and the thesis that difference must finally be subordinated to identity is reflected most clearly in his own brief, but interesting account of philosophical language. In this account, Hegel admits that when we first attempt to speak about an object, we stand over against it as an external content of cognition. The first moment of consciousness is external, and it brings us into linguistic contact with an object that lies outside ourselves. However, he also claims that when we focus on the object, the language we use to articulate its nature alienates us from it, and that in the course of discursive articulation, the object itself vanishes into a tissue of abstract universals. Presumably, this is what occurs in the Socratic quest for abstract form and in the corresponding attempt to generate a set of abstract definitions. But Hegel finally suggests that just as there is a mode of experience that transcends the pictorial consciousness, there is also a mode of speaking that transcends the subject–predicate structure of ordinary language. If we begin with an object, designated by the subject of a declarative sentence, the object first appears as substantial and independent. And in the utterance of the sentence, the subject "passes over" into its predicates, vanishing into the logical ground of an abstract set of cognitive contents. Yet this merely abstract conclusion can be avoided when we notice that the sentence itself contains a speculative moment. In the utterance of the sentence as a whole, we move from subject to predicate; the predicate itself issues a counter-thrust that turns us back toward the subject; and in the use of the copula, we unite both moments in a single whole.[51] According to Hegel, the copula signalizes the fact that the subject does not merely "pass over" into its generic features, which then reverse this outward directionality by turning us back toward the subject, but that it also expresses itself through them as a unified phenomenon. It is true that the externality which obtains between the act of speaking and the events which pictorial language attempts to describe is reflected in the externality to be found between subject and predicate. Yet Hegel maintains that the Speculative Sentence is also the linguistic reflection of the move beyond representational experience. At both levels, externality is overcome through the articulation of a dialectical Whole which transposes both the real and the logical ground into a speculative unity. In the act of philosophical reflection and in the use of speculative language, the Speculative Good Friday of abstract opposition gives way to the Philosophical Resurrection of dialectical unity. At the linguistic level, it is this moment of unity which Hegel attempts to capture as a way of bringing the quest for wholeness to completion.[52]

The Artistic and Religious Resistance to the Philosophical Quest for Completeness

Hegel has suggested that both Christianity and his own philosophical system are attempts to overcome the defects of radical externality. In each case the contrast between the finite and the infinite has been transcended, resulting in the incorporation of both directionalities of the quest for wholeness within a larger unity. On the other hand, when philosophy attempts to move beyond the standpoint of religion and when it seeks to translate the pictorial language of religion into the systematic language of philosophical reflection, it should be expected that the religious consciousness would resist this transformation. From the standpoint of religion, pictorial language is not a defect, but an essential way of expressing the richness of the quest for wholeness and of preserving the irreducible dimension of difference between God and the world which is sometimes encountered on the human journey. Formulated in somewhat different terms, the presence of openness and otherness in the religious quest for wholeness demands the use of representational discourse. The pictorial language of religion preserves the aesthetic dimension of the human journey in the very richness of its own formulations, while the separation between subject and object which pictorial language presupposes is a reflection of the difference between God and the world upon which the religious consciousness depends. The mystery and the otherness of religion, which are essential ingredients in the development of the quest for wholeness, are reflected in the pictorial language of religion, and it is for this reason that religion will always resist Hegel's transformation of religious discourse into systematic terms.

The clearest expression of both these dimensions of religion is to be found in the Christian conception of creation *ex nihilo.* According to the Christian tradition, creation is a primordial aesthetic act that brings something new into being and that establishes a moment of irreducible difference between God and the world. The created product is new because it comes into being from nothing, and it is radically different from its source because the nothingness from which it springs stands in contrast with the power that brings it into existence. In both respects, the pictorial language of religion is the ideal vehicle for expressing the doctrine of creation, for pictorial language has an irreducibly aesthetic dimension, while its subject–object structure preserves the dimension of difference that the act of creation always presupposes. By contrast with this account, it is instructive to notice that Hegel's own description of the act of creation is formulated in much less radical terms. In his brief characterization of the nature of Christianity in the *Encyclopedia,* he claims that at the moment of creation, the second person of the Trinity *divides itself* into a subsistent duality — on the one hand, the realm of nature; on the other, the realm of finite spirit.[53] And in the *Philosophy of Nature* he says that Nature *is* the Son of God and that it merely appears to be a distinct realm, abiding in otherness.[54] It thus would seem that Hegel's description of the notion of creation already presupposes the unity of the Whole into which he attempts to transform the language of religion. His account is rather clearly pantheistic, does not include any references to the aesthetic moment of richness and indeterminacy, blurs the moment of difference between God and the world, and attempts to substitute a holistic account of the relation between God and the world for an account that preserves their irreducible difference. In all of these ways, Hegel simply overrides the structure of the language of religion, preparing the way for a systematic account that subordinates the moments of richness and difference to a larger quest for unity.

There is also a radical difference between the Christian account of the incarnation, death, and resurrection of Christ and Hegel's holistic version of the same process. According to the Christian tradition, the incarnation presupposes the original act of creation and is a downward movement in which the second person of the Trinity enters a finite realm with which he remains in radical contrast. Though Christ becomes a man, he is also God in human form, and this fact alone is sufficient to sustain the original distinction between God and the world expressed in the language of creation. It is true that in the death and the resurrection of Christ, he is reunited with the ground from which he came. However, in this process, the one who dies and is resurrected remains distinct from other finite beings and is also to be distinguished from the Father from whom he was begotten. The death of Christ is not simply the death of a particular stage of consciousness, but the death of the whole person. As a result, Christ is separated from others in his death in a much more radical way than the stages of consciousness are separated from each other in the quest for reflective completeness. In the second case, the death of the stages of consciousness lead by necessity to their resurrection in the next, while in the first case, the body of the crucified Christ is buried in the ground for three days, awaiting a miracle whose immediate source remains outside itself. The need for this unexpected intervention is reinforced by an earlier discontinuity between the Father and the Son. At the death of Christ, God turns his back on his Son; Christ exclaims, "My God, my God, why hast thou forsaken me?"[55] and as the crucifixion comes to an end, he dies alone, commending his spirit back to God only after he has claimed that it is finished.[56] If within this context resurrection is to occur, it can scarcely do so of necessity, but through a radical act of regeneration that is even more powerful than the original act of creation through which the world was brought into existence. Finally, when Christ rises from the dead, he appears to his disciples in a resurrection body, the strangeness of which prevents them from overcoming the moment of difference that obtains throughout the Christian story of redemption.[57] And when he ascends to the Father, he does not merge with him, but sits down at God's right hand as a distinguishable individual.[58] In the Christian tradition, wholeness is achieved, not by the subordination of difference to a larger unity, but through a recapitulation of these original events in a fashion that preserves both unity and difference. The Christian conception of unity is founded on the notion of imitation rather than inclusion, and it is this conception of imitation that is concretized in the pictortial language of our earlier discussion.

Of course, Hegel would reply that the pictorial language of religion must be reinterpreted in nonpictorial terms if the dominance of difference is to be overcome and if unity is to be achieved. In fact, he even suggests that pictorial language finally lacks philosophical significance and that it must be replaced altogether by systematic philosophical discourse. Hegel claims that

> philosophy puts thoughts, categories, or, in more precise language, adequate *notions*, in the place of the generalized images we ordinarily call ideas. Mental impressions such as these may be regarded as the metaphors of thoughts and notions. But to have these figurate conceptions does not imply that we appreciate their intellectual significance, the thoughts and rational notions to which they correspond. Conversely, it is one thing to have thoughts and intelligent notions, and another to know what impressions, perceptions, and feelings correspond to them.[59]

Apparently, Hegel believes that sensuous language is much too particular and imagistic to be universally accessible to the reflective consciousness, and that in the end it merely reflects one's accidental participation in a particular region of human experience. As he suggests with respect to the language of religion, we have on the one hand the edification, the ecstasy, and the ferment of enthusiasm that springs from the level of religious feeling; on the other hand, we have the cold march of necessity and the universality of conceptual thinking that springs from the philosophical demand for absolute comprehension.[60] Confronted with this contrast, Hegel himself chooses universality, claiming that philosophy must guard against trying to be edifying and that it must attempt instead to express the truth in systematic terms.[61]

In focusing upon the immediacy, the vagueness, and the imprecision of representational discourse, Hegel fastens upon a dimension of ordinary language that must not be overlooked. However, in doing so, he underestimates the role of metaphor as an irreducible element of religious discourse; fails to appreciate its value as a way of pointing to the openness of the quest for wholeness; and refuses to understand it as a way of moving beyond systematic philosophical discourse to an even richer notion of concrete reflection. The metaphorical dimension of the language of religion is not expressed in this form because it falls short of the quest for systematic unity, but because it wishes to transcend the confines of a system and to make an even richer contact with the ultimate dimension of human experience. The pictorial dimension of the quest for wholeness is what it is because of a wish to be true to the mystery and the power to be encountered on the human journey and because of the conviction that this can be done only in a figurative mode of discourse that reflects the richness of the human journey. However, it is also true that the Hegel of the foregoing quotation is underestimating the role of metaphor in his own system, for he clearly uses metaphorical expressions to enrich his own conceptual account of the philosophical quest for completeness. In fact, the frequent occurrence of metaphorical discourse in the *Phenomenology* gives Hegel's thought its initial richness and provides him with a linguistic medium in terms of which to make philosophy concrete. For example, Hegel claims that the *Phenomenology* is both a pathway to Science and a highway of despair.[62] And he compares the stages of the philosophical journey to the stations of the cross,[63] where we encounter the metaphors of the inverted world, the master–servant relationship, and the unhappy consciousness, each of which is a complex mixture of the bondage and the liberation to be experienced in the philosophical quest for complete comprehension. In his more mature and systematic writings, Hegel also claims that his *Logic* is an account of what God was doing prior to the creation of the world.[64] In this way, art and the aesthetic dimension of experience reemerge as crucial elements of his system, and Hegel gives us poetic access to the meaning of his thought, right at the center of the most abstractly dialectical element of his entire quest for absolute comprehension.

It is also important to notice that one of the central features of Hegel's thought is a concept which lays down the conditions under which the construction of metaphors is possible. I refer, of course, to the concept of *Aufhebung*. As we have indicated already, for an earlier stage of reflection to be experienced, or to be *aufgehoben,* is for it to be taken up, moved beyond, and preserved in some degree of tension within a later stage of reflection. But this is precisely what occurs in the construction of a metaphor. In metaphorical discourse, the ordinary meaning of a concept is taken up, conjoined with a different, sometimes even contradictory meaning, and held in tension with it to comprise a larger metaphorical unity.[65] That is to say, metaphors differ from literal expressions in much the same way that the ordinary conception of experience differs from Hegel's richer, more dialectical conception. In both cases, the sheer opposition between two terms is made more fluid, so that the first term is taken up, conjoined with the second, and held together with it to form a richer, more complex unity. Thus Hegel not only uses metaphors within his system as a way of enriching his thought, but also introduces a concept which is presupposed in their construction and which serves as the ground of both metaphorical representation and dialectical reflection. In fact, if Hegel's account of experience and our account of the construction of metaphors exhibit an analogical structure, it would seem that both metaphor and systematic reflection spring from a common source. The tripartite dialectical process is a categorial reflection of the process which occurs in the formation of metaphors, and at the most fundamental level it is this fact that gives Hegel's system its power and makes it possible for him to make philosophy concrete.

Despite their common origins, it is also true that crucial differences exist between metaphorical discourse and philosophical reflection. What is of primary interest at the metaphorical level is the power of the metaphor itself — its power to illuminate, to bring hidden connections into view, and to place us at the center of a way of thinking that is both in motion and at rest. Like the statues of Daedalus that we considered in our earlier discussion of Socrates, metaphors are fluid concepts. Their apparent motion points beyond themselves to a set of meanings that are suggested rather than articulated, while their unity is open-ended, always making it possible for us to engage in further interpretation. By contrast, what is most interesting about Hegel's system is the process of reflection it embodies and the determinate stages through which it moves in the quest for absolute comprehension. Though Hegel's system holds its elements both together and apart, its fundamental intention is to articulate the structure of a concrete process, stretched out in the attempt to comprehend the Whole. A living metaphor is a concrete unity, the richness of which points beyond itself. By contrast, a philosophical system is an overarching unity, the richness of which appears within it as a plurality of distinguishable stages. Thus, the crucial distinction between identity-in-difference and difference-in-identity emerges once more: if we remain within the context of the religious quest for wholeness and within the figurative language in which its concrete richness is expressed, the unity in question is always dominated by difference; while if we move beyond the context of religion to the context of philosophy, difference is always subordinated to identity in the form of systematic reflection.

The difference between these two forms of unity is of crucial significance in attempting to understand the religious resistance to the quest for absolute comprehension. By contrast with Hegel's quest for systematic unity, which attempts to move beyond pictorial language to a conceptual system, religion takes up the dimension of metaphor which points beyond itself and transforms it into an open-ended quest for wholeness. This open-ended use of language breaks beyond the limitations of a bounded system and points to the infinite richness to be discovered in the ultimate dimension of human existence. Moreover, the dimension of mystery and indeterminacy which the quest for wholeness exhibits, and which the metaphorical dimension of pictorial discourse makes accessible, becomes a window through which the religious journey can move in its encounter with a real ground. Just as the ocean opened up to Ishmael to allow him to return to his origins, so the indeterminacy and the richness of the metaphorical dimension open out to a beyond in which it is possible to confront a source of significance that stands outside ourselves. It is this encounter with what lies beyond that reverses the directionality of the outward journey and leads us back to the ground of our individual existence. Metaphor, understood philosophically, becomes a dialectical system whose elements are understood as internal constituents of itself. But metaphor, understood in religious terms, becomes a pathway that leads beyond the finite order to a real ground, which can in turn be represented imagistically in the analogical language of the religious tradition. The irreducibility of mystery and openness in the outward journey demands metaphorical discourse, while the irreducibility of otherness and the return to origins demands an analogical mode of speech that brings us into an intelligible relationship with a real ground. Formulated in somewhat different terms, the artistic and the religious resistances to Hegel reflect the two directionalities of our earlier discussion: the first direction expresses its resistance metaphorically by opening us up to a richness of meaning that can never be bounded by a completed system, while the second expresses its resistance analogically, bringing us into linguistic contact with a real ground that is related to us, but nevertheless stands in radical contrast with us. There are thus two prongs to the pictorial language of religion, one of which preserves the mystery of the quest for wholeness, while the other preserves the power of what is ultimate as it stands in contrast with us. This enriched notion of language, and the interplay it exhibits between metaphor and analogy, balance mystery, power, and intelligibility, subordinating neither of the first two elements to the philosophical quest for absolute comprehension.

For the religious consciousness, the concept of creation is a metaphorical expression. That is to say, it points to an aesthetic act in which something new is brought into being, the richness of which is expressed when the product is described as a creation. In this case, the original term in the metaphorical act of creation is God as he is in himself; the second term is the radical nonbeing with which he stands in contrast; while the third term is the infinitely rich product that both comes into existence and that points beyond itself in an indeterminate number of ways. This product is the metaphorical result of an act of creation, which is itself the metaphorical process that brings this new creation into being. However, we must also notice that the act of creation does not point to an overarching process, the elements of which are internal to itself, but to the real ground of the created order — a ground which creates *ex nihilo* and which remains substantially distinct from its created products. As a result, the original act of creation is not only a metaphorical act that generates a metaphorical product, but is also the ground of the contrast between God and the world which obtains after the created product has been brought into existence. The act of creation may thus be regarded as the metaphorical ground of the language of analogy that can be used to relate the product of creation to its own creative source. Though the original relation between God and the world is generated by a metaphorical act of creation, there is a real distinction between these two terms that can only be made intelligible by analogical discourse. As we have indicated already, the theological terms that make this analogical relationship determinate are expressed in the notions of the incarnation, death, and resurrection of Christ. Within this context God and man are related to one another in a process of redemption, but they also remain substantially distinct. The distinction in question can be expressed in pictorial language by claiming that God and man begin by being separated and that they are also separated, even in the end. And the Christian belief that the alienation of man from God has been overcome through a process of redemption can also be expressed by claiming that man returns to God, in that he becomes *like* God. However, the most important point to notice is that this likeness does not presuppose that man and God are fundamentally identical, nor that they are stages in a process of development that leads to an overarching unity. To the contrary, their reconciliation points to the positive relationship between identity and difference that the language of analogy attempts to express.

The analogical structure of the language of religion involves two levels of internally complex terms, each of which contains the mystery, the power, and the logos already present throughout our earlier discussion. The mystery of both God and man points to the infinite richness of the quest for wholeness which metaphorical discourse attempts to express; the power of both terms is a reflection of their real existence and is the ground upon which their ultimate difference is finally founded; while the logos which appears on both sides of this contrast makes the analogical connection expressed in the process of redemption intelligible to the finite consciousness. As we have indicated already, the separation of God from the world prevents the terms in question from becoming aspects of a larger whole. Unlike the merely internal difference which systematic reflection involves, the kind of difference to which analogy points remains external. However, it is important to remember that in the case of analogical predication, the moment of difference does not completely separate one term from another. Though the structural dimension of man points to his nature as a bounded, finite being, the power expressed in human existence is the feature in virtue of which he can move beyond himself toward the sustaining ground of his existence. Out of the mysterious richness of his own nature, this partially structured being moves toward a real ground by means of the power which is always present in the human quest for fulfillment. Of course, we can never succeed in fully comprehending the divine nature, for the mystery of the ground to which we turn points to the inexhaustibility of God and to the infinite depths out of which he creates the world. However, we are not utterly cut off from the ground of existence, for God's power brings him into real relation with the world, first through the act of creation and later in the act of reconciliation expressed in the incarnation, death, and resurrection of Christ. Man's going out of himself in his own metaphorical acts of creation, death, and resurrection is an analogical reflection of these primordial acts of God himself. Within the Christian tradition, it is in accepting these acts of God as paradigmatic, and in attempting to reflect their concrete richness in one's own particular situation, that one participates most fully in the divine logos that underlies the religious dimension of human existence.

Of course, Hegel will insist that the likeness between man and God which results from the finite individual's attempt to reflect his ground must be transformed into a larger unity. At a number of points, he implies that the difference between man and what is ultimate is only an appearance and that this difference can be overcome in the complete articulation of the absolute standpoint.[66] Those who object to this assertion are usually provoked into inarticulate resistance, while the individual reinstates his right to exist outside the dialectical process, merely through the stubborn refusal to be incorporated. However, it is absolutely essential that this refusal not remain at the level of an unmediated opposition, but that it also be given an intelligible expression. Sheer externality can be transcended, not only in Hegel's philosophical system, but also in the analogical language of the Christian tradition. For this reason, I have emphasized the fact that the comprehension of an element within a larger whole is only one of the ways of understanding the contents of consciousness, and that it is also possible to understand the relationship between subject and object in terms of the mirroring relationship that binds them together and holds them apart. The intelligible openness and otherness of the language of religion opens up a space in which the individual can not only stand in contrast with his creative ground, but can also come into an intelligible relationship with what remains outside himself. It is finally in terms of this mode of intelligibility that the religious consciousness resists Hegel's attempt to comprehend the pictorial language of religion and reinstates the value of images as a way of preserving the dimension of irreducible difference that arises within the real order.

Hegel's fundamental mistake is to overlook the fact that the language of religion has a form of its own. Like systematic reflection, analogical predication preserves both sameness and difference, but it does so without incorporating the differences between the terms about which it attempts to speak. Hegel moves too quickly from the claim that Christianity overcomes radical externality through a process of redemption to the transformation of the language of religion into the language of a comprehensive system. The language of Christianity has its own integrity: it preserves the sameness and the difference between man and God in a fashion that does not undermine the possibility of a real encounter between them and that enables the finite individual to participate in the absolute standpoint without being included within a larger totality. Hegel's philosophy does not simply differ in form from the language of the Christian tradition, but also differs in content. The one depends upon openness, otherness, and intelligible difference, while the other depends upon comprehension, internal difference, and the inclusion of what is intelligible within a larger unity. As a result, the determinate negation of Hegel's system needs to be balanced by the affirmation of difference that underlies the Christian tradition. Of course, the affirmation of difference can be mistakenly understood as reinstating a beyond which man can never reach — a permanent chasm that separates the individual from the ground of his existence. However, when it is understood properly, the language of religion points to the infinite richness and to the radical externality that are present in the here and now and to the fact that neither of these dimensions of experience can be exhausted by reflective discourse. The language of Hegel's system brings the beginning and the end of things into focus in the present moment, declaring that what is different is nevertheless identical and that what is beyond is nevertheless here. By contrast, the permanent truth in the language of religion is that it reminds us that what is identical is also different and that it will always remain beyond absolute comprehension. It is this fundamental insight that underlies the middle ground between fragmentation and completeness and that sustains the resistance of the language of religion to the encroachments of the language of the speculative system.

Openness, Otherness, and Systematic Reflection

The resistance of the quest for wholeness to Hegel's philosophical transformation of the language of religion reflects the belief that openness and otherness must be preserved if the meaning of wholeness itself is to be adequately articulated. The fragmentation with which we begin and the completeness we might attempt to attain must both be overcome by a wholeness that stands in between these two extremes and that exhibits an interplay among the openness, the otherness, and the intelligibility that are always present on the human journey. In the previous chapters we have attempted to preserve all of these dimensions by building our account around a series of stories and by using pictorial language to convey our systematic intentions. In that earlier discussion both metaphorical and analogical elements are contained as ways of giving us access to the human journey and of making the concrete richness of the quest for wholeness accessible in human terms. More specifically, the use of metaphor makes the openness of the quest for wholeness possible, while the use of analogy makes radical otherness accessible to us in an intelligible fashion. Taken together, these two dimensions of figurative discourse give us access to the meaning of the quest for wholeness and make it possible for us to engage in concrete reflection. However, it is also important to notice that a figurative dimension is to be found within the context of philosophical reflection, and more specifically, within the framework of Hegel's own philosophical system. Hegel not only uses figurative language to enrich and to illustrate his systematic account, but also presupposes a figurative element in the very account itself as an irreducible structural dimension. It is this fact that introduces the openness and otherness of the quest for wholeness into the structure of philosophical reflection and gives our earlier discussion of figurative discourse a systematic significance. In what follows, I shall attempt to generalize my earlier suggestions about the nature of figurative language by pointing to the place of metaphor and analogy within this larger systematic context. In the final analysis, it is the presence of both these dimensions within this larger setting that grounds our earlier attempts to engage in concrete reflection and that points to the presence of openness and otherness within philosophy itself.

The first indication that figurative language plays a crucial role in Hegel's system is to be found in the open-textured meaning of some of his most important philosophical expressions. For example, the concepts of subject and object, life, spirit, process, and the Whole are all metaphorical extensions from finite contexts and are applied as systematic terms without losing their essentially metaphorical significance. We have already observed that the traditional concepts of subject and object are modified in Hegel's revised conception of experience and that in the process, they become open-ended notions that develop through an ordered sequence of stages. The object of experience not only stands in contrast with an observing subject, but also exists in the sense that it stands outside itself and undergoes a process of development that leads from stage to stage in the attempt to attain philosophical completeness. But at this point, what is most important to notice is that this process is metaphorical in structure and that the openness of Hegel's conception of experience is grounded in the open-ended meanings of the concepts of subject and object with which it is concerned. The original objects of experience are able to undergo modification because they are already infinitely rich and because each is a partial expression of the mystery and the indeterminacy which is present in these objects from the beginning. In addition, when Hegel claims that this process of articulation is living, spiritual, and dynamic, he is using terms that usually apply only to a limited range of experience to apply to the world as a whole and to his overarching conception of experience that makes this world intelligible. To say that the world as a whole is a dynamic process of development is to use a cosmic metaphor, the richness of which stands behind any of Hegel's more particular attempts to articulate the significance of the Whole in systematic terms. It is in this sense that a metaphorical dimension lies at the foundation of Hegel's system and provides the ground of his quest for absolute comprehension.

Since metaphors are open-ended and since the concept of the Whole is a metaphorical extension from finite contexts of cognition, mystery and indeterminacy are present in the concept of the Whole as Hegel introduces it. The open-endedness of the concept in question is itself an indication of its infinite richness, which can never be displaced by any attempt to articulate its significance as a sequence of determinate stages. However, we have already observed that mystery is also the vehicle to radical otherness and that the intelligibility of what stands in contrast with us can be expressed in analogical terms. In fact, the stages generated by Hegel's philosophical quest for completeness can be regarded as a sequence of metaphors which are held together by analogical connections. Perceptual objects, theoretical entities, self-conscious beings, and the Whole itself, both abstract and dynamic, are not only metaphorical extensions of the original objects of experience, but are also made intelligible by the analogical connections that bind them together. That is to say, the developing stages of Hegel's philosophical quest for completeness, which is itself grounded in the use of metaphorical discourse, are held together by analogical connections, which in turn provide the superstructure for the interconnection of the stages of consciousness as a developing sequence. Of course, Hegel could claim that just insofar as the dialectical process issues in an ordered sequence of stages, the intelligible order of these stages is more fundamental than the metaphorical dimension they exhibit or the analogical connections that bind them together. Thus, it could be argued that the analogical relations in question merely constitute the skeletal form of the dialectical process and that the metaphorical stages of this process are incorporated fully within the Whole when that process finally culminates in Absolute Knowledge. However, to argue in this fashion would be to overlook the fact that indeterminacy is constitutive of the stages of the quest for wholeness, and that the analogical relations that bind these stages together also point to a real dimension of otherness that holds them apart. Formulated in somewhat different terms, the openness and the otherness of the quest for wholeness are irreducible dimensions of the human journey, and for this reason, it is impossible to reduce the quest for wholeness to the stages of a bounded system. What is needed is a way of speaking that points beyond the internal connections among a sequence of determinate stages; that reaffirms the value of the earlier stages of our discussion; and that explodes the Whole which attempts to include these stages as internal elements of itself. Only in this way can the mystery, the power, and the intelligible structure of the quest for wholeness be affirmed as equally fundamental, and only in this fashion can the richest dimensions of the human journey be expressed in philosophical terms.

The clearest indication that Hegel himself presupposes this more fundamental kind of discourse, and that he in this respect transcends the limitations of his own system, is to be found in the opening pages of the *Phenomenology*. At the beginning of his argument, Hegel claims that before a distinct subject can emerge in contrast with a perceptual object, a spatiotemporal framework must be presupposed as the fundamental context of reflection.[67] Objects of experience are not simply isolated phenomena, but also fall within a context, and this context is always presupposed in any attempt to understand the determinate contents of cognition. However, Hegel also suggests that only as this larger context develops do objects of experience emerge in contrast with subjects. A particular object is not only *in* space and time, but is also a function *of* space and time understood as a generative principle. As the point might be formulated in more systematic terms, the 'this' which finally congeals into an object of consciousness is not only part of a larger spatiotemporal framework, but is also a concatenation of a determinate 'here' and a determinate 'now' in a dynamic process of development.[68] Thus we find that the two directionalities of our earlier discussion are present in the emergence of objects of experience as contents of consciousness. On the one hand, these objects point beyond themselves to a larger context in which they can be understood; on the other hand, this framework can also be regarded as the originative ground that brings these objects of experience into existence. In our earlier discussion, we have focused our attention on the dynamic interaction between these two directionalities and upon the constant interplay between the spatial and temporal dimensions of the human journey, but only in what follows will it become clear that our commitment to figurative discourse can be articulated in these same terms. Metaphor and analogy are deeply rooted in the spatiotemporal structure of Hegel's system, and this structure, in turn, is a reflection of the inherent bi-directionality of the human situation. Of course, we have argued already that the bi-directionality of the human journey can never be reduced to an overarching unity and that Hegel is mistaken in his attempt to transform the quest for wholeness into a quest for complete comprehension. Nevertheless, we shall soon discover that space and time, metaphor and analogy, and the two directionalities of our earlier discussion lie at the foundation of Hegel's system and that they are the nonholistic ground out of which an adequate account of the quest for wholeness can emerge.

With respect to the temporal dimension of his system, Hegel tells us that if we focus our attention on a single temporal moment and attempt to analyze its meaning, it vanishes quickly into another, different 'now'. The original temporal moment does not remain stationary, but generates a second moment, which in turn generates a third until an entire temporal continuum comes into existence. The outward thrust of the quest for wholeness toward a larger world is thus grounded at the philosophical level by a dynamic process of emergence, the very elements of which constitute the temporal dimension of the human journey. However, the 'now' which generates a sequence of successors may also be regarded as the original metaphor which unfolds as a dynamic sequence of stages. As Hegel himself suggests, time unfolds of itself, and the task of the philosopher is simply to describe this bacchanalian revel of spontaneous generation.[69] It is as though time itself were an image of the original act of creation that stands behind the world, where in both cases, the metaphor of creation is the ground out of which the structure of the world emerges. The temporal sequence that comes into existence from the original 'now' is an image of its source, just as the created order is an image of its creative ground. The openness and the indeterminancy of the original temporal moment is reflected in the fact that the temporal continuum it generates is an open-ended Whole, which does not contain a last member and which cannot be brought to completion as a bounded totality. As a result, the original metaphor from which the temporal sequence emerges is connected analogically with an equally metaphorical product. In this case the openness and the indeterminacy of both product and ground are bound together by an imagistic relation.

On the other hand, Hegel knows that time simply in this trivial mathematical sense finally has no dialectical or philosophical significance. As an unending sequence of moments, it is a 'bad infinity' from which the conceptual consciousness has always turned away,[70] seeking instead a meaningful whole within which the quest for conceptual understanding can be brought to completion. In addition, Hegel is tempted to undercut the metaphorical and the analogical dimensions of the temporal continuum and to take a simultaneous step toward conceptual understanding by suggesting that the sequence of temporal moments can all be subsumed under an abstract universal. He claims that Nowness itself gives us the conceptual content of the many 'nows' and that Nowness as an abstract universal brings the meaning of this infinite multiplicity to focus for the conceptual consciousness.[71] In this way the existence of an infinite series of 'nows' becomes irrelevant from the standpoint of cognitive activity, for the conceptual content of the entire temporal sequence is made available in a single, abstract notion. As a result, the openness and the indeterminacy of the temporal continuum seem to be undermined by the typical philosophical appeal to abstract universality as a principle of intelligibility. Once again, the Socratic logos appears to dominate the mystery of the temporal continuum and to bring stability to the moments of time by an appeal to an unchanging standard. Once more, Cronus is put in chains by an abstract standard that spans all the modes of time and that binds them all together in the unity of philosophical discourse. Yet Hegel also knows that the dynamic element expressed by an unfolding sequence of 'nows' is not reflected in a merely abstract reference to Nowness. Since Nowness is a universal, while the temporal process is an unfolding sequence of particulars, the intelligible content of the movement from one 'now' to another must be articulated in more dynamic terms. Thus Hegel attempts to move beyond Socrates and to restore the dynamic open-endedness of the temporal process by suggesting that just as a sequence of 'nows' unfolds in a temporal series, so the reflective movement from a single 'now' to other 'nows', in terms of Nowness as their common content, is itself a sequential process. Moreover, he claims that this process is more primordial than the generation of the ordinary temporal sequence, for it brings together in a single context the 'now', a set of 'nows', the abstract category in terms of which they are understood conceptually, and the process of reflection in terms of which we move from one of these elements to another. Just as Socrates attempted to hold the forms, the gods, and men together in a single Whole, Hegel holds the form of time, the moments of time, and the process of reflection together in a larger unity. In this case, however, unity is not merely abstract and overarching as it was in the earlier Socratic proposal, permitting a conflict to reemerge among the elements it includes. To the contrary, it is both dynamic and intelligible, for it includes its elements as intelligible stages in the unfolding process of time itself.[72]

The process Hegel describes in the opening pages of the *Phenomenology* is not merely mathematical, for in addition to a series of temporal moments, it also contains the generic notion of Nowness itself. It is not only the movement from one 'now' to another, but the development of the 'now', through a series of 'nows', by means of a reference to Nowness itself that constitutes the intelligible structure of this process. Thus, when Hegel speaks about the temporal structure of experience, he does so in an extended philosophical sense, including as elements of his account both the moments of time as a mathematical sequence and the abstract structure that makes these moments intelligible. In fact, Hegel suggests that the process involved in articulating the meaning of a single 'now' can be generalized to the whole of experience and that time in the extended philosophical sense is a developing sequence of stages that exhibits an intelligible dimension. In this way Hegel moves beyond the opposition between time and abstract structure, attempting to unite the open-ended dynamism of temporality with the intelligible structure of philosophical reflection. However, it is important to notice that in bringing these two antithetical elements together, Hegel transforms the ordinary conception of time into a cosmic metaphor, the open-ended richness of which is generated by the opposition between the two dimensions it contains. The interplay between dynamism and form is not itself a form or a process, but the togetherness of the two elements that always points beyond itself to the need for further articulation. It is for this reason that the time which underlies Hegel's system is a metaphorical conception, the open-ended richness of which makes the quest for wholeness possible as a human journey. The stages through which this journey develops may also be regarded as a series of metaphors, for each of them displays the interplay between dynamics and form which characterizes the temporal process as a whole. The open-endedness of the concept of time which underlies Hegel's system is reflected analogically in the open-endedness of the stages through which it develops, and it is this fact which gives each of these stages its infinite richness. As Hegel himself suggests in both the preface and the final section of the *Phenomenology,* the stages of the temporal process he describes may be regarded as a picture gallery, where consciousness must linger indefinitely to exhaust the richness of content that each temporal stage displays.[73] But what is the status of this 'artistic' comment apart from the recognition that the stages of experience exhibit an irreducibly aesthetic dimension and that these stages are themselves the 'metaphors' from which thoughts and notions are to be extracted? It is finally this aesthetic dimension that lies at the foundation of Hegel's conception of time and experience and on the basis of which the richness of his account of the human journey is to be understood.

Of course, anyone familiar with Hegel's thought will recognize the fact that Hegel himself would resist the philosophical implications of these suggestions. To carry them to their logical conclusion would be to place openness and indeterminacy at the heart of his system, while Hegel himself always insists on the absolute completeness of his quest for philosophical comprehension.[74] Time as Hegel uses the term is a metaphorical conception, for he extends the merely mathematical meaning of temporality to the philosophical level and holds together the antithetical conceptions of dynamics and form within a single open-ended conception. Yet in claiming that the process of philosophical articulation can be brought to completion, Hegel attempts to subordinate the openness at the center of his system to an overarching unity that includes all the stages of experience as internal elements of itself. Unlike mathematical time, which never comes to an end, Hegel claims that philosophical time can be brought to a final culmination. And he claims this because he believes that philosophy can give a complete account of all the categories necessary to understand the whole of experience.[75] As we indicated in the first section of this chapter, the opposition which arises between dynamics and form at one stage of experience is resolved by a determinate negation that issues in a new form, the completed sequence of which constitutes the complete categorial articulation of the whole of experience. However, even if it were true that all the categories of experience had been discovered, it still would be mistaken to conclude that logos had finally triumphed over the openness and indeterminacy with which experience begins. A complete list of categories is very abstract, and it is just the richness and the open-endedness of experience that such a list can never capture. Of course, the Hegelian might insist that his account is complete, not only in the categorial sense, but also as an articulated process, each stage of which has been made completely intelligible. However, such a claim simply overlooks Hegel's own admission that each stage of the process he describes is infinitely rich and that each of them can be lingered over indefinitely. But if this is so, it would be best to admit the implications of this assertion, both with respect to the claim to completeness and with regard to the task of concrete reflection. At the very least, this admission implies that openness and indeterminacy are just as fundamental as intelligible structure, which in turn suggests that the aesthetic dimension of experience cannot be subordinated to a larger conceptual unity. It is for this reason that we have built our own philosophical account around a series of stories and the figurative discourse they contain, rather than around the demand for scientific completeness. When a completed system contains elements that are partly indeterminate and open-ended, and when these same elements exhibit an infinite richness, the 'Whole' which includes them as 'parts' is not a whole in any ordinary sense. In fact, in figurative terms it is a 'Whole' that explodes from within, requiring a concrete richness of language that can never be achieved by categorial articulation.

As we indicated at the beginning of this section, Hegel suggests that the objects of experience are concatenations of spatial and temporal elements, and as we have just discovered, he uses the temporal side of the 'this' to develop the quest for wholeness as an outward journey. Hegel claims that the original 'now' falls apart into a sequence of moments, which together with a set of emerging categories, allows us to articulate the meaning of the objects of experience as objects of consciousness. As Hegel understands his own account, the *Phenomenology* is an ordered series of temporal stages that emerge from the original object, and which taken together, serve to bring our understanding of the objects of experience to completion. Hegel also claims that this series of stages unfolds of itself and that the task of the philosopher is simply to describe the process consciousness undergoes in its attempt to comprehend its objects. It is of course this claim that gives Hegel's thought the ring of necessity, for it is meant to indicate that the open-endedness of the temporal continuum will unfold of itself in a necessary pattern if the observer will simply allow it to do so without outside interference. In this way Hegel attempts to subordinate the open-endedness with which the quest for wholeness begins and the power with which it develops to a logos that brings it to a final culmination, giving the philosophical consciousness access to the meaning of the quest for wholeness as a quest for complete comprehension. But in the course of his account, what does Hegel say about the spatial dimension of the original objects of experience? The objects of consciousness are not only temporal, but spatial as well, and it would appear that space is equally as fundamental as time in giving us access to the meaning of the experiential process. But does the 'here' with which consciousness begins fall apart into a sequence of many 'heres' by analogy with the development of the 'now' into a temporal continuum? And in this case also, does the philosopher merely observe the process as the development of a necessary sequence that finally leads to complete comprehension? It is in attempting to answer these questions that we can finally reach the most fundamental level of Hegel's system, and through a critique of it, can lay the systematic foundation for our earlier discussion.

Hegel attempts to develop the spatial dimension of his system by claiming that the 'here' is not an intelligible unity in itself, but that like the 'now', it is part of a larger continuum. The intelligibility of a single spatial element depends upon its place within a larger spatial context, and it is this larger context which constitutes the overarching framework within which the quest for wholeness develops. Moreover, Hegel claims that the intelligibility of these spatial moments is a function of Hereness as an abstract universal and that Hereness is the intelligible unit under which these separate 'spaces' are collected.[76] Yet Hegel also suggests that the 'here' does not fall apart of itself into a plurality of spatial units, simply requiring the philosopher to observe the process understood as a necessary sequence. To the contrary, he says that we must first 'turn around' if the 'here' with which we begin is to become a different spatial region.[77] Space does indeed constitute a continuum of elements that may all be subsumed under Hereness as an abstract universal, but we move through space by turning here and there, and not simply by being carried along in the rush of temporality. In this crucial respect, space differs radically from time. In the case of time, development from moment to moment occurs spontaneously, and the process that develops can simply be described by the philosophical observer from an external point of view. But in the case of space, the observer must become active in the philosophical process, moving from place to place in order to make it possible for space to unfold its experiential richness. In our earlier discussion, this need to turn around and to move from place to place was conveyed most profoundly in religious terms. In the previous chapters, Ishmael turned toward the ocean to escape the threat of death and to come to terms with his fragmented condition; Abraham turned away from his familiar surroundings to make a journey into an unknown land; Moses turned aside from his customary activities to observe the burning bush and to listen to the voice of God; Socrates turned away from custom and tradition toward a new understanding of piety in which stability was to be found amidst the flux of experience; and at the end of his conversation with Socrates, Euthyphro turned back toward his origins as the sustaining ground of his existence. In all of these cases, space appears as a primordial conception and as a region that becomes accessible to us only through our own religious activity.

The need to turn from one place to another, which movement

through space requires, points to a dimension of radical otherness that can never be included in a larger Whole. Just as every stage of the temporal process we have considered is infinitely rich, so there are an infinite number of places to which the reflective consciousness can turn in its attempt to find the wholeness it seeks. And in each case it is necessary to make a decision about which place will be chosen as the focus of our reflective attention. The need to make a decision points to the religious dimension of the quest for wholeness and to the external contrast between one place and another, while the infinity of places points to the fact that these externally related elements can never be included in an overarching unity. We have already emphasized the fact that every stage of the temporal quest for wholeness can be understood in terms of the open-ended indeterminacy of metaphorical discourse. From the side of time, it is this initial richness that places an aesthetic dimension at the heart of Hegel's system and that finally makes it impossible for him to bring the quest for wholeness to completion. But now that we have turned to the concept of space as a primordial conception, it is possible to suggest that this concept introduces a religious dimension into Hegel's system and that it underlies the experiences of those who have become aware of something ultimate as radically distinct from themselves. The externality of space provides the scaffolding within which religious experience occurs, and it is the irreducibility of the spatial dimension of experience that makes the religious aspect of the quest for wholeness possible as a human undertaking. Finally, the emergence of the concept of space as a primordial conception suggests that the philosophical demand for intelligibility can be satisfied without needing to transform the quest for wholeness into a quest for complete comprehension. This can be understood by noticing that the relationship between one moment of experience and another is an analogical relation and that it is the analogy between one metaphorical moment and another that both binds them together and holds them apart. The analogy in question allows for the intelligibility of experience, but it does so without assuming that all of these elements can be collected as parts of a larger totality. There is thus a dual reason for rejecting Hegel's drive toward systematic completion, one of which springs from the infinite richness of the stages of experience and the other of which rests on the radical externality that holds these stages of experience apart. The metaphorical openness of the stages of experience allows them to open out toward one another, while the analogical otherness of these same elements allows them to be connected without being included in an overarching unity.

Of course, Hegel might reply that just as time in the trivial mathematical sense must be subordinated to a more fundamental philosophical conception, so the conception of space as a domain of real externality must be transformed into a larger, more inclusive unity. In fact, he claims on more than one occasion that space is empty and lifeless[78] and that it is at best the skeletal structure of a dynamic process that must be brought to completion at the standpoint of absolute knowledge. His earlier attack on representational discourse as an inadequate mode of speech and his claim that the language of religion can be comprehended in philosophical terms are a reflection of the belief that space finally plays a secondary role within a larger temporal system. Hegel's philosophical conquest of representational discourse presupposes that the spatialized language of religion can be transposed into temporal terms and that the spatial separation between one term and another can be transcended in a series of stages that constitute a necessary, scientific progression. However, what Hegel overlooks in attempting to subordinate space to time is the fact that the categories he articulates not only develop through time, but are also 'positioned' in space. Philosophical development presupposes 'positionedness', and the completion of the dialectical process does not issue merely in an ordered sequence of stages, but in the recovery of a place for each of them to stand. As I have suggested already, the integrity of these places is secured by the analogical relations that bind them together and hold them apart. Moreover, these regions cannot be reduced to stages of an overarching process, for the metaphorical openness of each place and the analogical otherness that connects one place with another serve to undermine the quest for complete comprehension. In fact, it is the irreducibility of openness and otherness that underlies the empirical possibility of the 'here' in contrast with the 'now' and to which the figurative language of our earlier discussion has attempted to point in representational terms.

At the most fundamental level, the concept of place creates the ontological nexus that makes our earlier discussion possible and that makes it necessary for us to use figurative discourse in our attempts to engage in concrete reflection. All the characters in the previous chapters stand at different places, and each is able to undertake the quest for wholeness in his own unique fashion because the place where he stands is distinct from every other place within the ontological continuum. From the place where he begins, every character opens out to undertake the human journey, but because this journey brings him into relation with other places, the one who undertakes it must be prepared to confront what stands in radical contrast with him. To be positioned is to be able to move beyond one's starting point on an outward journey, but to encounter other places is to come face to face with a dimension of radical otherness that will always attempt to preserve its own integrity. As I have suggested already, the place where experience begins is a concatenation of a 'here' and a 'now', and both dimensions must be taken into account if we are to give an adequate description of the human journey. The metaphorical openness of time allows the quest for wholeness to unfold as an outward journey, while the analogical otherness of space brings us into relation with a real ground that requires us to make a response of absolute receptivity. Of course, this means that the metaphorical and the analogical elements of our earlier discussion, and the aesthetic and religious dimensions they reflect, are necessary aspects of our attempts to engage in concrete reflection. These figurative uses of language are not simply representational elements of discourse that can be reformulated in systematic terms, for they are themselves reflections of the spatiotemporal structure of this larger systematic context. Figurative language is rooted in the spatiotemporal framework within which Hegel's system is developed, and for this reason it is an indispensable element in the philosophical attempt to come to terms with the human quest for fulfillment.

The two directionalities of our earlier discussion are human reflections of our need to take both spatial and temporal dimensions into account, but they also give us the most decisive reason for using imagistic language as an essential element in our earlier account. The first directionality is essentially temporal, and it unfolds with the metaphorical power of an outward journey toward a larger world. By contrast, the second directionality is essentially spatial, terminating in an analogical relationship between the one who undertakes it and the sustaining ground of human existence. But when we attempt to bring these two directionalities together, as we have done to some extent in every chapter, they can finally be related to one another only as mirror images and hence not as parts within a larger Whole. The outward and the backward journeys that occur within the ontological nexus have different directional orientations, and it is this difference of directionality that finally eludes the systematic drive toward complete comprehension. As we found at the end of our discussion of

Plato's *Euthyphro,* difference of directionality can only be made intelligible in imagistic terms, which makes it clear once more than our use of imagistic language is rooted in the very structure that the quest for wholeness exhibits as a human phenomenon. If the openness of the quest for wholeness requires metaphorical articulation and if the otherness to be encountered on the journey is to be made intelligible by an analogical relation, the bi-directionality of the quest is to be understood in imagistic terms, which is itself a final reflection of the fact that figurative discourse is an indispensable element of our systematic discussion.

The ontological nexus within which our figurative use of language is rooted gives us a new sense of ground and makes it possible for us to engage in concrete reflection within a systematic framework. In our earlier discussion, we have spoken about the objects of experience as the ground of cognition and about the structure of those objects as the logical ground in terms of which they can be comprehended in abstract terms. In addition, we have spoken about God as the ground of existence and about Hegel's attempt to take all three of these earlier conceptions up into a systematic Whole, understood as the holistic Ground in which each of them can be given a determinate place. But now that we have moved to the concept of place as the interplay between the spatial and the temporal dimensions of experience, it is possible to suggest that this concept is a new ground, allowing for the metaphorical openness and the analogical otherness of a real community, the unity of which is made possible by a series of analogical connections. Because the concept of place has a metaphorically temporal dimension, it captures the richness of life and the open-ended dimension of the human quest for fulfillment. But because this same concept is analogically spatial, it also points to the analogical unity of an ultimate and irreducible plurality. In both cases, this Place of places is the philosophical standpoint from which this book has been written and out of which the plurality of worlds that we have considered has arisen. In fact,this new sense of ground is the source of the metaphorical and the analogical elements that have made our earlier discussion possible. For this reason, figurative language is not to be confined to the initial stages of the quest for wholeness, but is to be found within the very structure of the philosophical language that must be used to understand our earlier discussion in systematic terms. As the point might be formulated in a somewhat different way, openness and otherness are the *topoi* of systematic reflection,[79] and it is out of these places that the imagistic language of our systematic project has emerged in order to make it possible for us to engage in concrete reflection.

When the Whole is understood as a Place of places rather than as an overarching unity, the single world which Hegel attempts to comprehend is transformed into a plurality of worlds, each of which is a reflection of the quest for wholeness from a certain point of view. Moreover, just as wholeness stands in between fragmentation and completeness, this plurality stands in between a series of philosophical fragments and a completed system that attempts to subordinate these worlds to itself as constituent elements. In fact, Hegel's own comment about the way in which the stages of experience can be understood as a picture gallery can be extended with even greater force to characterize the chapters of this book. Each of our attempts to understand the quest for wholeness is a world of its own, and it is posible to find wholeness within each world as an infinite expression of the human journey. Yet even though each of us lives within only one world primarily, it is also possible for us to live in other worlds by participating in the imagistic relations that bind them together. The chapters of this book are neither isolated individuals, a fragmented plurality, nor a completed totality, but are a sequence of attempts to reflect the human journey from a series of analogically related perspectives. Just as the characters who undertake the human journey open out toward a larger world, so the chapters of this book open out toward one another; and just as these same characters must confront a dimension of radical otherness, so these chapters retain their own integrity as a plurality of interconnected worlds. The critique of Hegel with which we conclude our discussion therefore points self-referentially in two directions: on the one hand, it explodes the Whole as an overarching context within which the quest for wholeness can be brought to completion; on the other hand, it locates the openness and the otherness within Hegel himself that serves to ground our own project as a plurality of worlds. It is this analogical nexus upon which our earlier discussion depends, and it is this plurality of worlds that makes it possible for us to undertake the quest for wholeness in philosophical terms.

In one of Hegel's early letters, Kojève tells us that

> he speaks of a period of total depression that he lived through between the twenty-fifth and thirtieth years of his life: a 'Hypochondria'...that was so severe as 'to paralyze all his powers,' and that came precisely from the fact that he could not accept the necessary abandonment of Indi-

viduality — which the idea of Absolute Knowledge demanded. But finally he surmounted this 'Hypochondria.' And becoming a Wise Man by that final acceptance of death, he published a few years later the First Part of the 'System of Science,' entitled 'Science of the Phenomenology of the Spirit,' in which he definitively reconciles himself with all that is and has been, by declaring that there will never more be anything new on earth.[80]

In this book I have tried, by contrast with Hegel, to preserve the moments of openness, otherness, and individuality, not by demanding the emergence of something new in the Absolute, but by pointing to the newness and the individuation that are present there already in the Place of places and in the figurative discourse that makes this Place accessible. In the process, I have suggested that hypochondria can be overcome, not by bringing the quest for wholeness to completion, but by standing in the middle ground between fragmentation and completeness and by participating in a series of images that can bring finite fulfillment to the human soul. In fact, we have discovered that Hegel's own attempt to understand the world as a whole requires him to tell a story of his own and forces him to resort to figurative uses of language in order to convey his fundamental insights. From the perspective of the present undertaking, it is finally his use of metaphorical and analogical discourse that lies at the foundation of his system and that allows his thought to be a concrete expression of the human spirit. Of course, Hegel is not Ahab in search of the white whale, nor is he the Ishmael who recovers his origins and brings his life to unity in narrative discourse. He is not Abraham who loses his son, only to find him again, nor is he Moses at the burning bush waiting to hear the name of God, which was to serve as the foundation of his fragmented existence. And of course, he is neither Euthyphro nor Socrates, caught up in dialogic interaction about the meaning of wholeness and attempting to come to terms with both the Ground and the Whole as they relate to the pressing problems of the human situation. Yet strange as he is, Hegel also appears as a character in our attempt to understand the meaning of wholeness, for in both figurative and conceptual language, he lays the foundation for a real plurality of worlds, one of which is constituted by his own philosophical system. In this way, Hegel helps us find a place to stand that is neither old nor new, but the foundation for the existence of a human community.

Notes

Introduction

1. *Augustine: Confessions and Enchiridion,* trans. Albert C. Outler (Philadelphia: Westminster Press, 1955), pp. 172–3.
2. Eccles. 3:1–8.
3. Cf. the discussion of these conceptions and of their relations to one another in Paul Tillich, *The Courage to Be* (New Haven and London: Yale University Press, 1952).
4. G. W. F. Hegel, *Phenomenology of Spirit,* trans. A. V. Miller (Oxford: Clarendon Press, 1977), p. 2.
5. Ibid., pp. 75–76.
6. *The Comedy of Dante Alighieri: Hell,* trans. Dorothy L. Sayers (Baltimore: Penguin Books, 1949), p. 71.
7. *Leibniz, Discourse on Metaphysics,* trans. Peter G. Lucas and Leslie Grint (Manchester: University of Manchester Press, 1953), pp. 18–22.
8. Cf. ibid., pp. 14–15.
9. *Letters,* trans. L. A. Post, in the *Collected Dialogues of Plato,* ed. Edith Hamilton and Huntington Cairns (New York: Pantheon Books, Bollingen Foundation, 1961), 341c–d.

Chapter 1

1. References to the novel will appear throughout the chapter in parentheses, citing the standard edition of Melville's work: Herman Melville, *Moby-Dick,* ed. Harrison Hayford and Hershel Parker (New York: W. W. Norton, 1967).
2. Gen. 21:8–14.
3. Gen. 15:1–5.
4. Ibid.; Gen. 12:1–3.
5. Gen. 16:1–4.
6. Gen. 17:18.

7. Gen. 21:9–11.
8. Gen. 21:12–13.
9. Jon. 1:1–17.
10. 1 Kings 21:20–24; 22:37–40.
11. 1 Kings 18:21–40.
12. Job 1:14–19.

Chapter 2

1. Gen. 12:5.
2. Ibid.
3. Gen. 12:3.
4. Gen. 15:1.
5. Gen. 15:2–3.
6. Gen. 15:4.
7. Gen. 15:6.
8. Gen. 16:1–17:22.
9. Ibid.
10. Gen. 12:10.
11. Gen. 17:18.
12. Soren Kierkegaard, *Fear and Trembling* and *The Sickness Unto Death* (Garden City, New York: Doubleday, 1954), pp. 46, 51, 57.
13. Gen. 22:1–2.
14. Gen. 22:1.
15. Gen. 22:6, 8.
16. Elie Wiesel, *Messengers of God: Biblical Portraits and Legends* (New York: Pocket Books, 1977), p. 77.
17. Wiesel at least suggests this way of understanding the story in his remarkable book about the Hebrew tradition. See *Messengers of God*, pp. 102–103.
18. Erich Auerbach, *Mimesis: The Representation of Reality in Western Literature*, trans. William R. Trask (Princeton, N.J.: Princeton University Press, 1953), p. 8.
19. Ibid., p. 9.
20. Ibid.
21. Ibid., p. 10.
22. Ibid., pp. 11–12.
23. Gen. 22:9.
24. Gen. 22:10.
25. Gen. 22:11–12.
26. Gen. 22:19.
27. See also Wiesel, *Messengers of God*, p. 97.
28. See especially the episodes relating to Jacob, Esau, and Rebekah in Gen. 27:1–40.
29. Gen. 25:26.
30. See Gen. 27:1–40 and Gen. 30:25–31:55.
31. See New American Standard Bible notes for Gen. 25:26.
32. Gen. 25:29–34.

33. Gen. 27:1–29.
34. In Gen. 25:23 God predicts that one of the twins and his descendants will be stronger than the other, but he does not say which one, nor does he indicate until later that the result is an expression of his will.
35. Gen. 32:28. See note for this verse in the New American Standard Bible.
36. Gen. 33:1–15.
37. Gen. 33:1.
38. Gen. 33:4.
39. Gen. 26:3–4; 35:11–12.
40. Gen. 29:31–30:13.
41. Gen. 37:3.
42. Ibid.
43. Gen. 37:23–28.
44. Gen. 37:29–35.
45. Gen. 45:1–8.
46. Gen. 45:16–47:12.
47. Gen. 45:17–47:12.
48. Exod. 1:7–2:2.
49. Cf. Hegel's claim that this relationship is never transcended in the Hebrew tradition in George William Friedrich Hegel, *Lectures on the Philosophy of Religion*, vol. 2, trans. E. B. Speirs and J. Burden Sanderson (New York: Humanities Press, 1962), p. 206.
50. Exod. 1:1–2:10.
51. Exod. 2:6–10.
52. Exod. 2:7–9.
53. Cf. the citation in Martin Buber, *Moses: The Revelation and the Covenant* (New York: Harper and Brothers, 1958), p. 28.
54. Exod. 2:11–12.
55. Exod. 2:13–14.
56. Exod. 2:15.
57. Exod. 2:15–22.
58. Exod. 3:2–5.
59. Exod. 3:5.
60. Exod. 3:6.
61. Ibid.
62. Exod. 3:7–10.
63. Exod. 3:11.
64. Exod. 3:12.
65. Exod. 3:13.
66. See Buber, *Moses: Revelation and Covenant*, pp. 48–49.
67. Exod. 3:14–15.
68. Wiesel, *Messengers of God*, p. 198; Exod. 16:35; Deut. 34:7; Acts 7:23, 30, 36.
69. Exod. 4:10.
70. Exod. 4:14–16.
71. *Basic Writings of St. Thomas Aquinas*, vol. 1, ed. Anton C. Pegis (New York: Random House, 1945), p. 131.
72. Ibid., pp. 131–132.

202 • NOTES

73. See Buber, *Moses: Revelation and Covenant,* pp. 51–52 and John Courtney Murray, *The Problem of God* (New Haven: Yale University Press, 1964), p. 8.

74. Ibid., p. 9.

75. Exod. 6:3. See also notes for this verse in the New American Standard Bible, and in *The International Standard Bible Encyclopaedia,* vol. 2, ed. James Orr (Grand Rapids, Mich.: Wm. B. Eerdmans, 1957), pp. 1266–67.

76. *International Standard Bible Encyclopaedia,* vol. 2, ed. Orr, p. 1265.

77. W. F. Albright, *From the Stone Age to Christianity* (Garden City, N.Y.: Doubleday, 1939), pp. 198ff.

78. For a detailed defense of this conception of God, see Robert C. Neville, *God the Creator: On the Transcendence and Presence of God* (Chicago: University of Chicago Press, 1968).

79. Buber, *Moses: Revelation and Covenant,* p. 51 and Murray, *Problem of God,* p. 13.

80. Buber, *Moses: Revelation and Covenant,* pp. 52–53 and Murray, *Problem of God,* pp. 9–10.

81. Exod. 26:31–33; 28:1–3; 29–30.

82. Exod. 19:1–2, 17–25; 24:15–17.

83. Exod. 32:1–4.

84. Exod. 32:19.

85. Exod. 34:1–28.

86. Deut. 20:7–12.

87. Deut. 32:48–52; 34:1–6, 10.

Chapter 3

1. See the Stephenus numbers in the standard edition of Plato's collected works.

2. Plato, *Euthyphro,* trans. Harold North Fowler (Loeb Classical Library; Cambridge, Mass.: Harvard University Press, 1914), 2a–b; 3e–4a. Further references to the *Euthyphro* will appear in the text in parentheses and will refer to this edition, though some of the translations are my own.

3. *Plato's Euthyphro, Apology of Socrates, and Crito,* ed. with notes by John Burnet (Oxford: Oxford University Press, 1924), p. 3.

4. Ibid., p. 2.

5. See Numa Denis Fustel de Coulanges, *The Ancient City,* trans. Willard Small (Garden City, N.Y.: Doubleday), pp. 11–223, esp. p. 99.

6. Ibid., pp. 21–33.

7. The Lyceum referred to here is a location in the city of Athens and is not to be confused with the name of the philosophical school later founded and presided over by Aristotle.

8. See especially *Plato's Euthyphro, Apology, and Crito,* pp. 5–6.

9. Fustel de Coulanges, *Ancient City,* pp. 21–33.

10. Ibid., p. 96.

11. Ibid., pp. 34–39.

12. Ibid., pp. 86, 114.

13. Fustel says that in the ancient family, the judicial power of the father

was absolute: "He could condemn to death like the magistrate in the city, and no authority could modify his sentence." Ibid., p. 93. See also pp. 86, 88.

14. Again, Fustel tells us that in the ancient world, for a man to bear witness against one of his own family was an act contrary to religion. Ibid., p. 104.

15. Ibid., p. 83.

16. Hesiod, *Theogony,* trans. with an intro. by Norman O. Brown (Indianapolis and New York: Liberal Arts Press, 1953), pp. 56–57.

17. Ibid., pp. 57–58.

18. Ibid., p. 66.

19. Ibid., pp. 64, 66–67, 71.

20. Ibid., p. 79.

21. Ibid., pp. 17–25.

22. See R.E. Allen, *Plato's "Euthyphro" and the Earlier Theory of Forms* (New York: Humanities Press, 1970), p. 40.

23. Ibid.

24. E.g., G. E. Moore, *Some Main Problems of Philosophy* (New York: Collier Books, 1962), pp. 72–74, where the point is made with reference to propositions.

25. Oskar Seyffert, *Dictionary of Classical Antiquities,* rev. and ed. Henry Nettleship and J. E. Sandys (New York: Meridian Books, 1956), p. 171.

26. Ibid.

27. Ibid.

28. Plato, *The Republic,* vol. 1, trans. Paul Shorey (Loeb Classical Library; Cambridge, Mass.: Harvard University Press, 1935), 434d–445b.

29. Ibid., 502c–509c.

30. Plato, *Cratylus,* trans. H. N. Fowler (Loeb Classical Library; Cambridge, Mass.: Harvard University Press, 1926), 396e–397a.

31. See Paul Tillich, *The Courage to Be* (New Haven and London: Yale University Press, 1952), p. 11.

Chapter 4

1. *Hegel's Science of Logic,* trans. A. V. Miller (New York: Humanities Press, 1969), pp. 106–108.

2. G. W. F. Hegel, *Phenomenology of Spirit,* trans. A. V. Miller (Oxford: Clarendon Press, 1977), pp. 479–493.

3. Ibid., pp. 11, 13–14.

4. Ibid., p. 55.

5. Ibid., pp. 52, 55.

6. Ibid., p. 46.

7. Ibid., pp. 47–49.

8. Ibid., pp. 51, 55–56.

9. Ibid., pp. 55–56.

10. Ibid., p. 54.

11. Ibid.

12. Ibid., p. 55.

13. Ibid., p. 54.

14. Ibid., p. 51.
15. Ibid., p. 55.
16. Ibid., pp. 111–119.
17. Ibid., pp. 11, 13–14, 50–51.
18. Ibid., p. 3.
19. Ibid., p. 50.
20. Ibid., p. 51.
21. Ibid., pp. 18–19, 51.
22. Ibid., p. 51.
23. Ibid., p. 16.
24. Ibid.
25. Ibid., pp. 16–17.
26. Ibid., pp. 67–79.
27. Ibid., pp. 111–119.
28. Ibid., pp. 139–145.
29. Ibid., pp. 364–409.
30. George Wilhelm Friedrich Hegel, *Lectures on the Philosophy of Religion*, vol. 1, trans. E. B. Speirs and J. Burden Sanderson (New York: Humanities Press, 1962), p. 1.
31. Ibid., vol. 3, pp. 1–151.
32. Ibid., vol. 2, pp. 178–188.
33. Ibid., p. 176.
34. Hegel, *Phenomenology of Spirit*, pp. 416–424.
35. Hegel, *Philosophy of Religion*, vol. 2, pp. 172–173.
36. Ibid., p. 229.
37. Ibid., pp. 239–241.
38. Hegel, *Phenomenology of Spirit*, pp. 439–453.
39. Isa. 53:4–6.
40. *Hegel's Philosophy of Mind*, trans. William Wallace (Oxford: Clarendon Press, 1892), p. 300 and Hegel, *Phenomenology of Spirit*, pp. 453–478.
41. 1 Cor. 15:54–55.
42. Hegel, *Phenomenology of Spirit*, pp. 462–463.
43. Ibid., p. 463.
44. Ibid., pp. 484–485.
45. Hegel, *Philosophy of Religion*, vol. 3, p. 148.
46. Hegel, *Phenomenology of Spirit*, pp. 492–493.
47. Ibid., p. 11.
48. Ibid., pp. 52–53 and *Hegel's Science of Logic*, pp. 455–456.
49. Hegel, *Phenomenology of Spirit*, p. 55 and *Hegel's Science of Logic*, pp. 456–458.
50. Hegel, *Phenomenology of Spirit*, pp. 56–57 and *Hegel's Science of Logic*, pp. 472–474.
51. Hegel, *Phenomenology of Spirit*, pp. 37–39.
52. G. W. F. Hegel, *Faith and Knowledge*, ed. and trans. Walter Cerf and H. S. Harris (Albany: State University of New York Press, 1977), pp. 190–191 and Hegel, *Phenomenology of Spirit*, p. 38.
53. *Hegel's Philosophy of Mind*, p. 300.
54. *Hegel's Philosophy of Nature*, trans. A. V. Miller (Oxford: Clarendon Press, 1970), p. 13.

55. Matt. 27:46.
56. John 19:30.
57. John 20:19, 26.
58. Mark 16:19.
59. *The Logic of Hegel,* 2nd ed., trans. William Wallace (Oxford: Oxford University Press, 1892), p. 7.
60. Hegel, *Phenomenology of Spirit,* pp. 5, 13–14, 35, 43.
61. Ibid.
62. Ibid., p. 49.
63. Ibid.
64. *Hegel's Science of Logic,* p. 50.
65. Cf. Carl R. Hausman, *A Discourse on Novelty and Creation* (The Hague: Martinus Nijhoff, 1975), pp. 99–110.
66. E.g., see Hegel, *Philosophy of Religion,* vol. 2, p. 349.
67. Hegel, *Phenomenology of Spirit,* pp. 58, 62.
68. Ibid., pp. 59–60.
69. Ibid., pp. 27, 54, 63.
70. *Hegel's Science of Logic,* pp. 137–143.
71. Hegel, *Phenomenology of Spirit,* pp. 60, 62.
72. Ibid., pp. 63–64.
73. Ibid., pp. 17, 492.
74. Ibid., pp. 50–51.
75. These categories are implicit in the *Phenomenology* and are developed explicitly in the *Science of Logic.*
76. Hegel, *Phenomenology of Spirit,* pp. 61–62.
77. Ibid., pp. 60–61.
78. Ibid., pp. 26, 27.
79. I owe this way of formulating the point to conversations with my colleague, Donald P. Verene. For his own discussion of the concept of place, see his recent book: Donald Phillip Verene, *Vico's Science of Imagination* (Ithaca and London: Cornell University Press, 1981), pp. 166–192.
80. Alexandre Kojève, *Introduction to the Reading of Hegel,* trans. James H. Nichols, Jr. and ed. Allen Bloom (New York and London: Basic Books, 1969), p. 168.

Index

Abraham: and the sacrifice of his future, 60; his silent obedience, 61, 80. *See also* Isaac

Abram: as creator of a new nation, 53; his degeneration, 52, 55-56; as a divided consciousness, 52; as father of a new world, 51; his fragmentation, 53; his name changed to Abraham, 56; his rejection of tribalism, 51; and tribal unity, 52

Absolute comprehension: and human wholeness, 8

Abstract reflection: limits of, x; value of, xii. *See also* Concrete reflection

Abstract structure: of the quest, 7-8

Abstracts: and abstractions, 9

Act: and state, 127

Ahab: his conception of power, 37; his destruction, 39; his lack of logos, 37; his lack of wholeness, 26; his quest for wholeness, 37; as a reflection of the white whale, 37-38; his relationship with Moby Dick, 36; his self-accentuation and his quest for completeness, 38

Ahab and Jezebel, 33

Alienation, 27, 48, 58

Analogy: in the Bible, 107; between Daedalus and Euthyphro, 137; in the dialogue, 149; between Euthyphro and Zeus, 108, 111-12; Euthyphro's use of, 103, 107-8, 119; and externality, 181; with God, 179; in the Hebrew tradition, 66-67; in Hegel's system, 183, 190-94, 197; and Justice, 142; between Justice and Goodness, 140;

language of, 179; and otherness, 178-182; and perspectivism, 196; between religion and philosophy, 168; in religious language, 178, 180-81; Socrates' use of, 119-20; unity of, 151, 153. *See also* Metaphor

Ancient family, the: and continuity, 101

Ancient Greece: family religion in, 100-101, 101-2; social and political life of, 97, 110

Anywhere, somewhere, nowhere, 23, 24, 117

Aquinas, Saint Thomas: his interpretation of the name of God, 82-83; and theoretical discourse, 82

Art: openness of, 154; its relation to religion, 48, 50; its richness, 154; transition from, 48

Artist, the: and the water, 20-21

Athens: as location of the *Euthypho*, 97; religious court in, 98

Attention: meaning of the word, 143

Auerbach, Erich, 61-62

Augustine, Saint: *Confessions*, 1-2

Because: the symmetry of the word, 125

Biblical stories; and origins, 11

Binding, the, 62

Blackness: as image of negation, 28; resists comprehension, 30

Book of Ecclesiastes, the, 2

Book of Job, the, 45-46

Bulkington: as an image of the white whale, 30

Categories: in Hegel's system, 189

Cato: and self-destruction, 26; and self-hatred, 25
Christianity: and Greek religion, 162-63; as highest expression of religion, 162-63; and Judaism, 162-63
Circularity: of philosophical reflection, 148
Coffin: and individuation, 48; of Queequeq, 42; its relation to custom and tradition, 42, 44-45; as symbol of death, 45; as symbol of life, 43; warehouses, 18, 43,
Coffin, Peter, 28, 43
Communication: and sacred space, 74
Community: of temporal moments, 76
Completeness: Hegel's quest for, 159, 161. See also Quest for wholeness; Whole, the; Wholeness
Concrete reflection, xi; as completed system, 12; and figurative discourse, 193; Hegel's concept of, 161; as mirroring, 16, 82. See also Abstract reflection
Concrete richness: of the quest, 8
Confessions (Augustine), 1-2
Consciousness: forms of, 158; as a third term, 157-58
Contradiction: in Euthyphro's position, 132, 136, 143
Conversation: linguistic result of Jacob's, with God, 80; between Moses and God, 78
Covenant: God's with Abram, 56, 66
Cratylus (Plato), 146
Creation, 166; as an aesthetic act, 173; ex nihilo, 173; as a metaphorical act, 179 See also Ground
Cronus, 187; and Euthyphro's father, 111; and Time, 109-11; and Zeus, 108

Daedalus: and the Cretian Minotaur, 137-38; and Icarus, 137; as a sculptor, 136; and Socrates, 137; statues of, 137
Dante: Divine Comedy and the two directionalities, 5
Death: of Christ, 163, 166; as a determinate negation, 160; and Euthyphro's predicament, 98; Hegel's concept of, 160; and mystery, 160; and origins, 160; and philosophy, 160; and power, 160; of Socrates, 149
Definition: genus-species form of, 142, 144; stable, 116
Degeneration: of the Hebrew people, 90
Dialogue: reflective dimension of a, 95

Difference; and abstract reflection, 126; and the act of creation, 173; and analogy, 180; between Christianity and philosophy, 168; and concrete reflection, 153; in a dialogue, 95; of directionality, 150; of directionality and images, 195; external, 180; between the Father and the Son, 174; fundamental sense of, 127; between God and the world, 173, 180; Hegel's view of, 153; in identity, 177; and images, 181; intelligible, 182; internal, 158-59, 182; as radical opposition, 152; and unity in the dialogue, 170. See also Otherness
Directionality: reversal of, 129
Divine abyss, the: mystery of, 33
Divine Comedy (Dante), 5

Egypt: Hebrews at home in, 68-69
El Shaddhi, 84
Elijah: Biblical prophet and character in Melville's novel, 33
Elohim, 84-85
Encyclopedia (Hegel), 173
Essence: identical with Being, in God, 83
Eternal present, the: as present, 88
Euthyphro: his abrupt departure, 145; and his claim to wisdom, 102, 115; description of, 101; and Dionysius, 100; his discomfort in the city, 100; and exact knowledge, 111; and the house slave, 98; as image of Zeus, 108, 112, 113, 145-46; as a model, 108, 113; and the Olympian gods, 114; and Olympian religion, 100, 102-3; his return to his origins, 147; his servant, 98; his violence, 98-99, 108
Euthyphro (Plato): as aesthtic unity, 96; and Hegel, 170
Euthyphro's father: and Cronus, 111; and Uranus, 110
Experience: Hegel's concept of, 156-57, 183; traditional conception of, 155-56

Family: and strangers, 104
Fate, 164
Figurative language: rooted in space and time, 194
Fragmentation: as a break in continuity, 112; as a break with the past, 112; caused by separation, 3; as degeneration, 64; and finitude, 8, 9; gods as a reflection of, 120; of ignorance, 105; as internal modification, 1; as lack of